CONCORDAT OF AGREEMENT: SUPPORTING ESSAYS

Concordat of Agreement: Supporting Essays

Edited by
Daniel F. Martensen

AUGSBURG
Minneapolis

FORWARD MOVEMENT PUBLICATIONS
Cincinnati

CONCORDAT OF AGREEMENT: SUPPORTING ESSAYS

Scripture texts are from the New Revised Standard Version Bible, copyright 1989 by the Division of Christian Education of the National Council of the Churches of Christ in the United States of America. Used with permission.

Library of Congress Cataloging-in-Publication Data
Concordat of agreement : supporting essays / edited by Daniel F. Martensen.
    p.   cm.
    Essays presented at the Lutheran-Episcopal Dialogue, series III, 1983-1991.
    Includes bibliographical references.
    ISBN 0-8066-2667-4 (pbk. : alk. paper)
    1. Episcopal Church—Relations—Evangelical Lutheran Church in America—Congresses. 2. Evangelical Lutheran Church in America--Relations—Episcopal Church—Congresses. 3. Episcopacy--Congresses. 4. Christian union—Congresses. 5. Anglican Communion—Relations—Lutheran Church—Congresses. 6. Lutheran Church—Relations—Anglican Communion—Congresses. 7. Lutheran-Episcopal Dialogue (3rd : 1983-1991). "Toward full communion" and "Concordat of agreement." I. Martensen, Daniel F. II. Lutheran-Episcopal Dialogue (3rd : 1983-1991)
BX5928.55.E95C66 1995
280'.042—dc20   94-44791
                                               CIP

The paper used in this publication meets the minimum requirements of American National Standard for Information Sciences—Permanence of Paper for Printed Library Materials, ANSI Z329.48-1984.   ∞™

Manufactured in the U.S.A   AF 10-26674

99   98   97   96   95   1   2   3   4   5   6   7   8   9   10

CONTENTS

FOREWORD

One of the challenges facing every theological dialogue between differing traditions is to bring the membership of the sponsoring churches to the same level of agreement already reached by the participants in the dialogue. How does a group that has been intimately involved in scholarly discussion for several years bring others to an appreciation of its conclusions and recommendations?

It has been customary for official dialogues to issue statements and progress reports to update their parent bodies regarding agreements reached and steps that might be taken as a result. What those statements and reports often lack, however, are the studies and documentation that led to an evolving consensus, and the shared experience that developed among the participants over the months and years of the dialogue.

The Lutheran–Episcopal Dialogue, Series III (LED III), met from 1983 through 1991. Three very significant documents were produced and made available to the churches: *Implications of the Gospel* (1988), *Toward Full Communion* (1991), and *Concordat of Agreement* (1991). What have not been available are the many scholarly papers and the animated discussions evoked by them. The essays that follow attempt to share with a wider audience of Lutherans and Episcopalians the significant theological and historical material that helped the participants in LED III reach the conclusions and recommendations reflected in those documents of 1988 and 1991.

These essays represent only a portion of those originally presented at the dialogue sessions. Space required that a selection be made. Each contribution helped the movement of the dialogue toward its assigned goal. Though the printed word can never reproduce the excitement and persuasive power of the conversation prompted by the presentations, it will place before the membership of our churches the foundational documents leading to most of the conclusions and recommendations of the dialogue.

We would have preferred that this present collection be published first, providing the basis for *Implications of the Gospel, Toward Full Communion*, and the Concordat. Unfortunately, this was not practical at the time. However, the dialogue is now able to present a dozen of the more than thirty papers presented at its meetings.

We, the co–chairs of LED III, urge the members of the Evangelical Lutheran Church in America and the Episcopal Church, U.S.A. to read all of the published material issued from LED III as a whole, beginning with this book of essays and then continuing with *Implications of the Gospel, Toward Full Communion*, and the Concordat. Such a sequential reading would have the advantage of following the chronological flow of the dialogue itself, and would greatly assist an understanding of the resulting conclusions.

In grateful recognition of the work of the authors of these essays and of all the participants in LED III, we are pleased to commend this book for study, discussion, and our churches' final determination in their ecumenical journey together.

Paul Erickson
William Weinhauer
Co–chairs, Lutheran-Episcopal Dialogue, Series III, 1983–1991

PREFACE

Toward Full Communion and *Concordat of Agreement*, which propose the establishment of full communion between the Episcopal Church, U.S.A. (ECUSA) and the Evangelical Lutheran Church in America (ELCA), were completed in 1991. Both churches are presently encouraging and facilitating churchwide study of that proposal. It is anticipated that action by both church bodies will be taken in 1997.

The essays included in this volume were developed over the course of the sessions of dialogue that ran from 1983 to 1991. Selection of the essays was determined by the relationship of the material to specific questions now being posed to our respective U.S. churches and worldwide communions as the study and reception of *Toward Full Communion* and *Concordat of Agreement* continue.

This preface is intended to assist readers in the effort to place the dramatic developments in U.S. Lutheran/Episcopal relationships in a broader context. Two dimensions of that context are to be addressed here. The first is the historical; the second includes the documentary results of global or other regional dialogues that are related to the U.S. situation.

THE HISTORICAL DIMENSION

Sporadic contact as well as geographical and cultural isolation marked the relationship between Anglicans and Lutherans from the sixteenth to the twentieth centuries. Since the turn of the century things have changed. In almost all the places where Anglicans and Lutherans live in close proximity, the two communities have fashioned some kind of relationship. Serious theological dialogue has developed in many settings.

Both the documentation from and the personal experience of those who have engaged in dialogue reflect the fact that Lutherans and Anglicans are in basic agreement about most of the important ecumenical theological issues, issues such as the role and/or authority of the Scriptures, the sacraments, and the creeds. Recurring themes in

9

the regional and international dialogues have been those relating to the gospel, the nature of the church, and areas of common witness and service.

The North Atlantic world has been the arena within which the most definitive documents and proposals for full communion have developed. Asia and Africa, however, have seen dramatic and important developments in Anglican–Lutheran relations. The East Africa Church Union Consultation is the most important example of this serious bilateral work. Even though neither union nor full communion resulted from these efforts, in East Africa and Southern Africa the relationship between the two communities has become very close as they have faced the common challenges of witnessing together against injustice, working for peace, and engaging in common mission.

GLOBAL AND REGIONAL DEVELOPMENTS

Series III of Lutheran-Episcopal Dialogue in the U.S. seriously took into account developments at the international level, particularly two documents and the experience that produced them. These documents remind us of the fact that Anglicans and Lutherans are each part of an ecclesiastical nomenclature at the world level, i.e., a Christian world communion. For Lutherans it is the Lutheran World Federation; for Anglicans, the Anglican Consultative Council. Yet authoritative, binding decisions in these communions can be made only by churches at the regional or national level.

The Cold Ash Report

In 1983 a working group appointed by the Anglican Consultative Council (ACC) and the Lutheran World Federation (LWF) produced a document in which the basic marks of full communion were described; it also affirmed that full communion was the goal of Anglican/Lutheran dialogue. The report said that the churches in communion would remain ecclesiastical bodies with their own identity. They would, however, make provision for common ministry, life, and corporate witness. The Cold Ash Report has had a powerful impact on present discussions of and proposals for the establishment of full communion, and it is in agreement with the statements of unity of the ECUSA and the ecumenical policy of the ELCA.

The Niagara Report

Convergence and consensus among Anglicans and Lutherans on a wide range of basic theological questions has been accomplished. The fact of the episcopacy stands as a hurdle on the track ahead. Just how formidable it is remains to be seen. It was this challenge that was addressed by the 1987 consultation sponsored by the ACC and the LWF, resulting in *The Niagara Report*.

Niagara lays out some concrete possibilities for ways to overcome the differences between the Anglican and Lutheran understandings of ministry and oversight, and it thereby provokes the churches to take action.

At the heart of *The Niagara Report* and the LED III proposals for full communion is a fundamental assertion. The issue of Episcopal succession is to be seen as one part of the historic self–understanding of the church in light of its total mission in the world. Continuity in mission, and "apostolic succession" as a part of it, is a mark of the church as a whole rather than being just one element in its doctrine or ministry. The hope is that by placing the issue of episcopacy in its proper ecclesial context, fruitless argument and debate will be avoided, i.e., polarization between those accenting Lutheran concerns about succession in doctrine and those lifting up the Anglican emphasis on succession in episcopacy.

The Porvoo Common Statement

In 1989, conversations that had occurred periodically over the years were begun once again between the Church of England and the Nordic, Estonian, and Latvian Lutheran churches. Later other British and Irish Anglican churches as well as the Lithuanian Lutheran church were involved in the dialogue. The Porvoo Common Statement, the official report of these conversations, was published in 1993.[1]

"Full Communion" as a phrase is not used in the Porvoo statement. However, if the proposals in Porvoo were adopted, all the components basic to full communion would be realized. Porvoo and the Concordat, if adopted by all the churches involved, would produce similar relations between Anglicans and Lutherans in northern Europe and in the United States. *A Commentary on "Concordat of Agreement"*[2] includes a chapter in which a detailed comparison is made between the Porvoo statement and the Concordat.

CONCLUSION

We hope that our churches will be able to engage in careful, responsible study and discussion of the ecumenical challenge before us. God willing, we will make decisions that will affirm the inseparable link between the unity and the mission of the church at a crucial point in our history.

Daniel F. Martensen

ABBREVIATIONS

ACC   Anglican Consultative Council

AP   Apology of the Augsburg Confession

BC   *The Book of Concord. The Confessions of the Evan-
                gelical Lutheran Church.* Trans. and ed. Theodore
                G. Tappert. Philadelphia: Fortress, 1959.

BCP   *The Book of Common Prayer according to the Use of
                the Episcopal Church.* New York: Church Hym-
                nal Corporation, 1979.

BEM   *Baptism, Eucharist and Ministry.* Faith and Order
                Paper No. 111. Geneva: WCC, 1982.

BS   *Die Bekenntnisschriften der evangelisch-lutherischen
                Kirche.* 3rd. rev. ed. (Göttingen: Vandenhoeck &
                Ruprecht, 1930).

CA   Confessio Augustana (Augsburg Confession)

Cold Ash   *Anglican-Lutheran Relations: The Cold Ash Re-
                port.* London: Anglican Consultative Council;
                Geneva: LWF, 1983.

Concordat, the "Concordat of Agreement." In *"Toward Full
                Communion" and "Concordat of Agreement": Lu-
                theran-Episcopal Dialogue, Series III.* William A.
                Norgren and William G. Rusch, eds. Minneapo-
                lis: Augsburg; Cincinnati: Forward Movement,
                1991.

Ecumenism   *Ecumenism: The Vision of the Evangelical Lutheran
                Church in America.* A Policy Statement Adopted
                by the Evangelical Lutheran Church in Amer-
                ica, August 31, 1991. Chicago: ELCA Office of
                the Secretary, 1991.

13

ECUSA	The Episcopal Church, U.S.A.
ELCA	The Evangelical Lutheran Church in America
Implications	William A. Norgren and William G. Rusch, eds. *Implications of the Gospel. Lutheran-Episcopal Dialogue, Series III.* Minneapolis: Augsburg; Cincinnati: Forward Movement, 1988.
LED III	Lutheran-Episcopal Dialogue, Series III
LW	*Luther's Works.* J. Pelikan and H. Lehmann, gen. eds. St. Louis: Concordia; and Philadelphia: Fortress. Vols. 1(1958)–55(1986).
LWF	The Lutheran World Federation
LWF 32	*Lutheran Ecumenism on the Way.* LWF Documentation 32. Geneva: LWF, 1993.
Niagara	Anglican-Lutheran International Continuation Committee, *The Niagara Report: Report of the Anglican-Lutheran Consultation on Episcope, Niagara Falls, September 1987* (London: Anglican Consultative Council; Geneva: LWF, 1988).
Porvoo	"The Porvoo Common Statement." Occasional Paper no. 3. The Council for Christian Unity of the General Synod of the Church of England. Also printed in *Together in Mission and Ministry: The Porvoo Common Statement with Essays on Church and Ministry in Northern Europe.* London: Church House Publishing, 1993.
SA	Smalcald Articles
TFC	"Toward Full Communion." In *"Toward Full Communion"* and *"Concordat of Agreement"*: *Lutheran-Episcopal Dialogue, Series III.* William A. Norgren and William G. Rusch, eds. Minneapolis: Augsburg; Cincinnati: Forward Movement, 1991.
TFC & Concordat	William A. Norgren and William G. Rusch, eds. *"Toward Full Communion"* and *"Concordat of Agreement."* Lutheran-Episcopal Dialogue, Series III. Minneapolis: Augsburg; Cincinnati: Forward Movement Publications, 1991.

WA	Martin Luther, *Luthers Werke*. Kritische Gesamtausgabe ("Weimarer Ausgabe"). Weimar: Böhlau, 1883—)
WA Br	Martin Luther. *Luthers Werke*. Kritische Gesamtausgabe ("Weimarer Ausgabe"). Briefwechsel. Weimar: Böhlau, 1930–).
WCC	The World Council of Churches

1

The Gospel and the Institutions of the Church with Particular Reference to the Historic Episcopate

by

L. William Countryman

A New Testament scholar may perhaps be forgiven for beginning from a New Testament text, even if it may at first appear to have very little direct bearing on the subject at hand. Indeed, it is partly for this reason that I choose it, for I suppose that if we aim at some kind of rapprochement between two widely varying perspectives, we must search for some larger perspective that could include them both without doing violence to either. Whether this essay succeeds in so ambitious a task or not, it is the only way I can see to tackle the issues.

My text is from Jesus' high–priestly prayer:

> I ask not only on behalf of these, but also on behalf of those who will believe in me through their word, that they may all be one. As you, Father, are in me and I am in you, may they also be in us, so that the world may believe that you have sent me (John 17:20–21).

This is not a text about church unity in the usual sense. It is about something both more and less difficult, both more and less attainable. It speaks of a mystical union that is not only a union between a single human reality and the divine, not only the flight of the alone to the alone, but also a union among all who are in union with God. The unity of Father and Son in the godhead is the model for this unity of believer with believer—and also the source from which it flows.

To speak in this way is to speak of what the Jesus of the Synoptic Gospels calls the kingdom of God, or of the heavens, and what the

Jesus of John's Gospel calls himself: "I am the way, and the truth, and the life. No one comes to the Father except through me....Whoever has seen me has seen the Father" (John 14:6, 9). It is to speak not only of the means of salvation, as when we speak of justification through faith, or of the cause of salvation, as when we speak of God's grace, but of the goal of salvation in the communion of perfect love within God and among God and humanity.

Paul, too, makes the same point:

> Love never ends. But as for prophecies, they will come to an end; as for tongues, they will cease; as for knowledge, it will come to an end. For we know only in part, and we prophesy only in part; but when the complete comes, the partial will come to an end (1 Cor. 13:8–10).

This means, I believe, that everything in our present experience is but a pointer or, perhaps, a means toward that consummation which Paul describes as "the complete" (*to teleion*). This is not to invalidate prophecy or tongues or knowledge—all of which Paul both criticizes and vindicates in this same epistle—but rather to relativize them. Ultimately, for Paul as for John, there is but one "this-worldly" value that can hold its place in the consummation: the love that binds God to us, us to God, and us to one another:

> And now faith, hope, and love abide—these three; and the greatest of these is love (13:13).

The greatest is love, because it alone holds its place forever. Faith may give way to sight, hope to realization; but there is no more perfect replacement for love. Our love may no doubt be purified, but it does not give way to something else.

Paul, of course, was speaking in eschatological terms, and I have followed him. The Jesus of John's Gospel, however, does not limit himself in quite the same way. He does not pray "that they may all be one" in the world to come or in heaven, but "that they may all be one," pure and simple. In this respect, John was voicing a concern highly characteristic of early Christian literature in general: that the gospel should be (and even must be) manifested in a *united* community of faith. Our forebears of the first and second centuries did not find that easy to achieve; but the wonder is that they thought it necessary or important to pursue at all. Such a concern was very nearly unexampled in their world.

The Jewish nation had a certain political and legal unity, of course, and that was, likely, one source of the early Christians' concern, since they used Israel as a metaphor for their own identity. But the Jews were a national entity, not a voluntary association of believers, not a "religion" in the modern sense. If we look at the Hellenistic and Roman background of the early churches we find that with the single exception of the theatrical guilds, there was no form of voluntary association that rose above the most purely local level of organization.[1] Nor was there any preexisting model for an ecumenical (i.e., empire-wide) voluntary organization such as the church, which stressed unity of belief and life, set itself apart with characteristic rites, and fostered its ecumenicity by the way it structured its institutions.

The point I am making is this. The earliest Christians believed that the loving unity of human beings with one another, in and with and under God, was the point and goal of the proclamation of the gospel. They found it necessary that the church should not only proclaim such a goal in words, but also express it in its life—so far as that might be possible in the conditions of the present world. Thus the life of the church, even in its institutional aspects, had from the beginning a theological and soteriological drive behind it. This does not suggest that everything that came out of this impulse was therefore right or necessary, or that an institution can ever adequately embody the transcendent truth that inspired its creation. But it does suggest that, to understand early Christian institutions, one must see them as social expressions of theological convictions.

The unity of love as the goal of salvation came to be expressed in the church through four main institutions, each of which has roots in the New Testament era, but reached classic definition only in the second and later centuries of our era. They are, in roughly the order of their reaching classical form: (1) the ritual complex centered on the dominical sacraments, (2) the threefold (apostolic) ministry, (3) summary statements of Christian belief (creeds), and (4) the New Testament canon. The second of these, the ministry, provides the focus for this essay; but we would likely place it in a false perspective if we failed to note that it developed as part of a larger socio–historical process, that it never stood on its own, and that it was an integral expression of a community life that was also being realized simultaneously in other ways.

It should be useful to outline briefly what is known of the development of each of these four institutions:

(1) The dominical sacraments of baptism and Eucharist were understood to have been authorized by Jesus himself, whether in his

ministry (John 4:1; 6:54; 1 Cor. 11:23–26 and parallels) or after his resurrection (Matt. 28:16–20). It does not necessarily follow, however, that the earliest Christians automatically knew exactly what to do with these rites or how to interpret them. Some have argued that the Gospel of John is at least skeptical of them (cf. 6:54 with 6:63). However that may be, it is clear that the Eucharist, at least, did not at once reach its classic form. In 1 Corinthians 11, Paul speaks of it as a full meal, with the opportunity for drunkenness. At some point, the rites of bread and wine were separated from the full meal—a fairly radical innovation—and probably moved to another time of day. The rest of the meal perhaps formed the foundation of the Agape, which therefore carried with it much of the same meaning as the Eucharist. The result is that in the *Didache* it is difficult to be sure whether the prayers provided are meant for the one or for the other; even in the third century, other foods could still be offered at the Eucharist, and the Agape could itself be seen as an "offering" (Hippolytus, *Apostolic Tradition* 5–6, 26). In brief, an initial impetus ascribed to Jesus himself developed over several centuries before achieving the classic pattern still in use.[2]

Similar developments took place in connection with baptism, though here one would have to broaden the perspective to ask not only how the rite was altered but also how its boundary functions changed with the shift from a largely Jewish to a largely Gentile church, as well as with the development of the catechumenate and, later, of the *disciplina arcana*. The rigorous and highly developed catechetical system of, say, the Jerusalem church in the fourth century would have been quite different from what was being done there in A.D. 37 or 38.[3]

(2) In the area of ministry, also, we see a fairly long and complex process of development. At least two basic social impulses contributed to the shape it began to take. One of these was simply the need for any human community to have some degree of internal articulation. The early Palestinian communities may have continued the existing Jewish practice of acknowledging certain people as elders. Acts 6:1-6 tells us of the innovation of a Board of Seven with specialized responsibilities for welfare. The Pauline communities at first depended heavily on charismatic persons for leadership and service (as did the communities described in the *Didache*); but Paul also urged them to pay special attention to certain persons of long standing in the church and of greater stability (e.g., 1 Cor. 16:15-18). Eventually, what appear to be official titles make their appearance (Phil. 1:1), and post–Pauline developments (see 1 Tim. 3:1–13, Titus 1:5–9; cf. *Didache*

15.1–2) included a steadily increasing regularization of the ministry. By the early second century, one finds the threefold ministry of bishops, presbyters, and deacons unmistakably articulated in the letters of Ignatius of Antioch; and by the last quarter of the century, this appears to have become the classic shape of Christian ministry everywhere—even in a conservative stronghold such as Rome.[4]

The other strand in the development of the early Christian ministry is quite different and originally more or less distinct from the question of functional articulation of the community. It was a matter, rather, of the personal mediation of discipleship. For a variety of reasons it is difficult for us to grasp the importance of this element in first-century Christianity. Most, if not all, of us have been educated in the context of an image such as "the marketplace of ideas"; discipleship in Jesus' world tended to emphasize rather the image of "the one great teacher." There was a concentration on the individual and the personal in a way that might make us uncomfortable. In addition, for the earliest Christians, the absence of any distinctly Christian scriptures intensified their reliance on living persons. The scriptures of Israel were, of course, taken over and expounded upon within the Christian community; but they did not speak the gospel without assistance. (The story of Philip and the Ethiopian eunuch, Acts 8:26–40, offers a vivid example of this.) If one wanted access to the gospel in its simplicity—the message of, by, and about Jesus—one could not turn to written documents; one had to seek out appropriate persons. (Given the oral bias of ancient Mediterranean culture, one might continue to do so even after written documents became available; cf. Papias of Hierapolis and his preference for the "living and abiding voice.")[5]

It was thus the apostolic quality of certain individuals—their ability to put one in touch with Jesus himself because of their own favored relationship to him—that also determined the significance and value of the ministry for the earliest Christians. Paul's claims for himself as a genuine, if belated, apostle are a case in point (1 Cor. 15:1–11; 2 Cor. 10–12). Since he could not claim to have been a disciple during the earthly ministry of Jesus, he needed to stress his being called by the risen Lord. Still, it is the element of personal contact and authorization that puts a foundation under everything else, not only Paul's right to a hearing, but the very right of the local church to exist. The whole life of the Church flows out of the personal link with Jesus formed by the apostles. With the death of the apostles, the churches did not simply abandon the notion of personal links with Jesus. Even if they had wished to do so, what substitute for them did they yet have? Instead, they interpreted their ministries as carrying on this linkage as well as serving the function of articulating the life of the community. They could express this in various ways, but the two most important were the notions of succession through delegation of authority (the Pastorals, *1 Clement*) and succession in the teaching office (Irenaeus). By the early third century, at the latest, some sort of tactile succession was the normal public sign of this succession.[6]

(3) As with the dominical sacraments and the ministry, the development of short summaries of Christian faith has its roots in the New Testament era. I would not see the early hymnic elements in Paul's letters (e.g., Phil. 2:6–11) in this light; they are more celebratory than definitive. But the terse summary of Pauline theology in Titus 3:3–7 could readily have served as a kind of touchstone of orthodoxy. Similar motives led to the production, in the second century, of the *regula fidei* or *kanon aletheias*, a kind of oral tradition designed to elucidate the contents of catechesis and to rule out Gnostic and Marcionite theologies. By the late second century, one finds another similar device: baptismal responses elaborated—especially in the article on the Son—with a summary of cardinal points of belief. These responses, in turn, apparently provided the basis for the fourth-century baptismal creeds, solemnly "handed over" to catechumens in the *traditio* and repeated by them in the *redditio*. Beginning with Nicaea in 325, church councils also began to produce creeds and other brief formularies (e.g., the Chalcedonian Definition), more as theological tests than for liturgical purposes.[7]

These summary statements arose in response to specific needs in the interpretation of the gospel, especially needs arising out of sharp theological disagreements. That in itself is enough to explain why Jesus himself did not offer such summaries and why they first appear only rather late in the New Testament era. It also explains why they are not more comprehensive than they are. While the Chicago–Lambeth Quadrilateral describes the Nicene Creed as "the sufficient statement of the Christian Faith," we cannot take that to mean exactly the same thing as "containing all things necessary to salvation"—a phrase reserved for the Holy Scriptures. Such summaries have a more limited purpose, namely, to exclude certain lines of development felt to be fundamentally antagonistic to the gospel itself. They are intelligible only as arising out of and putting limits on the teaching functions of the living church community. It is natural, then, that these summaries should arise and reach their classic forms only over a period of several centuries.

(4) Of these four major institutions of the earliest Christian communities, probably the last to arise and certainly the last to reach definitive form was that of the New Testament canon. Indeed, it is said that the East Syrians have not to this day accepted more than 22 books, so perhaps the question has yet to be closed definitively.[8] The earliest evidence we have pointing to the formation of a New Testament canon comes from the Second Epistle of Peter and the work of Marcion, both dating to around A.D. 140. It would be another two centuries, however, before the standard modern list would emerge. One often sees the date 367 for this list, but that is only its first datable occurrence, not the end of the process of development. Not until the tenth century, it seems, can one rely on finding the book of Revelation included in an average Greek New Testament manuscript. And some of the sixteenth–century reformers, most notably Luther, felt that the question was not finally closed.[9]

The New Testament canon had, of course, a variety of functions: it helped focus the church's teaching and preaching and provided specifically Christian readings to stand alongside the scriptures of Israel in public worship. It offered a written deposit of the apostolic teaching that could balance the continuing oral tradition, with its tendency to rework material in terms of the church's changing context. By its increasingly fixed form, it thus became a kind of counterweight to the developments of sacrament and ministry. On the other hand, it was distinct from the credal development in being more diffuse (thus countering the tendency to reduce the faith to a few controverted issues) and more closely tied to first–century language and concerns.

I have sketched the history of these four institutions not because the material is unfamiliar; it is familiar to us all in greater or less detail. I am seeking rather to make a point about their comparability with each other: while they performed a variety of tasks, not one of these institutions has reached us exactly as it left the lips and hands of Jesus. The dominical sacraments were reorganized and fitted into a developing community structure. The ministry was adapted to needs and occasions quite different from those of Jesus' immediate following of disciples. The message of Jesus was reformulated in the short credal summaries to protect it from unwarranted developments, and in a scriptural canon to provide a fuller point of reference in writing. Each of these developments gave the Christian church a sense of its own identity and continuity—continuity with its founder and continuity within itself, in both space (among its scattered congregations) and time (with its own past).

These four institutions do not, of course, exhaust the social reality of the early Christian communities, for there were many other things going on in their life, some of them institutionalized to a similar degree. The scriptures of Israel, for example, formed a significant institution within early Christianity, though there has never been full agreement as to the exact canon of the Old Testament. And most early Christians insisted on the importance of a variety of social activities to which they ascribed religious significance, including care for the poor and the stranger, chastity, and refusal of idolatrous worship (even when this meant martyrdom). Without discounting the importance of these, I think it would still be true to say that these four institutions (sacraments, apostolic ministry, creeds, New Testament canon) were the cardinal ways in which the church "constructed" itself—that is, drew its boundaries and articulated itself in relation to its source in the gospel.[10]

Now to the point of all this: What is the relationship of such institutions to the gospel itself? Jesus' own ministry was not marked by a high degree of institutionalization; indeed, some of his most characteristic modes of expression were calculated to undermine rather than reinforce institutions. The parable calls hearers out of the familiar into a new way of understanding and living. The paradox and hyperbole serve to deny our ordinary view of reality and substitute a new one focused on the kingdom of God and on Jesus' own person and message. Jesus' religious preference for the company of the irreligious serves to disconnect faith from conventional piety.[11] How then do we turn from such a person and such a gospel to the institutional life of a human community and somehow let the latter be a vehicle for the former?

The answer, I suppose, is that we do it imperfectly, and yet we have to do it. Communities do not survive without institutionalization. The critical question is not whether there will be institutions. There will be. The question is how they will go about pointing to the gospel, which stands as the fountainhead of the life of this community. I should like to suggest that each of the four institutions I have been speaking about have a characteristic use in the proclamation of the gospel—and a characteristic set of abuses. The two are entangled with one another, and it is perhaps impossible to separate the good and bad once and for all in the context of our human and social existence.

The social functions of our institutions are perhaps easier to agree on than their theological necessity. The two great sacraments, for example, have provided a ritual objectification of the most basic patterns of faith (most especially the pattern of death and resurrection). Through their engagement with the physical and temporal aspects of reality and with each believer as an individual, they serve to provide a certain direction to our life as Christians, and to point always toward an underlying pattern of reality of which we would otherwise find it easy to lose track. Yet it is precisely the element of objectification in the sacraments that opens them to our characteristic abuse of them, namely to substitute them for the reality to which they point, to treat them as ends instead of means.

The creeds, in turn, serve their social function by focusing the gospel with reference to a particular challenge. They are not comprehensive statements of the Christian faith, but rather highly selective summaries, usually designed to exclude certain lines of theological development. As with sacraments, the temptation is to substitute them for the larger reality and thus, in the case of creeds, to let orthodoxy become a matter of subscribing to correct formulae rather than a matter of being in a faithful and worshipful relation to God through our Lord. The danger is to reduce all Christian theology to a polemical exercise.

The scriptures of the New Testament serve as a literary concretization of the first age of faith, so that we can preserve some kind of direct communication with it; without the canon, we would find the development of the church over the centuries moving us further and further from the original. Worse than that, we would probably have lost, in the period of emerging orthodoxy, much of the early richness and pristine energy of the gospel. Yet, having once concretized that earliest period of the faith, we are from then on tempted to misuse the New Testament canon by substituting the written letter for the living voice of the Spirit, by treating the past as a blueprint for the present, or by seeking in the Scriptures the capstone of faith rather than its foundations.

What is true for canon, creed, and sacraments, is also true of their contemporary institution, the threefold ministry in apostolic succession. The abuses of this institution are of a similar kind and arise in a similar way—by mistaking the institution for an end rather than a means. The ministry may be (and often has been) mistaken for the church whose life it serves to articulate—even to the extent of implying, in some theories of orders, that the ministry can exist without the church (though not the church without the ministry). Again, the ministry can be mistaken for the gospel that it is intended to convey. In this way, the ministry (or a certain portion of it) may be assigned a kind of absolute teaching authority over against the people of God, or the ministry may be seen as a kind of sacramental conduit serving to validate sacraments, or as an independent charism guaranteed by God alone and drawing nothing at all from the church.

Absus autem non tollit usum. A formal, distinct ministry is still found in most Christian traditions because it continues to do what it was created to do: articulate the communal reality of Christian existence and offer a sacramental concretization of our continuity in the gospel. Different ways of constructing the ministry, however, will communicate different interpretations of these realities. If one looks at the second- or third-century patterns, one finds them dominated by a threefold ministry in apostolic succession. What did this pattern say about church and gospel?

In one sense, this represents a simple functional structure: the function of local presidency came to be vested in a single person, the bishop; the function of counsel was vested in a college, the presbyters, who could also act on behalf of the bishop when and as delegated; the administration of daily life was vested in deacons working under the bishop. Naturally, such a functional division of labor would have to change periodically through history, as the needs and presuppositions of society changed; and that is exactly what happened. The resident bishops of Iona (who were effectively subject to the abbot, a presbyter),[12] the politicized prince–bishops of the Holy Roman Empire, the missionary bishops of the American frontier, contemporary bishops struggling with the bureaucracy of the office—all were functionally different from one another, as well as from the second–century bishop–martyr of Smyrna, or from the urban bishop of the third century, who kept the church treasury in his house, directed the only general social-welfare program in town, and acted as patron of widows and host to Christian travelers.

In another sense, however, it is a symbolic rather than functional structure we are looking at. This is clearest in terms of the rites of ordination, first detailed for us in *The Apostolic Tradition* of Hippolytus—an early third–century work, but one of a deliberately conservative cast.[13] Briefly summarized, the system worked thus: a bishop was elected by the congregation, but only the other bishops present (presumably from neighboring towns) laid hands on him, with a prayer that associated the office with the apostles as precedent (*Apost. Trad.* 2–3). A presbyter was ordained by the bishop "while the presbyters touch him," with a prayer alluding to the seventy elders consecrated at Mt. Sinai (8). (Confessors, however, became presbyters without ordination, 10). A deacon was ordained by the bishop alone with a prayer that apparently took Jesus as the type of this office (9).

One did not lay on hands to call persons to other ecclesiastical functions (11–15).

What does such a system say about the symbolic relationship between ministry, church, and gospel? It makes the bishop the focal point of continuity, both in space and time—elected by the local congregation, but ordained by episcopal colleagues from other congregations, with specific reference to the continuation of apostolic authority. The bishop was thus an intersection of the local and the ecumenical, the contemporary and the historic/apostolic. The presbyters were a purely local body that was self–perpetuating, but only in cooperation with the bishop. (Hippolytus refused to grant them any power to ordain, but he was forced to deny the apparent import of the rites themselves in doing so, 9.5–8.) Deacons were individuals in direct relation to the bishop. In other words, the bishop was ordained in a way that made the office a symbolic focus of the unity of the church as no other office was.

This does not mean that the chain of tradition or the unity of the church's life is or ever has been simply identical to the succession of the Christian ministry; that would be to confuse sign and reality. It would be equivalent to saying that Jesus is "really absent" everywhere that he is not "really present" in the sacrament. The historic episcopate or the threefold ministry does not exhaust the functions of ministry in the church, but offers a sacramental expression and elucidation of the nature of that ministry. One trusts that ordained ministers do indeed retain a share in the total ministry, but the distinctive function of ordination is rather to point to the ministerial nature of the whole body, to its articulation of its own life in the present and to its continuity with Christ through the long chain of people who have heard and then proclaimed the Gospel.

All four of the distinctive early Christian institutions are social expressions that *point* to the gospel as the originating fact of the Christian community. Not one of them, however, is simply *identical* with the gospel; and, accordingly, not one of them can be regarded as indispensable to the life of the Christian church. Churches have existed or do exist that omit one or more of the four. Indeed, the latest of the four, the New Testament canon itself, scarcely reached reliable and final form before the tenth century; and there have been occasions since when one or another group of faithful people have felt it necessary, for reasons of abuse, to reject one or another of these institutions. The Religious Society of Friends does not practice any external sacraments at all; nor do they have a stated ministry or creeds. To deny that they are an expression of the church, however, would be most problematic. A group whose faithfulness to Christ in the gospel has placed them in the forefront of efforts to care for the oppressed and needy and to resist the reign of violence has a right to be understood as "church." If we should deny them that, we would be coming perilously close to the kind of double-talk that characterized the Inquisition:

> Heretics are recognized by their customs and speech, for they are modest and well–regulated. They take no pride in their garments, which are neither costly nor vile. They do not engage in trade, to avoid lies and oaths and fraud; but live by their labor as mechanics—their teachers are cobblers. They do not accumulate wealth, but are content with necessaries. They are chaste and temperate in meat and drink....(*Liber contra Waldenses* 7).[14]

No one institution, however venerable, can be understood to be of the *esse* of the church; only the gospel is that. (And this is uttered by a professor of New Testament, who may be presumed to have a vested interest in at least the canon of that document).

Thus during the Protestant Reformation there were those, such as the Quakers, who felt that the sacraments could not be purified and so rejected them. There were others, like Luther, who felt that the question of canon should be reopened, perhaps to the detriment of such books as James and Revelation. There have been those, like Alexander Campbell at a later date, who felt that credal formulae were so prone to abuse that they could only be discarded (though, truth to tell, he may have been attacking the Westminster Confession more than the ancient creeds). And it is no surprise that there have been occasions in the history of the church when good and faithful people have thought the existing ministry beyond salvaging—when, indeed, the existing ministry has actually made itself an enemy of the gospel and effectively resigned from the church. The church certainly does not cease to exist by the loss of any of these institutions.

That being clearly understood, however, we do not so easily resolve the question of when it is best to retain them, when best to reject them, or when best to resume them again. There is something in us that would like to have a church life as absolute in its clarity and simplicity as the godhead. Either a thing is indispensable to the existence of the church, we could then say, or else it ought to be dispensed with. Or, in a less intransigent mood, we might say, "Either a thing is indispensable, or it is *adiaphoron*—and therefore not worth much attention." Such an approach, however, seems to me to miss the fundamental ambiguity that the life of the church shares with the life of all human communities: it is the most useful thing that is most readily abused. To bring the gospel within reach is to subject it to the possibility of being seized and misused.

The historic episcopate finds its place in the life of the whole church not because it is indispensable, nor because it is a functional convenience (though it is at times), but because it is a presentation on the sacramental plane of that unity which is the goal of the gospel. It therefore points beyond itself to the gospel and to the life of the church that flows out of the gospel, and also toward the life of the world to come, where the consummation of the gospel is effected. It does so not by guaranteeing that bishops will be good at their assigned tasks—or even that they will do good as opposed to harm, but by setting up a curiously physical and historical network of persons that proclaims that all Christian community is a succession of dependencies on one another, stretching back to the original discipling of particular people by the incarnate Word. Not, once again, that this succession comes to us through the bishops alone, but that they are the focal image that tells us over and over what our nature as church is.

To break the episcopal succession does not mean that one breaks the succession of the life of the church. If the latter is broken, the church will cease to exist; if the former is broken, the church will simply lose one pointer to its own nature. In the context of the continental Reformation, it seemed right and, at times, necessary to many leaders of undoubted faith and ability to let the historic episcopal succession be broken. It is not necessary or appropriate to second-guess their decisions. Let it be taken for granted that it was the right course at those places and times. The effect of such action, at least as pursued within Lutheranism, was not to extinguish all ministerial succession, but either to begin a new episcopal succession associated with the Reformation, or to transfer the function of ministerial succession entirely to the presbyters. In this way, something new was created that has its own value. It may not, however, do exactly the same task as the older succession, if only because the older succession had already been in universal use for at least thirteen centuries. The new mode of succession therefore embodies not only a continuity with the Reformation, but also a break from what went before. Such a message may have meant one thing in northern Europe in the sixteenth century, when it seemed impossible to extricate the use of the historic episcopate from its abuse.[15] It is apt to mean something else at a further remove in time and space. The question for Lutherans and Anglicans together may be whether both successions can be embodied in one ministry, with the increased richness signified in a continuity that has been both broken and reclaimed and thus witnesses to its own transcending.

I have deliberately sought, in this discussion, to avoid the quasi-metaphysical categories sometimes used in the past, such as "validity" or "fullness" of ministerial orders. Such terms are, I think, unanalyzed and sometimes verge on the magical. I do, however, think that the things being discussed are real: that the historic episcopate contains an element of the proclamation of the gospel not contained in the Reformation successions—and vice-versa. The historic episcopate declares to us that the gospel is not only an idea or a proposition or a proclamation, but the animating force of a living community communicated over and over again from one person to another. The bishop, in this succession, is thus a living image of the unity of the faithful in and with God, a unity yet to be consummated but already at work in us across the barriers of time and space. The Reformation successions also have a message for us: that the gospel is always transcendent and never merely identical with any of the institutions to which it has given rise among us; if the institutions fail, that does not mean that the gospel has failed nor that the church has ceased. God remains perfectly free to make new beginnings with people. The two successions, then, are not merely identical in what they signify. Yet neither do I see that they need be antithetical. If we can recognize that the Spirit has given utterance to each, then we will want to find ways of sharing and preserving both messages.

2
AUGUSTANA 28 AND LAMBETH 4:
EPISCOPACY AS ADIAPHORON OR NECESSITY
BY
ROBERT J. GOESER

An essay on the historic episcopate focusing on an either/or of *necessity* or *adiaphoron*[1] must be constructed primarily on the grounds of doctrinal theology. If the focus is defined, however, as a comparison of Augustana 28 (CA 28) and Lambeth Quadrilateral 4, the study becomes more historical. I am taking the way of a historical essay to provide the context for raising the doctrinal issues.

TO THE DIET OF AUGSBURG

As early as 1523—before the Lutheran reform received princely acceptance in Saxony—Luther wrote publicly about church, episcopacy, ministry, and ordination. In the tract, *De instituendis ministris ecclesiae*, Luther wrote to the Utraquists in Bohemia regarding their situation, where episcopal ordination was becoming fraught with great difficulties. So long as the papal bishops refused to provide them with ministers of the Word—would give them, instead, ministers who would obliterate the Word and destroy the church[2]—the assembly of the church had to elect those fit to be ministers of the Word and bishops. They could then be ordained before the whole congregation and acknowledged as ministers and bishops.[3] (These bishops could then select leaders responsible for visitation and so create an evangelical archepiscopate).[4] Unless ministers were selected their church would perish, for the church is born and nourished by the Word of God; without proclamation of the Word it ceases.[5] Luther wrote that they need have no scruples about such actions; they were the church, for the church is marked by the Word of God and knowledge of Christ, not by outward customs.[6] Quite evidently Luther maintained that the church originates in the Word and that the Word is also its gift and responsibility. The Word is antecedent to any order, and the institution of the ministry of the Word belongs to the church as a whole and not to a right of episcopal succession.

Luther envisioned the situation of the Utraquists as one about to be realized within the German evangelical movement. In a sermon of 1524, he observed that ordained ministers were dying out, while the bishops would ordain only those who denied the gospel.[7] As time moved on, it would be necessary to ordain evangelical pastors.[8] The ordination would be into a ministry different from that to which the bishops ordain.[9] He concluded:

> To ordain is not to consecrate. If, therefore we know a pious man, we single him out, and, by the power of the Word which we have, we bestow on him the authority of preaching and administering the sacraments. This is to ordain.[10]

In another sermon of the same year he commended a ministry of preaching the Word of God that was different from that which the bishops established.[11]

More important than the issue of ordination is the different understanding of ministry that was being expressed. The ministry is the ministry or office of the Word, where Word is the means of grace, and sacrament is derived from Word. This is in contrast to the sacerdotal ministry of sacrifice (the mass) and of the sacramental system. Ordination is not a consecration conferring power and defined character which mediate sacramental grace; it is the assurance of a call to proclaim. The whole theology of sacrifice and merit incorporated into the sacramental system was in conflict with a ministry of the Word and its understanding of grace, faith, and Christ[12] as gift.[13] To say this is to recognize that the evidence is supplied not by the few passages addressed above, but in the burden of Luther's writings from 1519 on, which center around the rediscovery and proclamation of the Word as the means of grace.[14] It is there also in the ongoing critique of the ministry of priest, bishop, and pope, which sounds at times like an attack on ordained ministry itself.[15]

A similar view of the dependence of church and ministry on the Word is explicit in Melanchthon's writings. In the *Iudicium de iure reformandi* (1525) he responded to the question of whether the evangelicals were right in promulgating their teachings before these were corroborated by the prelates, and whether they were to be criticized as heretics.[16] His answer was that they had first submitted to the hierarchy in informing the leaders of false doctrine and practices.[17] Since the papacy and bishops had responded with scorn, persecution, and tyranny, it was the task of the preachers—because of their ministry (the *Predigtamt*)—to preach about faith in Christ—the central doctrine of Christian teaching—and defend the truth.[18] Melanchthon next wrote:

> On the other hand, when they say that they are the church and the church cannot err, so that whoever falls away from them falls from the church, they are easily answered. For we will not allow that papacy and bishops, monks and priests are the church—although among them are people who, belonging to the churches, do not give consent to their errors, but have a right faith. So Paul teaches in Ephesians 5 that the church consists only of those in whom the Word is urged and promulgated—there is church and no where else.[19]

Already in the *Loci* of 1521, Melanchthon distinguished sharply between the authority of the Word in the church and human laws or traditions of papacy or councils.[20] This continued to be a basic distinction in his thought and came to full expression in the Augsburg Confession.

There is record of at least two ordinations in Saxony before the Diet of Augsburg. George Rörer was ordained in the Pfarrkirche in Wittenberg in 1525, by the laying-on-of-hands by Luther. A contemporary recorded later that Rörer regarded the ordination to be *"nach Apostolischer Weise"* and believed his orders to have the same validity as those in Wittenberg possessed of episcopal ordination. There is record also of the ordination of Wencel Kilman in 1529. Whether there were other ordinations during the period is not clear. Luther's lament (December 1530) that there was such a dearth of faithful pastors and that they should, by proper rite (*proprio ritu*), ordain ministers suggests that there have been few ordinations and also assumes the possibility of a proper and regular ordination that is non-episcopal.

The expansion of evangelical teachings and the breakdown of episcopal supervision created a situation of irregularity and disorder demanding visitation undertaken by the state. The *Unterricht der Visitatoren* (1528) comes close to establishing a new church order. In the preface, Luther wrote of the care of the congregations and pastors effected by Peter, Paul, Barnabas, and others, through letters, visitations, and preaching. The episcopal office originated in such care for congregational teaching and life.[21] Now that the gospel was preached again—where formerly there was spiritual desolation—there was

33

need for right visitation.[22] Since the evangelical preachers did not feel called to this office, they had appealed to their prince to undertake this task out of Christian love, although according to his secular authority, he did not have this responsibility.[23]

The *Unterricht* assumes the establishment of the office of superintendent (*"Superattendant"*), whose duties are defined as overseeing pastors and congregations to ensure sound doctrine, true preaching of the Word of God and the gospel, and administration of the sacraments according to Christ's institution.[24] The pastors' lives should be such as to lead parishioners to a better life and in no way be an offense to them; their preaching must not arouse disorder or rebellion against the authorities.[25] In addition, the superintendents should examine candidates for the ministry, testing them in regard to both doctrine and life, to see if they are adequate to proper care and leadership of the congregations. This demanded careful attention, since in the past incompetent pastors had led so many astray.[26] The right of examination was not accompanied by the right of ordination—at least no such provision is articulated. Varying interpretations have been given for this "omission." Lieberg suggests that ordination was simply not observed—the call by the congregation (or the patron) and examination by the superintendent sufficed for installation into the office,[27] and Pfister assumes that the candidates were bound to an "orderly ordination."[28]

Whatever uncertainty there may be about details in the *Instruction*, it clearly constitutes the nucleus of a new church order—a territorial church that is catholic, evangelical (biblical), and ordered, in contrast to Anabaptists and "enthusiasts." Similar visitations and new orders were being carried through in other states in addition to Electoral Saxony.[29]

This development was deflected temporarily and the whole situation altered by two factors. (1) The concluding address of the Second Diet of Speyer (1529) instructed the states to implement the decisions of the Edict of Worms against the reformers. This reversed the formulary of the First Diet of Speyer (1526), which left enforcement of the Edict to the consciences of the princes and town councils. Only one elector, four secular princes, and fourteen cities protested the action. (2) The first call of Charles V for the Diet of Augsburg demanded defense of their position from the Protestants.

This situation posed the greatest danger so far to the Reformation cause; the possibility of putting down the heresy by political and military force seemed at hand. Common danger demanded political alliance by the evangelical states for survival, but who were to be included and what was to be the common statement of faith? Were the cities to be included along with the princes? They were among the first states to become evangelical, but their independence, hostility to bishops, republican political sensitivities, and concern for the community represented a Reformation different from that of the princes.[30] If the cities were included,[31] did this extend to Strassburg and the Swiss? Then, what would be the common statement of faith, since the new "churches" had been slow or hesitant to formulate confessional statements?[32]

While these issues were being mulled over, further instructions from the emperor, more irenic in tone, seemed to promise a place for open discussion of religious matters that might lead to legal recognition of the Reformation movement. Although Charles had not changed his attitude toward reform, and imperial issues were low on his dynastic priorities,[33] the Lutherans heard an offer of peace, politically and ecclesiastically. This was a strong appeal. In view of the disorder aroused by peasants, "enthusiasts," and Anabaptists, as well as weaknesses revealed by the visitations, order was needed. A new emphasis on office and regular order[34] was required, because the maintenance of order against the radicals was difficult when the magisterium-approved reforms were themselves irregular. The reforms had been carried through without episcopal approval and in opposition to episcopal supervision; according to imperial law, they were revolutionary actions.[35]

At this point, Electoral Saxony determined on a political move to gain legal recognition of reform in exchange for reintroduction or recognition of episcopal authority. Leadership was taken by Chancellor Brück, Melanchthon, the princes, Jonas, and Luther (the latter sometimes hesitatingly). It was a Saxon policy at first; the plan was not immediately convincing to Philip of Hesse, or to the cities that were all more or less strongly anti–episcopal. For Saxony—according to Maurer—the plan was overcompensation for the "revolutionary" reform.[36]

The first articulation of the new political move was the several statements of the Torgau Articles. The ordering and content of two of the Torgau documents is especially significant.[37] Document A begins with general comments on "the doctrines and ordinances of men." Assurance was given that the elector had not opposed customary church ordinances (although of human institution) because they could be observed without opposing the Holy Spirit. These ordinances were kept for "the sake of peace."[38] There were other human ordinances that could not be observed without sin. Then follow three brief sections: "Of the Marriage of Priests," "Of Both Forms," and "Of the Mass." These are followed by an article on confession and by two notable articles on episcopal jurisdiction and ordination. There is a most explicit statement that because of these ordinances (whose observance would involve sin) ministerial candidates of evangelical conviction could not and must not seek ordination from the bishops:

> Likewise because the bishops burden the priests with such oaths, as they cannot observe without sin, viz., not to preach this doctrine and not to be married, ordination cannot be sought from them; for such an oath is contrary to God, and we must obey God rather than men, as also the canons prescribe that the bishops are to be deserted who compel men to act contrary to God.[39]

Document B has the same ordering of articles in its first part: Article 1, "Of Both Forms in the Sacrament," Article 2, "Of the Marriage of Priests," and Article 3, "Of the Mass." Again these are presented as practices to which evangelical pastors or ordinands cannot subscribe (except by sinning). The next article is on ordination. Here the conclusion is even stronger than in Document A. Bishops were to give up demanding subscription to these godless practices and godless doctrines. If they did not, they were to be overthrown, and ordination granted in some *becoming way other than by the bishop*:

> There can be no better means for unity in these matters, than for the bishops to discontinue the oath and obligation, whereby, they bind those whom they ordain to godless doctrine and to a life without marriage; for thus they would remain in their dignity and government, and would obtain priests enough. But *if they will not discontinue them, they must be utterly overthrown.* For what is now taught and what is now arranged are of the same nature; and they will not burden themselves with such heathenish, dangerous and godless doctrine. And it will at last come to this, viz., that ordination will not be asked or received of bishops, *but as is otherwise becoming.*[40]

The language could not be more explicit. There is no suggestion of the necessity of episcopal ordination for valid ordination. An appropriate, orderly ordination will be sought by the evangelicals—without benefit of bishops. The language is remarkably similar to a lament by Luther in a letter of December 1530, regretting the lack of pastors and the need to ordain by an appropriate form: "*Magna ubique penuria fidelium pastorum ita ut prope sit, quo cogemur proprio ritu ordinare seu instituere ministros.*"[41] This language is a clear non–episcopal "*rite vocatus.*"

Document C defines the power of the keys as a spiritual, not secular, office, which consists of preaching the gospel, absolution, and administration of the sacraments. It is really the ministry of the Word as such and is not related to particular grades such as episcopacy or papacy. "This alone is to be the office of bishops *or* priests...."[42] "The Pope has no more power in the use of the keys than every other pastor...."[43] Maurer writes that nowhere had there been such a massive, radical critique of episcopal jurisdiction.[44]

The significance of the Torgau Articles—according to Maurer—is that they are the nucleus of the compromise plan the Saxons took to Augsburg. Put simply, that plan offered acceptance of limited jurisdiction of bishops in exchange for recognition of evangelical practices regarding communion in both kinds, the mass, and priestly marriage.[45] Without the recognition of these three matters there could be no reintroduction of episcopal jurisdiction (and a restricted jurisdiction, at that). The compromise plan was built into the second part of the CA and its principles governed the actions of the Saxon party at Augsburg. CA 28 is the evangelical concession in the compromise.

The Saxon preparations for the diet were more thorough than those of the other evangelical states. Where these states least followed the Saxon policy was at the point of episcopal jurisdiction. Philip of Hesse protested its restoration already on March 27, 1530.[46]

Nürnberg regarded the claims of the bishop of Bamberg to be fully broken, but it feared that at the diet he would seek to make restitution of episcopal power the condition for discussing matters of faith. On May 7, Nürnberger preachers, reviewing the whole situation, recommended complete rejection of episcopal jurisdiction.[47] Margrave George of Brandenburg–Ansbach, with a long–standing quarrel over the claims of the bishops of Würzburg and Bamberg, asked advice from the pastors.[48] The *Gutachten* of the Franconian pastors affirmed the right of secular authority to reform the church and to abolish the inherited episcopal power. They argued that according to Scripture there is no qualitative difference between the bishop and pastor, and the bishop has no special power of ordination.[49] The bishop has no legal power of ruling; his only power is the Word—which stands not at his disposal, but is to be preached. Again, the called servants of the Word are "*episcopi seu pastores.*"[50]

The final form of the confession at Augsburg included more, of course, than the compromise plan. Its content was partly determined by the atmosphere at Augsburg. Eck had come intent on pressing the most damning case against the reformers. His method was to take extreme statements from Luther and others out of context and place them in juxtaposition with statements by Zwingli, Anabaptists, and enthusiasts. Everyone was lumped together, including religious radicals and those promoting disorder and rebellion. Lutheran views thus led to the rejection of sacraments, catholic doctrine, and ordered ministry; they ended in civil disorder.[51]

Melanchthon needed not only to establish that Lutherans were catholic in doctrine; he had to exclude from the label "Lutheran" everything to the left—Zwingli, Anabaptists, peasants, and civil disorder. Hence the references in the CA especially to the Anabaptists. This situation coincided precisely with the time when Saxony was beginning to prosecute Anabaptists. A letter by Melanchthon (1530) dealing with the Anabaptists is summarized in this way by Oyer: "Melanchthon replied that all Anabaptists were to be treated with utmost severity, no matter how blameless they might appear. All Anabaptists rejected some of their civil duty; and if they were indulged by the magistracy, they took advantage of leniency to build upon seditious ideas until they actually provoked insurrection."[52] Melanchthon then drew a connection between the Anabaptists, the Zwickau prophet Storch, Müntzer, and the peasants' revolt. He "was certain that revolution was their (the Anabaptists') ultimate goal irrespective of pious pretension or peaceful bearings."[53] He regretted his earlier mildness in opposing the elector's desire to put Storch to death, and he criticized Brenz's much milder evaluation of the Anabaptists.

There was much talk at Augsburg about the disorderly peasants as well—political rebellion. And Melanchthon was no friend of the peasants. He was more severe in attitude to both peasants and Anabaptists than was Luther. This background helps to explain the highly conservative character of the CA.

The actual proceedings at Augsburg need not detain us. Melanchthon clung doggedly to the compromise plan but allowed more and more concessions to Rome. On July 4 he wrote to Campeggio, modifying the plan by offering obedience to the Roman church and the papacy, respect for the hierarchy, and assurance of the agreement of the teachings of the CA with the Roman church. The conditions required for the obedience would be minor, involving insignificant ritual matters.[54] Maurer calls this action a total distortion and inversion of the Saxon plan, thus hopelessly discrediting the whole policy.[55] In fact, Rome's response to Campeggio indicates that there was never the slightest possibility of the plan succeeding. The whole program underlying the second part of the CA was really a dead letter when presented. By the end of August the plan was clearly shattered.

The question of episcopal jurisdiction was at the center of the ensuing criticism of Melanchthon and Brück. On August 29, Philip of Hesse sent instructions to his advisors in Augsburg and a letter of complaint to Luther in which he attacked the Saxon policy thoroughly. Giving authority to the bishops would bring the gospel to an end. *("...die Bischöf, über unser Prediger Richter sein lassen, die sie ohn Zweifel mit lange leiden wurden, so wurde dardurch das Evangelium niddergerruckt und die alten Missbrauch widderumb ufgericht, welchs wir gar keins wegs gemeint oder gesinnt sein anzunehmen."*[56]) The theologians from Hesse took a similar stand; observing the absence of a true gift for office among the bishops, they remarked that the sheep of Christ would be thrown to the wolves again.[57]

The margrave of Brandenburg was also strongly anti–episcopal, but did not join the anti–Saxon criticism because he was too dependent on Saxony politically. The Lüneberg delegation joined in the criticism, however. Nürnberg's leaders were especially critical. Hieronymus Baumgärtner, an old friend of Melanchthon, wrote that no one at Augsburg had done more damage to the evangelical cause than Melanchthon.[58] Lazarus Spengler wrote to Luther that presentation, examination, and approval of pastors by the bishops would lead to an uprooting of the gospel, so that finally no evangelical pastors would be left.[59] Finally, Matthäus Alber of Reutlingen wrote that revived episcopal authority would give *"dem antichristen das sceptrum wider in die hand."* How, he asked, can they recognize as shepherds those who have shed blood like wolves? The time before a general council was called would be used to stamp out the evangelicals.[60]

Thus by the end of the negotiations at Augsburg, the states signing the CA (with the exception of electoral Saxony) had all disavowed the compromise plan, and had—in effect—rejected the second part of the Augustana insofar as bishops were concerned. Maurer writes of the end of the Diet: "Die Bishchöfe erscheinen als die blutigen Tyrannen, die die Predigt des Evangeliums verfolgen; die Unterwerfung unter ihre Iurisdiktion bedeutet die Verleungnung des Evangeliums und den Verzicht auf seine Ausbreitung."

INTERPRETATION OF CA 28

We examine now the text of CA 28, keeping in mind two observations by Maurer: (1) it is not an article of doctrine (*"daß CA kein Lehrartikel ist; weniger noch als anderswo können hier verbindliche dogmatische Erklärungen erwartet werden"*) but a program of negotiation; and

(2) the teaching on the two kingdoms provides the theological basis of the program.[61] We recognize that Document C of the Torgau Articles was expanded into CA 28 and that the most basic meaning of the article is the proper separation of the spiritual and temporal realms. The spiritual realm is the power of the keys and it must be carefully set off from temporal power. The article constitutes a fundamental critique of the whole medieval confusion of the spiritual and the temporal: of the church's use of temporal power to establish its authority and influence. The church had also distorted the power of the keys by introducing demands that were in excess of or opposed to the Word of God; these were then laid on the conscience as necessary for salvation. Two-thirds of the article is devoted to enumerating the burdens the bishops had placed on the people, which exceeded what is commanded by the Word. Thus the article—while recognizing the bishop—consists almost totally of a critique and corrective of ecclesiastical power—specifically episcopal power. (It is important to recognize that it is the whole regimen of the papal church that was being questioned, but the compromise plan demanded that it be posed in terms of the office of bishop).

The corrective was stated carefully by defining the power of the keys. This consists of "the power or command of God to preach the gospel, to remit and retain sins, and to administer the sacraments."[62] "This power is exercised only by teaching or preaching the gospel and by ministering the sacraments either to many or to individuals depending on one's calling."[63] It is briefly elaborated on as the ministry of Word and Sacrament, forgiveness, rejection of doctrine contrary to the gospel, and excommunication (excluding "from the fellowship of the Church ungodly persons whose wickedness is known").[64] This description is given when commenting on the jurisdiction of bishops. This, of course, is also the description of ministry in CA 5. Thus the power of the keys is nothing different than the understanding of *Predigtamt* in contradistinction to a priesthood of sacrifice, which had been fundamental to Lutheran teaching from 1519, with Luther's new understanding of Word and faith. Just this distinction was articulated clearly in article 13 of the Apology, where the ministry of Word, Sacrament, and forgiveness is described as the ministry contrasted with the priesthood of sacrifice. ("Thus priests are not called to make sacrifices that merit forgiveness of sins for the people, as in the Old Testament, but they are called to preach the Gospel and minister the sacraments to the people.")[65]

Since we must conclude that the power of the keys is the ministry of Word and Sacrament, then the statement (in the German version) that "According to divine right, therefore, it is the office of bishop to preach the Gospel, forgive sins, etc."[66] cannot refer to a *de jure* understanding of episcopacy and episcopal power.[67] It can only refer to the ministry of the Word as divinely instituted, as the next sentence makes explicit: "All this is to be done not by human power but by God's word alone."

Most decisive in understanding this matter is the full statement of Torgau Articles Document C, which includes this crucial passage:

> Thus the power of the keys is now only spiritual government, the preaching of the Gospel, the reproof and forgiveness of sins, and the administration of the sacraments. This alone is to be the office of *bishops or priests*.[68]

This section concludes by maintaining:

> ...since the keys are nothing else than the preaching of the Gospel and the administration of the sacraments, *the Pope has no more power in the use of the keys than any other pastor*.[69]

Thus CA 28 is affirming the *Predigtamt*—the one office of Word and Sacrament. It is recognizing bishops but, in fact, ascribes nothing peculiar to the episcopal office and power. There is no description of supervision, of the responsibility for ordination—only what is common to the *Predigtamt*.

The Lutheran position became explicit in the Smalcald Articles and the Treatise on the Power and Primacy of the Pope. In the latter, Melanchthon wrote:

> The Gospel requires of those who preside over the churches that they preach the Gospel, remit sins, administer the sacraments, and in addition, exercise jurisdiction, that is, excommunicate those who are guilty of notorious crimes and absolve those who repent...it is evident that this power belongs by divine right to all who preside over the churches, whether they are called *pastors, presbyters, or bishops*.[70]

Melanchthon then referred to the opinion of Jerome that the grades of ministry are by human, not divine authority.

Ordination is not a right restricted to bishops, although formerly this power was the main distinction between bishop and pastor.

> But since this distinction between bishop and pastor is not by divine right, it is manifest that ordination administered by a pastor

in his own church is valid by divine right. Consequently, when the regular bishops become enemies of the Gospel and are unwilling to administer ordination, the churches retain the right to ordain for themselves. For wherever the church exists, the right to administer the Gospel also exists. Wherefore it is necessary for the church to retain the right of calling, electing, and ordaining ministers.[71]

A similar explication was given by Melanchthon in the *Loci Communes* of 1555. He responded to the question that had been raised about whether ordination without sanction or consecration by bishops is valid.

Although the name and title of the bishops and the custom with regard to the consecration be kept, it is nevertheless basically invalid to create in the unintelligent a hallucination. The *persecutors* of the gospel are *not bishops* [italics in original] and should be regarded as exiled (cf. Galatians 1:6–24). The ceremony of the consecration, as customarily practiced by bishops, is wrong and full of error, in the same way as masses for the dead and the consecration and transubstantiation of the bread.

But there is a true way of maintaining the vocation and confirmation, or consecration, of preachers. St. Paul ordered Titus to arrange for and to ordain priests here and there in the cities. From this it is clear that true shepherds of souls are commanded, when preachers and shepherds of souls are needed, to obtain in the churches qualified persons and ordain and confirm them laying on of hands and prayer.[72]

For Melanchthon there was a succession, but it was doctrinal and not episcopal. In the major work *De Ecclesia et autoritate verbi dei* he wrote:

These words seriously warn us that we should not think of the church as though it were a worldly state and that we should not measure it by the succession of bishops or by the rank and place of pontiffs, but we should hold that the church is to be found among those who retain the true doctrine of the gospel.[73]

A few paragraphs later he added that we must not think carnally

and imagine that the church is a state of pontifs and which bind it to the regular succession of bishops, just as empires consist of the regular succession of princes. But the church is constituted in another manner. For its assembly is not bound to regular succession, but to the word of God. The church is born again where God restores the doctrine and confers the Holy Spirit. Paul in Ephesians witnesses that in this manner churches are guided and preserved and not by ordinary succession.[74]

Fraenkl explains that ordinary succession meant for Melanchthon having a "legal" ecclesiastical claim, not a sacramental or salvific reality. "On the contrary, though he knew the sacramental character attributed to this succession by Roman theologians, he saw in it the very opposite of a vehicle of grace."

The meaning was doctrinal succession, not episcopal succession, and for Melanchthon doctrinal succession involved a whole view of the church. The church began at creation with Adam. It is a reality brought into existence in history by the Word of God; it did not begin as something instituted by Christ. Since the church is the life of a people in history, the succession is not a direct line, but a zig-zag. Over and over again the church has been unfaithful to the Word, and the true church may be a suffering remnant. Yet the church is visible; were this not so, its catholicity would be undermined. The Word is constantly renewed and judging the church. Melanchthon paid great tribute to the early church (a kind of consensus of the first five centuries), but in it, too, there was error. The Word, not the authority of the church, must be the judge. Melanchthon spoke of the church as a *coetus scholasticus* to suggest that doctrinal transmission resembles the transmission of learning. Doctrine, however, includes living proclamation of the Word and not merely *"reine Lehre."* Nonetheless, the very conception contributes to a later scholastic view of doctrine as propositional truths.[75]

ANGLICAN EPISCOPACY AND RELATIONS WITH OTHER CHURCHES

As we turn to Lambeth it seems fitting to tarry a bit longer in the sixteenth century and provide some background for nineteenth-century developments. Basic to the English settlement was the "godly prince," who made possible the reformation, and with the model of the Old Testament godly ruler, became head of the church and a substitute for the papacy. The prince enabled retention of episcopacy, but the new church was basically reformed, as evidenced by the understanding of the church in the *Articles*. As in the Augustana and Calvin's *Institutes*, the church was defined as a congregation of the faithful where the pure word is preached and the sacraments duly administered (art. 19). Again, consistent with Luther and Calvin, the church has power to deal with faith and practices (ceremonies) but never contrary to the Word of God (art. 20). There was recognition, of course, of the common evangelical concerns of English and continental churches. For example, Cranmer sought a consensus in addressing Calvin, Melanchthon, and Bullinger in the hopes of a synod where agreement could be reached on the sacrament and other doctrinal matters (significantly, the question was not one of order).[76]

The Puritans raised the issue of order as well as ceremonies, and Whitgift and Jewell defended the episcopacy for its universality and long history in the church. Yet succession was significant for doctrine rather than person or place. Jewell argued: "Succession, you say, is the chief way for any Christian man to avoid antichrist. I grant you, if you mean the succession of doctrine."[77] Moreover, Whitgift maintained that there is equality of ministry regarding Word and Sacrament, and Jewell was clear that in Scripture, bishop and priest are one—a position maintained by the fathers as well.[78] The distinction between bishop and priest was a matter or orderliness and custom in the church (especially in respect to ordination); it did not exist "by the truth of God's ordinance".[79]

Hooker's notable defense against the Puritans (so important for the emergence of Anglicanism) was marked above all by a significant biblical interpretation, shared in part by Whitgift. Most basic to his critique of Cartwright was the insistence upon the distinction between doctrine and practice with respect to biblical authority.[80] The Scriptures are forever valid and authoritative in doctrine—in all that is necessary for salvation. The revelation given in Scripture concerns the doctrine of salvation and ethical demands. Order, practice, and ceremonies—these matters are relative to the New Testament times. They are not forever binding in the church. With great historical perception Hooker recognized that there is not a full presentation in the New Testament of all the practice of the early church, and, besides, there are different stages within the New Testament development itself.[81] The scholar cannot, therefore, deduce from the New Testament one binding church order. Not only is the *New Testament* not unified (because it was responding to changing situations), but in the history of the *church*, changing situations demand changes in practice. Order and practice are established not only by appeal to Scripture, but to reason and tradition (history) as well. "Even so, the necessity of polity and regiment in all churches may be held without holding any one certain form to be necessary in them all."[82] Yet Hooker believed that the church has been ruled by bishops since apostolic times—but episcopal origin is apostolic and not dominical.[83]

In the early seventeenth century a different understanding of episcopacy was articulated. In the face of aggressive critique from Puritans and Geneva, as well as from the Roman church, a *de jure* doctrine of episcopacy was developed by Saravia, Bilson, Bramhall, Taylor and others. It maintains a divinely ordered distinction between bishop and presbyter. Episcopacy is of divine appointment, necessary for the church. It ranks among the *credenda* of the church. Succession is necessary in government as well as in doctrine. Bishop Hall wrote, "...that government whose foundation is laid by Christ, and whose fabric is raised by the apostles, is of divine institution."[84] There is thus a direct succession from Christ, through the apostles and the fathers, to present bishops.

Even so explicit a doctrine could be modified, however. So Bramhall and Hall did by distinguishing between the essence and the perfection of the church. For the former, episcopacy was not absolutely necessary, but for the latter it was. This distinction helped the Caroline divines to continue recognizing the ministries and churches of the continental Reformation.

Lancelot Andrewes wrote:

> Nevertheless if our form be of divine right, it doth not follow from thence that there is no salvation without it, or that a church cannot exist without it. He is blind who does not see churches consisting without it; he is hardhearted who denieth them salvation.[85]

At the same time he wrote to Peter Du Moulin:

> You ask whether your churches have sinned in the matter of divine authority. I did not say that. I said only that your churches lacked something which is of divine authority; but the fault is not yours but that of the evil of the times.[86]

The last clause was consistently a basis for recognizing the foreign churches—circumstances prevented their adoption of episcopacy.

Especially pertinent for this dialogue is the following observation of Archbishop Laud:

> For in Sweden they retain both the thing and the name; and the governors of their churches are, and are called, bishops. And among other Lutherans the thing is retained, though not the name. For instead of bishops they are called superintendents, and instead of archbishops, general superintendents. And yet even here too these names differ more in sound than in sense. For bishop is the same in Greek that superintendent is in Latin. Nor is this change

45

very well liked by the learned. However, Luther, since he would change the name, yet did very wisely that he would leave the thing, and make choice of such a name as was not altogether unknown to the ancient church.[87]

This quotation raises a significant question. Does episcopacy consist primarily in function rather than in succession?

On the basis of this recognition of foreign churches there is evidence that at least two continental ministers with presbyterian ordination held benefices in the Church of England without re–ordination.[88]

The relations with continental churches took distinctly different forms in the eighteenth century and involved Lutherans in particular. I begin first, however, with the correspondence and policies of Archbishop Wake. He wrote to various continental churches and their leaders, recommending a policy of intercommunion when church members were present in the other land; for example, English persons communing in Dutch and Swiss churches, and Dutch and Swiss communing in English churches.[89] In some sense this grew out of the response by Oxford University to the church at Geneva, which felt that, at an academic exercise there, aspersions had been cast on the Swiss church. Both the complaint and the response expressed respect for the order of the other church (although the Oxford response lamented the lack of episcopacy at Geneva).[90]

Anglican-Lutheran relations in India were the result of the new Protestant foreign missionary zeal. Developing out of the sending of German Lutheran missionaries to the Danish colony of Tranquebar, eventually about sixty missionaries with Lutheran ordination served the S.P.C.K. from 1728–1825. As chaplains to the East India Co. they administered Word and Sacrament to Anglican Church members; more directly under S.P.C.K. auspices they served English, Indian, and Eurasian congregations. The sacraments were celebrated, and the Book of Common Prayer and the Anglican Catechism used, although Lutheran services of worship were also used. The Lutheran missionaries also ordained native Indians with full approval of the S.P.C.K.[91] The Church Missionary Society also used Lutheran (and Reformed) missionaries.[92]

In the American colonies there were especially close relations between the Swedish Lutherans and the Anglicans. There was common practice of intercommunion, frequent pulpit exchange, and even service by one minister in a congregation of the other church when there was a pastoral vacancy. Indeed, Acrelius wrote that "every

Swedish minister upon his return home received from the Society in London (S.P.G.) thirty pounds sterling for the services which he had performed among the English churches here."[93] Intercommunion and pulpit exchange were less frequent between the German Lutherans and the Anglicans; nonetheless, Muhlenberg wrote:

> Our nearest and best friends and well wishers are the upright, pious teachers, elders and members of the established church....Their articles of faith have been extracted from the Word of God as well as ours....their explanations of their articles of faith are as good Evangelical Lutheran as one could wish them to be; in a word, the doctrines of the English established church are more closely allied to ours than those of any other denominations in the whole world.[94]

THE TRACTARIAN MOVEMENT

The tractarian movement confronts us with quite a different understanding of episcopacy from that which we have so far examined, especially after the varied and latitudinarian views of the eighteenth century. Writing of the origins of this movement, Storr rather simply and directly points to three factors: political, theological, and general.[95] Both the political and theological can be put fairly specifically. A series of acts reflective of an ascendant political liberalism—including the Roman Catholic Emancipation Act (1829), the Reform Bill of 1832, and the suppression of ten bishoprics of the Irish Church—was evidence that the state, with its liberal, secular values, did not recognize the integrity of the church—of its doctrine and its order. Keble's famous sermon at Oxford on "National Apostasy" was an outraged response to the suppression of the Irish sees, but it expressed deeper concerns about state interference in the life of the church when the state was no longer the "godly prince." The threat of and the response to theological liberalism cannot be pinpointed so nicely, but the threat was there. The development of "higher criticism" in Germany seemed to threaten biblical inspiration and revelation, as well as long-held beliefs on the miraculous. New theologies with starting points not in revelation, but in natural things—feelings or the moral sense— seemed to endanger theological or ecclesiastical orthodoxy. In England itself, the thought of men like Thomas Arnold constituted a liberalism that questioned the meaning of the church as a divine institution and made of both doctrine and institution a far more human affair. In addition there was the general threat from changes in the world: social, economic, educational, and, not least of all, from the impact of science and technology.

To some, at least, there seemed no adequate resources in the church to counter these threats. The evangelicals lacked an intellectual theology and institutional sense; the "Noetics" at the university did not perceive the seriousness of the theological issues; and the old high–church party was not relevant to the new issues.

The tractarians sought an authority in the church that could be a defense against these elements of the modern world. The doctrine of episcopacy seemed to supply the needed certainty. In the first of the *Tracts for the Times* this focus is evident.

It is plain then that he (the bishop) but *transmits;* and that the Christian ministry is a *succession.* And if we trace back the power of ordination from hand to hand, of course we shall come back to the apostles at last. We know we do, as a plain historical fact: and therefore all we, who have been ordained clergy, in the very form of our ordination acknowledged the doctrine of the *Apostolical succession.*

And for the same reason, we must necessarily consider none to be really ordained who have not *thus* been ordained.[96]

From this basic position follow three other points:

(1) that participation in the body and blood of Christ is essential for the maintenance of the Christian life and hope in each individual; (2) that this participation is communicated to individual Christians *only* by the hands of the Apostles' successors and their delegates; (3) that the successors of the Apostles are those who descend from them in "straight line by the imposition of hands, and that their delegates are the priests whom each has commissioned."[97]

How confident Newman was regarding the succession is evident from the following passages.

As to the fact of the Apostolical Succession, i.e., that our present Bishops are the heirs and representatives of the Apostles by successive transmission of the prerogative of being so that is too notorious to require proof. Every link in the chain is known from St. Peter to our present Metropolitans.

By reason of the Bishop's appointment of the Ministers of the Word, it is through him that the news of redemption and the means of grace come to all men. "I, who speak to you concerning Christ, was ordained to do so by the Bishop; he speaks in me—as Christ wrought in him and as God sent Christ. Thus the whole plan of salvation hangs together."[98]

With this view of succession, sacrament, and salvation, the tractarians could of course arrive only at a reinterpretation of the Thirty-Nine Articles—and of the sixteenth century—that minimized and criticized the Reformation elements. A further consequence was a quite different evaluation of continental ministries and sacraments. They could no longer be honored. Newman wrote:

With this reflection before us, does it not seem to be utter ingratitude to an astonishing Providence of God's mercy...to attempt unions with those who have separated from the Church, to break down the partition walls, and to argue as if religion were altogether and only a matter of each man's private concern?[99]

Brilioth speaks of the "static view of the church" that obtains in the Tractarian understanding of succession and tradition. The faith that is the "treasure and life of the church" is what is formulated in the Apostles' and Nicene Creeds. All other formulations are secondary. The faith had thus been defined once and for all in the early church.[100]

To return to the observation that political and theological liberalism were major stimuli for the emergence of Tractarianism, one may quote Froude from a letter of 1833.

His notion is, that the most important subject to which you can direct your reading at present is the meaning of canonical obedience, which we have all sworn to our Bishops; for this is likely to be the only support of Church Government, when the State refuses to support it.[101]

Newman wrote late in life that they "took refuge in *succesio apostolica* and all that goes with it, 'not only because these things were true and right but in order to shake off the State.'"

The threat of theological liberalism is put rather remarkably in the following passage from W. Palmer's *Treatise on the Church of Christ: Designed Chiefly for the Use of Students in Theology.*

I have spoken throughout of the foreign reformation as of a thing that has passed away. Lutheranism and Calvinism are indeed now little more than matters of history for the feeble and lifeless relics which they have left behind, and which still bear their names, are but painful memorials of systems whose imperfections and faults, whatever they might be, were dignified by a holy ardour and zeal for God and God's revelation....Overrun by the audacious impiety of neologism, an infidelity which clothes itself under the name of Christianity in order to inflict a more grievous wound on faith, or sunk into the deadly lumber of Socinian and Arian Apostasy, Lutheranism and Calvinism, as religious systems, seem to have nearly perished in the countries where they arose.[102]

Most illuminating of the threat of theological liberalism is the intellectual odyssey of Pusey. Early in his career at Oxford he became interested in the writings that attacked Christian doctrines of revelation and biblical inspiration, as he had earlier been attentive to the arguments on Christian evidences. He began to confront the "higher criticism" from Germany. He sought resources to defend his theological and biblical orthodoxy, but found no help from the evangelicals, the old high–church policy, or even from his mentor Lloyd (who was still using Paley). How to battle unbelief? He determined to study in Germany for "the critical and scientific part of divinity." There he met disillusionment. The very scholars who were to be the defenders of orthodoxy had themselves given up belief in the miraculous. Yet he found resources: Schleiermacher's theology of feeling (although Pusey regarded him as a virtual pantheist), Tholuck and his theology of experience, and the mediating theologians. He returned from Germany believing that he could bring science (biblical scholarship) and piety together.[103] He subscribed to the interpretation given by the mediating theologians to the relation between Luther, orthodoxy, pietism, and rationalism in Lutheranism. In fact such a view was important to two volumes he published on German theology. Then came disenchantment. Those whose views he had championed he came to regard as rationalists. The outcome of biblical science could only be a human system unconnected to the inspired minds of the biblical authors. His definition of religious rationalism included "all who would make the historical and critical study of Scripture the foundation of their divinity."[104]

The new answer he found was in the fathers. In the patristic allegorical understanding of Scripture he found its spiritual meaning and unity. This became the point of contact with the Tractarian movement, but it also brought him to an "ecclesiastical authoritarianism."[105]

There seems justification for the following evaluation by Brilioth.

One may therefore be fully justified in assuming that it was the pressure of the political situation, as above described, more than anything else—the necessity of finding a firm and unshakable foundation for a theory of the Church which could defy the assaults of the age, something objective in the deepest sense to put as a breakwater against what was regarded as the inundation of liberal subjectivism, and also a short watchword as a signal and a standard in the hourly struggle—which made them catch at the principle of Apostolic Succession, sever it from the complex of ideas which gives it its correct import, and give it a formulation, the somewhat violent simplification of which was made possible by the absence of all disposition to a critical view of history. So it was strategic rather than religious reasons which gave the idea of Apostolical Succession its dominant place in the static Church conception of Neo–Anglicanism.[106]

LUTHERAN AND ROMAN CATHOLIC DEVELOPMENTS

Hermelink—in a major work on modern church history—has identified parallel reactions to modern thought in Roman Catholicism and Lutheranism.[107] In resisting the aftermath of the Enlightenment, secularization, and nineteenth-century liberalism, Catholicism returned to curialism, papal ultramontanism, and emphasis on the priestly order. Lutheranism resisted the same forces with an attachment to an earlier definition of doctrine.[108] In both instances, what was sought was a place of objective truth, certainty, and authority. In one case it was found in papal infallibility, in another in a doctrine including infallible Scriptures. Was not the Tractarian appeal to apostolic succession a comparable response?

There are significant parallels in nineteenth-century Lutheranism to the Anglican developments already sketched. Here, too, one may perceive a threat from the state as well as a threat from modern thought and theology. The attempt of the Prussian king in 1817 to effect religious unity in his land by an imposed union of the Lutheran and Reformed churches, with a changed church order, called forth resistance. Among Lutherans, especially, the response involved a renewed sense of Lutheran identity in contrast to confessional indifference (one thinks of Klaus Harms' *95 Theses*); it could also take the form of separatism—the separation of orthodox Lutherans from rationalistic or unionist state churches. The threat from modern thought was, at first, simply the older rationalism in and outside the church.

One response was a new pietism called the *Erweckungsbewegung,* whose most notable theologian was Tholuck (to whom Pusey was attracted).[109] He was given a professorship at Halle in order to oppose the dominant rationalism there. He himself had an awakening experience, and the experience of regeneration became the center of his theology, which was primarily concerned with sin and grace: scriptural teaching corresponds to the human situation and the need of rebirth; this situation is a kind of proof of divine revelation. Tholuck saw in Kant, Fichte, Schleiermacher, and the romantics—with their attention to an area of moral responsibility and religious feeling separated from the quantitative realm of causation—elements of thought that he could relate to an experiential theology of sin and grace. His theological writings consisted mainly of biblical commentaries that were scholarly and edifying. His theology was no narrow confessionalism; he had little interest in the confessional writings.

There was a stimulus, however, from Tholuck and the Awakening that merged with the reaction to the Prussian Union, producing a Lutheran theology that tried to reject much modern thought by returning to seventeenth-century scholasticism. Perhaps the most influential figure was Hengstenberg,[110] who was not at first so self–consciously Lutheran, but who, in bringing together pietism and orthodoxy, always had as a central goal the opposition to rationalism. He saw his task as rooting out all "rationalistic" or modern influences in theology, including those stemming from Schleiermacher and the mediating theologians. The enemy was especially the new critical biblical scholarship, for central to his thought was a rigid biblical literalism and the conflict between Scripture (revelation) and reason. He sought in the Scriptures and the doctrine of the church a certainty and objectivity that could withstand the vagaries of modern thought.

There were, in fact, a large number of theologians sharing in general a return to the theology of the seventeenth-century Lutheran dogmaticians.[111] The heart of their theology was the doctrine of verbal inspiration of Scripture, which they regarded as the Lutheran doctrine of revelation. They rejected all historical-critical study of Scripture. This theology included a wide range of the characteristic Lutheran dogmatic positions of the seventeenth century. Out of many names, I mention only two. Heinrich Schmid was the author of the *Doctrinal Theology of the Evangelical Lutheran Church: Exhibited and Verified from the Original Sources,* basically a compilation of what was taught by the orthodox Lutheran dogmaticians. It was used in various Lutheran seminaries in America as recently as a few decades ago. Wilhelm Löhe[112] represented the more churchly side of this theology. He regarded seventeenth century scholastic theology as "a step in advance of the confessions," said that "dogmatics is above history" (like Manning's "dogma is above history"), and held that the essence of the Christian life consists of such acts as confirmation, absolution, the Lord's Supper and ordination.[113]

This kind of theology stamped American Lutheranism (with few exceptions) from 1850 on. In an extreme form one church leader had not only the highest regard for the power of the pastor and the superintendent, but regarded only members of orthodox Lutheran congregations as really sure of salvation. For most Lutherans, intercommunion and pulpit fellowship were a form of evil. For most Lutherans the goal was to build a *"rechtgläubiges Zion."* Most would have judged Muhlenberg and his associates harshly for their "unionism." An illustration especially appropriate to this dialogue is the Episcopal experience of ecumenical conversations accompanying the Chicago Quadrilateral. Presbyterians and Lutherans were approached in "dialogue." The conversations with the former lasted for some years and broke down over the question of order. The conversations with the latter continued only a short time and broke down over doctrine; the Lutherans wished to make the Augsburg Confession and not the Quadrilateral the starting point of discussion.[114] For Lutherans today to have responded to the Lutheran–Episcopal Dialogue in the way they have done constitutes a tremendous shift in attitude and practice.

Different Anglican theologians repeatedly refer to scholarship and an approach to and study of history as characteristic of Anglicanism. It is sometimes used as a point of difference with Roman Catholicism: historical scholarship vs. authority. Lutherans share a commitment to history and to historical method. What does this say to the question of dogma, to the search for objectivity, certainty, and authority? What does it say to *episcopal* and *doctrinal* succession?[115]

In an essay in volume six of the Lutheran–Roman Catholic Dialogue, Burgess[116] surveyed the background of Vatican I in terms of resistance both to modern thought and political liberalism. The method was increased centralization of power in the papacy, to control theological thought and ecclesiastical practice as rigidly as possible. Although this included breaking down the quasi–autonomy of national developments such as Gallicanism, the enemy was primarily modern thought, since that might encroach on theology and life and practice in the church. The secularized state was also a threat. Neothomism became the thought pattern on which various control systems were based. "According to this way of thinking, truth tends to be clear and static; there is little place for change and historical thinking. To know God is to know the doctrines that he has revealed. Where can these doctrines be found? The answer is: in Scripture and tradition, and the Roman Catholic Church preserves and teaches these doctrines." [117] The dogma of 1854, the "Syllabus of Errors," and the dogma of papal infallibility—these are defensive moves against modern thought and life. They are forms of a reactionary resistance, but they raise the question of whether they were necessary. Must Vatican I be a timeless model for the church?[118]

This survey raises a larger question, namely of the struggle in ecumenical discussion to deal with issues formulated in the defensive posture of the church in the nineteenth century. Put differently, must not the understanding of catholicity be expressed more in terms of mission, responsibility to the world, and ethical community—an apostolicity of the people of God moved by God's Word rather than one restricted to doctrine and order?

3

TEACHING AUTHORITY IN THE CHURCH: THE GOSPEL, THE CHURCH, AND THE ROLE OF BISHOPS— SOME ANGLICAN REFLECTIONS

BY

JOHN H. RODGERS, JR.

INTRODUCTION

As one begins an essay for this third round of Lutheran–Episcopal Dialogue, one can't help but give thanks for the distance we have traveled together, for the unity that we have discerned in the substantial matters we have discussed, and for the prayers and urgings that accompany us and our labors from around the world (i.e., the International Anglican–Lutheran Discussions Report of 1972, the Report of the Anglican–Lutheran Joint Working Group, and the words of the presidential address of the archbishop of Canterbury on the occasion of Luther's 500th anniversary; the strongest urging, of course, comes to us from the dominical and apostolic words of Holy Scripture). Surely we have every good reason to be expectant of God's provision and guidance for us in the days ahead.

The purpose of this essay is to sketch the way teaching authority is conceived and functions in the Episcopal church, and to discuss in particular the place of the bishop(s) in the exercise of that authority.

COMMON GROUND

The Gospel

If we take 1 Cor. 15:1–11 as a clear, early statement of the apostolic gospel—or, as the apostle calls it, "the gospel," which he claims all the apostles preached (1 Cor. 15:1, 3, 11)—several factors stand out:

(1) There are certain historical features or facts that are essential to the gospel, such as Jesus and his suffering, death, burial, resurrection, and appearances to specific witnesses. These features are simply given "once for all."

(2) There are theological assertions about these facts, such as "Christ died for our sins," and "the gospel." The message of the gospel involves apostolic teaching as well as historical facts centering in the meaning of the death and resurrection of Jesus.

(3) There are witnesses mentioned. The Old Testament Scriptures witness to and find their fulfillment in the gospel. The gospel records events that happened "in accordance with the scriptures," thus the biblical tradition itself is a witness to the gospel. In addition, the apostles themselves were witnesses, indeed, eyewitnesses of these things and became proclaimers of the gospel by the words they preached, taught, and wrote. Thus the gospel took written shape, forming the center and chief part of the apostolic or New Testament writings, which were later recognized as the second part of the canon of the church, through which Christ by his Spirit exercised that authority in heaven and on earth that had been committed to him until the end of the ages.

(4) The authority of the gospel is referred to in the words, "through which also you are being saved," and "of first importance," and also "so you have come to believe." Lutherans and Anglicans have referred to this as the Word of God heard and believed in the power of the Spirit. The gospel's authority is not an authority that can be objectively proven or externally enforced, but must be personally perceived and heard in the heart by the grace of the same God who has, indeed, provided and offers the gospel.

From the above comments several things follow:

(a) There is fixed content to the gospel; there is only one apostolic gospel. It is a "given" in both the sense of being fixed and not to be changed, and also in the sense of given by grace.

(b) This gospel must be passed on, transmitted: "I handed on...what I in turn had received."

(c) There is a *hic et nunc* event of hearing and believing that is not passed on but is the authoritative saving work of the Spirit of God, giving and sustaining faith in the hearts of believers.

Since there are aspects of both transmission and encounter to the Word of God as gospel, these aspects ought not be opposed to one another, but should rather be seen as complementary aspects of the gracious coming of God to us in history, time, and space. To play the two against one another is wrong. To speak of the encounter, for example, without the content and transmission (or succession) is docetic; on the other hand, to speak of the content and transmission without the encounter in the Spirit is pelagian, formalistic, and often authoritarian.

The Church

What is true of the gospel is also true of the community of the gospel, the church. The church has transmissive, objective, and institutional aspects, as well as believing and responsive aspects. On the one hand, it is true to say that the church is God's people as a community in history, moving through time in visible succession from apostolic origins. On the other hand, it is true to say that the church "happens" as faith is awakened and as brothers and sisters worship in faith, build one another up in love, hope, and common life, and reach out to their neighbors in mission and service. It would seem perverse to set these aspects against one another, and reductionistic to ignore either side. (The Lambeth Quadrilateral was an Anglican attempt to indicate the main lines of transmission or apostolic succession that are instrumentalities and means used by the Spirit of God to sustain, enable, and continue the church in its life, work, and history. The fact that these instruments of transmission constantly need to be locally expressed, adapted, interpreted, and made alive in the Spirit need not imply that they are without genuine significance. All of them—the canon, the creed, fixed liturgies for the sacraments, and the orders of ministry—bear evidence of historical development, and each contains a certain sheer "givenness" in the early church that is impossible to totally "rationalize." Their perseverance in the universal church speaks on their behalf as given by the Spirit and as expressive of the nature of the church, as well as being serviceable to the life, witness, and work of the community of the gospel, or so Anglicans believe and testify. The purpose of this essay is to indicate some of the reasons why Anglicans so testify in the sphere of the teaching office and the role of bishops.)

Teaching Authority

The church lives in fellowship with God by grace received in faith through the Word, as mediated in and through the means of grace made effective in the Spirit. There are the chief means of grace: preaching, teaching, and sacraments, and the informal ways the Spirit applies the law and gospel and exhortation to the hearts and lives of God's people.

Teaching authority in the church refers to what should be, and may be spoken in the name of God as official preaching and teaching of the church. It raises the question of the sources of such teaching, who may do such teaching, and how the church tests—and oversees—its teaching.

It seems to me that in the basic understanding of the gospel, the church, the means of grace, and teaching authority, Anglicans and Lutherans are generally speaking on common ground.

ANGLICAN APPROACHES TO TEACHING AUTHORITY

How does the Anglican church go about answering the question of, or exercising, doctrinal discipline? What role does the bishop play in that discipline? Is this a "better way," and, if so, why?

Ordination Vows

Ordination vows include the following statements:

FOR A DEACON AND FOR A PRIEST

The bishop says, "Will you be loyal to the doctrine, discipline, and worship of Christ as this Church has received them? And will you, in accordance with the canons of this Church, obey your bishop and other ministers who may have authority over you and your work?"

The Ordinand answers, "I am willing and ready to do so; and I solemnly declare that I do believe the Holy Scriptures of the Old and New Testaments to be the Word of God, and to contain all things necessary to salvation; and I do solemnly engage to conform to the doctrine, discipline, and worship of The Episcopal Church" (BCP 526, 538).

The Ordinand also signs the above in the presence of the congregation, and it is also signed by witnesses.

OF A BISHOP

The bishop-elect declares, "In the Name of the Father, and of the Son, and of the Holy Spirit, I, *N.N.*, chosen Bishop of the Church in *N.*, solemnly declare that I do believe the Holy Scriptures of the Old and New Testaments to be the Word of God, and to contain all things necessary to salvation; and I do solemnly engage to conform to the doctrine, discipline, and worship of The Episcopal Church."

The bishop-elect signs this statement in the presence of all, and witnesses also sign (BCP 513). Other churches in the Anglican communion all use similar vows.

From these vows it can be seen:

(1) That the Scriptures are held to be the canon of the Church's teaching.

(2) The central theme of the Scriptures is seen to be God's great work of redemption of sinners in and through the gospel, and

(3) There are books of common prayer, official canonical disciplines and stated doctrine of the ECUSA to which the ordinand promises to conform his or her life, doctrine, and loyalty.

Teaching authority, then, would inquire as to the faithful harmony or correspondence between the actual teaching of the teacher, preacher, or published statement and the Scriptures and the doctrine of the ECUSA.

Sources of Anglican Doctrine

One might rightly ask where such "official doctrine" is to be found. We can state the following sources:

(1) The Holy Scriptures of the Old and New Testaments.

(2) The teaching stated in or entailed by the public services in the BCP, the chief didactic or doctrinal parts of which would be the ecumenical and catholic creeds and the catechism.

(3) The Constitution and General Conventions' official teaching, found in statements of the General Convention of the ECUSA, as well as theological perspectives implied in the Constitution and canons of the ECUSA.

(4) The doctrinal ethos of the church, found in the "historical" section of the BCP. This section includes the chalcedonian definitions, the Athanasian Creed, the Thirty–Nine Articles, the Preface to the 1549 *Book of Common Prayer*, and the Chicago and Lambeth Quadrilateral statements.

(5) Weighty public pronouncements. These include such things as the various statements of the several Lambeth Conferences, as well as a classic study entitled "Doctrine in the Church of England," a report of a commission presided over by Archbishop William Temple from 1922–37.

(6) Influential theological writings. Influential writings include those of the early fathers of the church, Reformation writers, the great

Tractarian writers, both Anglican and non–Anglican contemporary theologians, as well as other contemporary scholars.

Characteristics of Anglican Theology

If one were to look for characteristic motifs in the Anglican doctrinal ethos emerging from the above sources, one might characterize Anglican theology as gospel-centered, credal, and associated with the best scholarship and cultural knowledge of the day. (See "Appendix D" at the end of this essay.)

The following quotations from "Doctrine in the Church of England" illustrate these characteristics. They refer to the authority of Scripture and to the nature of assent to the doctrinal formularies of the church. First, with reference to the authority of "the Bible as a whole" (pp. 31–32):

> The Bible possesses authority for Christians on the ground that it is the classical literature of that progressive self–revelation of God in history which culminated in Jesus Christ.
>
> The Bible has been and is for the Christian Church the primary criterion of its teaching and the chief source for the guidance of its religious life.
>
> It further vindicates its authority by continuing to mediate to individuals the revelation which it records and by nurturing their Spiritual life.
>
> The fact the Church has accepted this particular body of literature as Canonical Scripture, invests in it as a whole with an authoritative character for all of its members.
>
> Nevertheless, the use made of the Bible as an authoritative source of teaching should be controlled by the following considerations:
>
> 1) The authority ascribed to the Bible must not be interpreted as prejudging the conclusions of historical, critical, and scientific investigation in any field, not excluding that of the biblical documents themselves.
>
> 2) Christian thinkers are not necessarily bound to the thought forms employed by the biblical writers.
>
> 3) The biblical writings display a wide variety of literary type. In using the biblical books as a standard of authoritative teaching, these facts must be taken into account. The supreme spiritual value of some parts of the Bible is not shared by all.

4) In estimating the relative spiritual value of different portions of the Bible, the standard is the mind of Christ as unfolded in the experience of the Church and appropriated by the individual Christian through His Spirit. That is to say the stages of biblical revelation are to be judged in relation to its historical climax.

"ON ASSENT" (pp. 38–39):

With a view to the avoidance of misunderstanding of what is said note, and elsewhere in this report, N.R., the Commission is desirous to place on record the following resolutions.

1. The Christian Church exists on the basis of the Gospel which has been entrusted to us.

2. General acceptance, implicit if not explicit, of the authoritative formularies, doctrinal and liturgical, by which the meaning of the Gospel has been defined, safeguarded, or expressed, may reasonably be expected from the members of the Church.

3. Assent to formularies and the use of liturgical language in public worship should be understood as signifying such general acceptance without implying detailed assent to every phrase or proposition thus employed.

4. Subject to the above, a member of the Church should not be held to be involved in dishonesty merely on the ground that, in spite of divergence from the tradition of the Church, he has assented to formularies or makes use of the Church's liturgical language in public worship.

The above considerations apply to the authorized teachers as well as to all other members of the Church: but the position of the authorized teacher is distinctive, and the Church has a right to satisfy itself that those who teach in its name adequately represent and express its mind.

5. No individual can claim to receive the teachers commission as a right, and the commission itself involves the obligation not to teach, as the doctrine of the Church, doctrine which is not in accordance with the Church's mind.

6. If any authorized teacher puts forward personal opinions which diverge (within the limits indicated above) from the traditional teaching of the Church, he should be careful to distinguish between such opinions and the normal teaching which he gives in the Church's name: and so far as possible such divergencies should be so put forward as to avoid offending consciences.

7. In respect of the exercise of discipline within such limits as the above resolutions recognize, great regards should be paid to the need for securing a free consensus as distinct from an enforced uniformity.

N.B. – Some members of the Commission, while not dissenting from these resolutions, are of the opinion that number six is by implication too wide a latitude, and would press more strongly the obligation resting upon all who hold office in the Church to believe and to teach the traditional doctrine of the Church.

It seems to this writer that some of the cautions listed above have been abandoned in more recent days in the Episcopal Church, and that in many congregations parishioners would have a hard time distinguishing between what they might identify as "the church's mind" and unusual interpretations given by the local clergyman or lay teacher.

A General Comparison of Anglicanism and Lutheranism

Looking over the above (with the exception of the place of the confessions, which for Anglicans are replaced by the BCP, it seems to this writer that the sources of Anglican doctrinal authority and Lutheran doctrinal authority have a great deal in common. The broad thrust of the theological ethos is similar, due to a common reformation sense of the darkening and noetic effects of sin, and hence a strong reliance on the gospel–centered biblical word and Holy Spirit to cleanse reason in things pertaining to God. In some of the Anglican tradition there has been a greater confidence in the dictates of "sound reason," but not to the exclusion of a strong sense of the place of the gospel, the Scriptures, and the Holy Spirit in theological teaching and personal faith. Another difference, of course, is that no single theological author has had the impact in Anglican theology that Luther's thought and writing has had and continues to have in the theology of the Lutheran church.

The Bishop's Role

What precisely does the bishop do in the whole realm of the church's teaching? How can the bishop and the bishops collectively function in this area?

SEVERAL STATEMENTS

The primates of the Anglican Communion meet regularly. In late April and early May of 1981 they met to take up the issue of authority. Their chief conclusions were stated in the document, "Authority in the Anglican Communion." This quotation is from the conclusion of that paper:

Practical Implications of the Anglican View of Authority

1. The Anglican Communion accepts and endeavours to practice the theology of dispersed authority as set out in the 1948 Lambeth Conference document, The Anglican Communion ("The Meaning and Unity of the Anglican Communion" pp 84–86). [See "Appendix A" at the end of this essay.]

2. Since that statement was written the Anglican Communion has evolved two further institutions to meet the swift changing circumstances in different parts of the world: the Anglican Consultative Council and the Primates' Meeting, within guidelines laid down by the Lambeth Conference.

Fundamentally these two institutions are consistent with the theology of dispersed authority, referred to above.

The Primates' Meeting expresses that special responsibility characteristic of the episcopate. The A.C.C. reflects the responsibilities characteristic of a synodically governed Church.

3. In Christ's one holy, Catholic and Apostolic Church, every member has, in virtue of his or her own baptism, his or her special vocation and ministry.

4. In the Anglican Church, the episcopate has a particular responsibility for teaching the faith, for encouraging promoting and maintaining the proclamation in word and deed of the apostolic gospel by and in the whole Church.

5. In a divided universal Church, the Anglican episcopate shares its peculiar responsibility with those called and chosen to exercise *episcope* in the totality of Christ's Church. The Anglican episcopate acknowledges that it has a special obligation to consult with leaders of other Churches and thereby to practise collegiality in a divided Church.

6. Anglicans recognise that all exercise of *episcope* entails personal loyalty to Christ, commitment to the poor and outcast, willingness to suffer for him, and an open appeal to the common conscience of fellow human beings.

7. In the continuing process of defining the *consensus fidelium*, Anglicans regard criticism and response as an essential element by which Authority is exercised and experienced and as playing a vital part in the work of the Holy Spirit in maintaining the Church in fidelity to the Apostolic Gospel.

Primates' Meeting
Washington D.C.
April 1981

The same interplay between dispersed authority and the central role of the bishop in connection with the teaching of the faith is seen in the restatement of the Lambeth Quadrilateral adopted by the last General Convention of the ECUSA (see "Appendix B" at the end of this essay).

DISPERSED AUTHORITY

Bishops in the Anglican Communion do not act independently of the whole body. When bishops gather at Lambeth, or in the Primates Meeting, or in a particular church in the House of Bishops, the authority of their common statements is persuasive and not juridical. In addition to this, there is much emphasis on the collegiality of the episcopal office, so that a particular bishop ought not simply go off on his own in matters that concern the whole church. (See "Appendix C" at the end of this essay.) Binding decisions are made only by the General Convention of the several national churches of the Anglican Communion, involving a representation of laity and clergy from the several dioceses. On the local level, the Diocesan Convention, with representation of clergy and laity from the several congregations of the diocese, makes binding decisions within the context of the decisions of the national church. It should also be mentioned that, in the exercise of the office of bishop within a diocese, major decisions most often require approval by committees that involve both lay and clergy representatives.

Episcopal Leadership and Responsibility in Teaching Authority

How then do the local bishop and the bishops together exercise leadership and responsibility with reference to teaching on the several levels of the life of the church? The following seem to be important ways in which the episcopate functions.

(1) Lambeth Conferences are an important source of Anglican thought and practice. They are not juridically binding but they are influential. In practice, it seems that little is done practically with the "reception" of the Lambeth Reports, and that attention should given to a more vital use of the Lambeth Conference findings.

(2) The Pastoral Letter of the House of Bishops of the Episcopal Church is read to all congregations annually and is a source of teaching.

(3) In the diocese, much depends upon the theological depth, vitality, and leadership of the bishop. He has a great deal more potential to influence the actual teaching and preaching of the diocese than many realize. (a) He can influence the place where his ordinands prepare for the ordained ministry. (b) He can personally teach and/or bring in teachers to speak to the clergy of the diocese. (c) He can sponsor and call for district or regional conferences during the church year. (d) He appoints members to a number of diocesan committees that can influence the "direction" of the diocese. (e) As he travels throughout the diocese making his annual parish visitations, he has opportunity to communicate his vision and understanding of the gospel and sense of direction and call for congregational and diocesan life and mission. (f) The bishop is required by the national canons of the church to "make a statement of the affairs of the diocese or missionary districts since the last meeting of the convention or convocation" which gives him an opportunity to address the entire diocesan convention, communicating his sense of vision and direction. (g) The bishop has a right, on serious grounds, to refuse "Letters Dimissory" to clergy wishing to enter the diocese, and can strongly influence the whole calling procedure of parishes, as well as appoint the vicar of mission churches. (h) The bishop has a strong say in who he will ordain, though he cannot ordain apart from the agreement of the Standing Committee of the diocese. (i) Finally, to put it negatively, there are specific provisions made in the constitutions and canons of the church to try bishops and clergy who fail in their responsibilities to the Church due to false teaching and/or immorality, etc.

In general the bishop is looked upon, by clergy and laity, as an influential leader in the diocese. A bishop who is a strong leader, not afraid to speak out and act out of love, can have a great impact when clergy and laity catch the same vision and follow him.

EVALUATION

Anglican Preference and Witness

The question arises, is this in any sense, a "better way"? Does this offer a significant advance over other ways of seeking to exercise doctrinal episcope in the life of the church? On the whole, Anglicans would answer yes for a whole range of reasons. Here are a few that stand out to this writer.

(1) Episcopal oversight in historic succession in the teaching of the church is the way the church has gone about its doctrinal encouragement and discipline from very early days. In unparalleled fashion it

symbolizes continuity and unity, both in the life of the church and in the realm of doctrine. Where it can be had in obedience to the gospel, it would seem wrong to abandon it or to imply that it is of little of no consequence.

(2) If Anglicans are to transcend congregationalism and speak of effective regional or diocesan leadership and oversight in the realm of preaching, teaching, and mission, then there is no effective substitute for the personal role of the bishop. If the office is not provided, either there will be no such leadership or it will happen unofficially and covertly, often without the kind of checks and balances that an open expression of "dispersed authority" provides.

(3) Committees cannot provide in one person the synthesis of pastoral relationship, oversight, and leadership that can be lived out by a person in the office of bishop. The coordination of dispersed authority through the office and personal relationships of the bishop holds forth the possibility of a richer and stronger influence for good and for change.

The office of bishop functions in a helpful way in dispersed authority in which the bishop's primary leadership is persuasive rather than juridical. It is important to realize that in Anglicanism the episcopate is not primarily viewed under the "institutional" model as described by Avery Dulles in *Models of the Church* (p. 169).

> In the institutional model, the priesthood is viewed primarily in terms of power; the three-fold power of teaching, sanctifying, and ruling is concentrated at the top, in the Pope and bishops. The bishop is given the fullness of hierarchical power, and the presbyterate is seen as a participation in the priesthood of the episcopacy. All the functions of the bishop or priest are juridicized. When he teaches, people are obliged to accept his doctrine not because of his knowledge or personal gifts but because of the office he holds. When he celebrates the sacraments, the priest exercises sacred powers that others do not have. According to some theories the priest's 'power of the keys' enables him at his discretion to supply or withhold the means of grace, and thus to confirm or deny what is needed for salvation—a truly terrifying power over the faithful. When the priest commands, he does so as one set over the faithful by Christ, so that to resist his orders is equivalently to rebel against God himself.

While Dulles goes on the say a word or two in defense of the institutional model of priesthood, he certainly does not advocate this view in the above form, and neither do Anglicans.

Anglican Practice—The Track Record

Anglicans (Episcopalians) can learn much from Lutherans and others in rethinking the office and role of the bishop.

(1) I am not convinced that we in the Episcopal Church have "locally adapted" the office in ways that allow the bishop the pastoral contact necessary to lead effectively by persuasion—as the view of "dispersed authority" envisions. Perhaps we are still too tied to the concept of the "lord bishop" to be fully comfortable with smaller dioceses, or to take the role of the suffragan bishop seriously. When one sees what the office of the episcopate demands of an individual, as it presently is institutionalized, it is a courageous person indeed who will hear the call to serve as a bishop in the Episcopal Church.

(2) I am not convinced that our present selection process is adequate in discerning gifts and recognizing the right person for leadership in the Episcopal office. At times the clergy and laity who share in electing the bishop fear strong leaders and gravitate toward one who will protect the status quo. It may well be that the increasing secularity of the West will force all of us Christians to ask more searching questions—of leadership and about our own witness and mission.

CONCLUSION

Anglicans have no theory of the episcopate that is required of all Anglicans. We have in fact never really agreed on a particular theology of the episcopate. We are, however, agreed on the fact and value of the historic episcopate, as expressive of the oneness of the gospel and the unity of the church in time and space, as well as an office that has unique potential for serving the gospel in the preaching and teaching of the church. If we have not done as well with this treasure as we might have we hope that the Spirit of the Lord will lead us into better ways, and pray that the Lutheran dialogues will be of help to us as we reflect on a proper local adaptation of this office. We hope also that we might convince the Lutherans that there is treasure here as well. To be sure, we have the treasure in earthen vessels. The episcopate in historic succession is an earthen vessel that we feel has the blessing of the Lord upon it. We seek to commend it to you.

APPENDIX A

Extract from the 1948 Lambeth Conference Committee Report on "The Anglican Communion," pages 84–86

The Meaning and Unity of the Anglican Communion

The world is in grievous disorder and needs to be restored to the order which God wills. A perplexed generation is in search of an authority to which to give its allegiance, and easily submits to the appeal of authoritarian systems whether religious or secular in character.

The question is asked, "Is Anglicanism based on a sufficiently coherent form of authority to form the nucleus of a world–wide fellowship of Churches, or does its comprehensiveness conceal internal divisions which may cause its disruption?"

Former Lambeth Conferences have wisely rejected proposals for a formal primacy of Canterbury, for an Appellate Tribunal, and for giving the Conference the status of a legislative synod. The Lambeth Conference remains advisory, and its continuation committee consultative.

These decisions have led to a repudiation of centralized government, and a refusal of a legal basis of union.

The positive nature of the authority which binds the Anglican Communion together is therefore seen to be moral and spiritual, resting on the truth of the gospel, and on a charity which is patient and willing to defer to the common mind.

Authority, as inherited by the Anglican Communion from the undivided Church of the early centuries of the Christian era, is single in that it is derived from a single Divine source, and reflects within itself the richness and historicity of the divine Revelation, the authority of the eternal Father, the incarnate Son, and the life–giving Spirit. It is distributed among Scripture, Tradition, Creeds, the Ministry of the Word and Sacraments, the witness of saints, and the *consensus fidelium*, which is the continuing experience of the Holy Spirit through His faithful people in the Church. It is thus a dispersed rather than a centralized authority having many elements which combine, interact with, and check each other; these elements together contributing to a process of mutual support, mutual checking, and redressing of errors or exaggeration to the many–sided fullness of the authority which Christ has committed to His Church. Where this authority of Christ is to be found mediated not in one mode but in several we recognize in this multiplicity God's loving provision against the temptations to tyranny and the dangers of unchecked power.

This authority possesses a suppleness and elasticity in that the emphasis of one element over the others may and does change with the changing conditions of the Church. The variety of the contributing factors gives to it a quality of richness which encourages and releases initiative, trains in fellowship, and evokes a free and willing obedience.

It may be said that authority of this kind is much harder to understand and obey than authority of a more imperious character. This is true and we glory in the appeal which it makes to faith. Translated into personal terms it is simple and intelligible. God who is our ultimate personal authority demands of all His creatures entire and unconditional obedience. As in human families the father is the mediator of this divine authority, so in the family of the Church is the bishop, the Father–in–God, wielding his authority by virtue of his divine commission and in synodical association with his clergy and laity, and exercising it in humble submission, as himself under authority.

The elements in authority are, moreover, in organic relation to each other. Just as the discipline of the scientific method proceeds from the collection of data to the ordering of these data in formulae, the publishing of results obtained, and their verification by experience, so Catholic Christianity presents us with an organic process of life and thought in which religious experience has been, and is, described, intellectually ordered, mediated, and verified.

The experience is *described* in Scripture, which is authoritative because it is the unique and classical record of the revelation of God in His relation to and dealings with man. While Scripture therefore remains the ultimate standard of faith, it should be continually interpreted in the context of the Church's life.

It is *defined* in Creeds and in continuous theological study.

It is *mediated* in the Ministry of the Word and Sacraments, by persons who are called and commissioned by God through the Church to represent both the transcendent and immanent elements in Christ's authority.

It is *verified* in the witness of saints and in the *consensus fidelium*. The Christ–like life carries its own authority, and the authority of doctrinal formulations, by General Councils or other–wise, rests at least in part on their acceptance by the whole body of the faithful, though the weight of this *consensus* "does not depend on mere numbers or on the extension of a belief at any one time, but on continuance through the ages, and the extent to which the *consensus* is genuinely free."

This essentially Anglican authority is reflected in our adherence to episcopacy as the source and centre of our order, and the Book of Common Prayer as the standard of our worship. Liturgy, in the sense of the offering and ordering of the public worship of God, is the crucible in which these elements of authority are fused and unified in the fellowship and power of the Holy Spirit. It is the Living and Ascended Christ present in the worshipping congregation who is the meaning and unity of the whole Church. He presents it to the Father, and sends it out on its mission.

We therefore urge the whole Conference to call upon every member of the Anglican Communion to examine himself in respect of this obligation to public worship.

We recognize that our fellow–Churchmen in some parts of the world do not always express themselves in worship according to Western patterns, and that they must have generous liberty of experiment in liturgy; and we therefore reaffirm Resolutions 36 and 37 of the Conference of 1920.

But we appeal to those who are responsible for the ordering and conduct of public worship to remember how bewildered the laity are by differences of use, and with what earnest care and charity they should be helped to take their full share in liturgical worship.

We consider that the time has come to examine these "features of the unity of the Anglican Communion" (Resolution 37, 1920) and the Recommendations of Committee IV of 1920.

APPENDIX B
Extract from the Journal of the 1982 General Convention

House of Deputies
On the tenth day, the Chairman of the Committee on Ecumenical Relations presented its Report #14 on Resolution A–47A (Principles of unity) and recommended concurrence with House of Bishops Message #120.

(A–47A)
Resolved, the House of Deputies concurring, That the 67th General Convention of the Episcopal Church re–affirm the Chicago–Lambeth Quadrilateral as found on pages 876–878 of the Book of Common Prayer as a statement of basic principles which express our own unity, and as a statement of essential principles for organic unity with other churches, and affirm the following as an explication of that basic document without denying anything contained therein: that

(1) The Holy Scriptures of the Old and New Testament are the word of God as they are witness to God's action in Jesus Christ and the continuing presence of his Holy Spirit in the Church, that they are the authoritative norm for catholic faith in Jesus Christ and for the doctrinal and moral tradition of the Gospel, and that they contain all things necessary for salvation.

(2) The Apostles' and Nicene Creeds are the forms through which the Christian Church, early in its history under the guidance of the Holy Spirit, understood, interpreted and expressed its faith in the Triune God. The continuing doctrinal tradition is the form through which the Church seeks to understand, interpret and express its faith in continuity with these ancient creeds and in its awareness of the world to which the Word of God must be preached.

(3) The Church is the sacrament of God's presence to the world and the sign of the Kingdom for which we hope. That presence and hope are made active and real in the Church and in the individual lives of Christian men and women through the preaching of the Word of God, through the Gospel sacraments of Baptism and Eucharist, as well as other sacramental rites, and through our apostolate to the world in order that it may become the Kingdom of our God and of his Christ.

(4) Apostolicity is evidenced in continuity with the teaching, the ministry, and the mission of the apostles. Apostolic teaching must, under the guidance of the Holy Spirit, be founded upon the Holy Scriptures and the ancient fathers and creeds, making its proclamation of Jesus Christ and his Gospel for each new age consistent with those sources, not merely reproducing them in a transmission of verbal identity. Apostolic ministry exists to promote, safeguard and serve apostolic teaching. All Christians are called to this ministry by their Baptism. In order to serve, lead and enable this ministry, some are set apart and ordained in the historic orders of Bishop, Presbyter, and Deacon. We understand the historic episcopate as central to this apostolic ministry and essential to the reunion of the Church, even as we acknowledge "the spiritual reality of the ministries of those Communions which do not possess the Episcopate" (Lambeth Appeal 1920, Section 7). Apostolic mission is itself a succession of apostolic teaching and ministry inherited from the past and carried into the present and future. Bishops in apostolic succession are therefore, the focus and personal symbols of this inheritance and mission as they preach and teach the Gospel and summon the people of God to their mission of worship and service. And be it further

Resolved, the House of Deputies concurring, That this 67th General Convention commend to the Anglican Consultative Council this commentary as an explication of the Chicago–Lambeth Quadrilateral to guide this Church in its ecumenical dialogues.

Motion Carried
The House Concurred
Communicated to the House of Bishops in HD Message #253.

APPENDIX C
(Bulletin #38, November/December 1979)

The Committee on Theology
The Committee on Theology of the House of Bishops, currently in the process of doing a comprehensive study of the place of Authority in the Episcopal Church (as requested by the House of Bishops Meeting in Kansas City in the fall of 1978) proposes now the following resolution on the subject of Collegiality:

Be it resolved that the House of Bishops adopt the following statement as an expression of its common mind:

Statement on Collegiality
The concept of collegiality, as a description of the relation of bishops with one another, has an historic basis in the exercise of *episcope* (oversight) in the Church.

The first examples of the collegial exercise of apostolic oversight are found in Scripture (cf. the Council of Jerusalem in Acts 15), and church history is full of examples of bishops taking counsel together on regional, national and international levels. Normatively, bishops have been guided in the exercise of their ministries by the decisions and counsel of other bishops.

Recent documents reflecting on the nature and exercise of episcopacy see each individual bishop as a member of a college of bishops. The 1968 Lambeth Conference of Anglican Bishops Report alluded to this when it wrote, "He can fulfill his role as focus of authority in his diocese only because his ministry is exercised in partnership with his brother bishops and with the regional and universal Church" (page 108). And Lambeth 1978 reiterates (page 76), "The bishop receives his authority from both Head and members and neither without the other. This authority is not to be exercised apart from the Church, that is, without collegial consultation at proper times with brother bishops, and without ensuring that it has support and consent of the rest of the church as far as possible." It is instructive to note the general agreement in this respect from as different points of view as those represented by the Anglican Roman Catholic International Commission (ARCIC) and the Consultation on Church Union (COCU).

The Canterbury Statement, issued by ARCIC, referring to Ephesians 4:12, states that Christian ministry is for building up the church, the body of Christ, the community of reconciliation. *Episcope* is the responsibility of the ordained ministry and a special responsibility of the bishop as he signifies and serves the unity of the church. In the ordination of a bishop the presence of at least three bishops and their action of laying hands on the new bishop is the means of his reception: "into their ministerial fellowship." As a result, "this new bishop and his church are within the communion of churches." In the Venice Statement, also issued by ARCIC, the role of the bishop is described as helping insure that the local church is "aware of the universal communion of which it is a part." The Statement goes on to say: For every bishop receives at ordination both responsibility for his local church and the obligations to maintain it in living awareness and practical service of the other churches.

A recent document by the Consultation on Church Union, speaking of the role of bishops, says, "Episcopacy is *collegial* in the sense that responsibility for the apostolic unity, continuity and mission of the whole church is the special obligation of the body—or "college"—of bishops. Though bishops are individuals responsible for the authenticity of the Church's confession and witness, no bishop is independent or autonomous in the exercise of this ministry. Just as, in a particular area or district, the bishop's work of oversight is carried out in fellowship with presbyters, laity and deacons, so with regard to the whole Church it is carried out by the bishops as a college, acting together with the representatives of other ministries. The college of bishops meeting for mutual counsel and operating on national or regional levels is, thus, an expression of the fact that the ministry of oversight is a single ministry shared by many individuals" (Emerging Consensus first draft #35c).

The issue of collegiality has come to have a special urgency in our day. The manner in which the church is being challenged to state and restate its position on a score of topics and the instant communication which makes the words of one bishop immediately accessible in every diocese place special burdens on episcopal collegiality. And yet the conditions of modern technology also offer bishops opportunities for consultation and mutual support such as never was possible in former ages. This is, therefore, an appropriate time to reassess the significance of collegiality and to build upon its implications for authority in the ministry of God's Church today.

Collegiality must sometimes take into account matters involving sharp differences of conscientious conviction. There are those who for one reason or another cannot endorse a majority view or even a fairly impressive agreement. There may be those who feel called by God to words and actions which go further than any present consensus; there may be some who find difficulty endorsing agreement already achieved. Collegiality involves a sensitivity to such persons and a patience and forbearance expressed in a willingness to listen, to communicate and to learn. On their part, bishops holding minority views will need to give whatever agreement has been achieved its due weight by remaining open to whatever of the truth and conviction such agreement represents. A problem of a different order is involved when a bishop, in the administration of the sacraments, acts without the authorization of the Church in which he was ordained. On such occasions the bishop does not act as an agent of his Church.

All this indicates the necessity of consultation among bishops whenever a bishop anticipates the need to act apart from the agreed position of the House of Bishops, or in a situation where no collegial guidelines have been set. By so doing we respect the integrity and unity of our own episcopal college and its relationship to the rest of the Church, maintaining "the unity of the Spirit in the bond of peace."

APPENDIX D

Statement: Moral and Theological Principles (The House of Bishops, 1983)

The Committee on Theology has been asked (H.B. Resolution B–16, 1981), to state the theological and moral principles by which this House makes decisions on matters of doctrine and discipline.

We, the House of Bishops, hold to the characteristic appeal of Anglicanism to *Scripture* as interpreted by church *tradition* and applied with *reason*. Scripture, reason and tradition penetrate each other. Scripture, for example, is not an ingredient of the Christian life standing completely outside reason and tradition; rather reason and tradition are found within its fabric. Holy Scripture is a lasting deposit of the living tradition of the early church, reasonably discerned under the guidance of the Spirit. In like manner, in Christian belief reason does not stand completely apart from Scripture and tradition; Scripture and tradition inform reason, and it must be admitted that human reasoning needs redemption just as much as any other human activity. It is within the tension of these three strands that Anglicans discern God's revelation of himself to his people. This three–fold approach seeks to maintain Catholic faith and practice while remaining open to the unfolding insights of other disciplines of human knowledge.

This House Affirms That:

The Holy Scriptures of the Old and New Testaments contain all things necessary to salvation, and in that sense are the ultimate standard of faith for this church. The Scriptures, written by the people of the Old and New Covenants, under the inspiration of the Holy Spirit, culminate in the life, teaching, death, and resurrection of Jesus and the proclamation of the Good News of the Kingdom of God for all people.

The Holy Scriptures contain a record of God's definitive revelation of himself to his people. We must recognize, however, that revelation has many ingredients. God infinitely transcends all human capacity to know and to express him; thus, even when human beings are inspired by God's grace, there is no adequate means for them fully to comprehend God's revelation of himself to them. God in himself always remains a mystery to his creatures, and the difference of God from us must never be compromised in our relations with him, or in our relations with each in his name.

The Source of all is beyond all. God reveals himself to us through many means:

1. Through events and deeds;

2. Through words and propositions;

3. Through symbols and images which cannot be reduced to words or concepts;

4. Through intimate personal experience of his presence;

Although it must be acknowledged that God surpasses all events, deeds, words, propositions, symbols, images, and personal experience.

Contributions from all the modes of revelation are found in the church's recognition and use of the Bible; thus the fact that the Bible, from one point of view, is itself a collection of propositions and is often referred to as the "word of God" should not mislead people into believing that the sentences of the Bible are by themselves God's revelation. Propositions about God, as everything used by God to communicate with human beings, terminate beyond themselves in the mysterious being of God himself. God's Word is a Person, not a book; the Person transcends all books, even the Bible.

Jesus is the (true) Word of God and sums up in himself the whole of God's self–disclosure for human beings (Col. 1:15; Hebrews 1:1–3). By the Holy Spirit, the church continues to hear the Holy Scriptures as God speaking to his people through his Son. The Church's essential endeavor in the exercise of its teaching office is to unfold the full extent and implications of the mystery of Christ, under the guidance of the Spirit of the risen Lord.

Holy Scripture needs to be studied and expounded continually because language changes and because the church faces problems which did not exist in biblical times or did not exist in the same forms. But expositions vary, and sin corrupts; the pure testimony of Jesus Christ, our only savior, is then endangered. The Holy Spirit, through means such as creeds, councils, and theological formularies, has provided guides for correctly expounding Holy Scripture. These are secondary guides, subject to the norm of Holy Scripture and they, like Holy Scripture, are also in need of expositions because language changes and new problems arise. Here too, God through the power of his Word and Spirit continues to lead and guide his church and directs the church's attention to Jesus Christ as proclaimed in Holy Scripture.

No endeavor of the church to express the truth can add to the revelation already given. The spirit who is to guide the Church into all truth (John 16:13) does so by enabling the community of faith to penetrate ever deeper into the Christ who is the way, the truth and the life (John 14:6). Moreover, since the Scriptures are the uniquely inspired record of the witness to divine revelation, the church's expression of that revelation must be tested by its agreement and consistency with Scripture. This does not mean simply repeating the biblical texts, but also delving into their deeper significance and unravelling their implications for Christian belief and practice. It is impossible to do this without resorting to current language and thought. Consequently the teaching of the church will often be expressed in words that are different from the original text of Scripture without being alien to or reducing its meaning. The church has always been engaged in this process, the first instance being the translation of the gospel from a Hebrew to a Greek culture. The church's centuries–long wrestling with the Scriptures and the culture in the power of the Holy Spirit has produced a rich store of experience. That resource is what we mean by tradition, which combines the permanence of the revealed truth and the continuous living out and exploration of its meaning in the world.

All members of the church share in expounding what Holy Scripture means for their faith and life, using their God–given reason in carrying out this task. Some individuals because of their authority, gifts or training are able to be especially discerning interpreting

Scripture for their time. Even those with special gifts, however, remain subject to the Scriptural norm of Christian faith and life as received and authenticated by the church.

The situation of the preacher is a paradigm for all members of the church who seek to proclaim the Gospel. One can begin with Scripture, seeking the insights of revelation, then take these to the human situation; or one can begin with a description of the human situation taking its dilemmas and ambiguities to God's word. Such kerygmatic and pre-kerygmatic preaching provides the model by which decisions are made with regard to matters of doctrine and discipline. The norm of Scripture whether it precedes or follows the analysis of the contemporary situation must always govern. This pathway between Scripture and the contemporary human situation is sometimes called the hermeneutical arch. For the purpose of interpretation this arch carries the church's tradition and human reason to either base and holds them in proper relationship.

Moral and ethical discussions (the problems relating to the environment, family life, divorce, abortion, human sexuality, life-styles, liberation movements, nuclear weaponry, genetic engineering, peace making and social justice among others) current in the church's life and witness today generally fall under the categories of the classical doctrines of creation (viz. Gen. 1; 2:15 ff; Isaiah 43:7 et al.), redemption from sin through grace (viz. John 3:16; 2 Cor. 5:18, 21 Gal. 4:4 ff; et al.) and the sanctification of human life through the working of the Holy Spirit (viz. John 16:1; 2 Cor. 5:17 Eph. 1:13f; 2:8f; et al).

The church's understanding of God's will can never be adequate without the evangelical witness in the arena of the moral and ethical issues of the times. As the church has always been most true to itself when engaged in mission to the world, so our witness must always be in and as a result of the church's participation in the ethical and moral crises of our times. The church's witness, therefore, requires that we speak out on these issues, to guide, to instruct, and to call for obedience to the Gospel. These statements have authority. However, the deepest level of authentic authority lies not in votes or pronouncements, but in the faithful assents and response as tested by the living experience of God's people.

This House affirms that its specific interpretations should be consonant with the received witness which Scripture bears to the new life given to us in Christ Jesus, the incarnate Word of God, when interpreted with the fullness described above.

4

BISHOPS AND LUTHERANS IN THE UNITED STATES

BY

JERALD C. BRAUER

This essay was originally prepared for an informal discussion between Lutheran and Anglican representatives in 1985. It was not
intended to be a carefully researched and properly documented historical analysis of the issue. Rather, its purpose was to provoke
discussion by presenting a series of generalizations that arose from
years of reading in Lutheran literature and from thinking about the
question from time to time. The consequence of such reading and
thinking is an overall impression that is articulated in a series of
generalizations that seek to make sense of why Lutherans in America,
unlike some of their Lutheran brethren, never adopted the office of
bishop until the formation of the Evangelical Lutheran Church in
America, and even then did not seriously consider seeking apostolic
succession for their bishops through the Lutheran Church of Sweden.

Most Lutheran churches in Europe have bishops of one type or
another. That is, at various points in their history, they have adopted
the office of bishop as part of their ecclesiastical structure. The Church
of Sweden has never been without bishops, and they can lay claim to
an unbroken apostolic succession (with perhaps a better case than the
Church of England). With such a background, it is curious that no
Lutheran group in America developed the office of bishop until
recently, when three of the groups (which formed the ELCA in 1988)
redesignated the offices of national and synodical presidents with the
title "bishop." Prior to this there had been no serious or sustained
effort in any of the Lutheran groups in America to adopt the office of
bishop.

The Anglican Church, both in England and in the colonies, had a particularly close relationship with the various Lutheran groups that came to America in the eighteenth century. There were a number of reasons for this special affinity, but the most important was the crowning of a Hanoverian Lutheran as George I, King of England, in 1714. He was accompanied to England by his chaplain, a German Lutheran clergyman, who maintained a voluminous correspondence with Lutheran pastors and theologians in Germany and who conducted German services for the king. The most famous royal chaplain, the Reverend Frederick Michael Ziegenhagen, served the first three Georges from 1722 to 1776, and was deeply committed to the work of Lutheranism in the sovereign colonies. Ziegenhagen had close connections with Halle, with various Lutheran consistories in Germany, and with many of the German Lutheran congregations in the New World. He was also an important link between the Church of England and the German Lutherans.

Although Lutherans made no move to adopt an episcopal system, a number of Lutheran ministerial candidates from the Colonies went to England to be ordained by English bishops, among them Peter Muhlenberg, the son of the American Lutheran patriarch, Henry M. Muhlenberg. They went not because they sought ordination through apostolic succession, but because they wished a legal ordination in order to minister in territories in the Colonies where the Church of England was established. To be sure, occasionally certain Lutheran pastors advocated union between the Church of England and the Lutherans in America in order to strengthen both sides. These advocates pointed not to the importance of apostolic episcopacy but to the similar liturgical services of both churches and to the similarities between the Thirty–Nine Articles and the Augsburg Confession. On neither side did episcopacy seem to be a requirement for fellowship or for unity.

If the vast majority of Lutherans who immigrated to America came from churches with bishops, and if Lutherans generally found themselves in close relationship with the Church of England in America, why, then, did they not adopt the episcopal system? This question admits no easy answer; however, it is worthy of serious consideration and speculation. The answer, necessarily, will be one of speculation because it is difficult, if not impossible, to document it historically. There is an old saying in Germany, *"Stadt Luft macht frei"* ("City air is liberating"), that has been adapted to the American scene by many historians; they argue that the American context tends to break down many of the traditions and institutions in which European immigrants had been raised. That is the typical answer given to the question concerning bishops and Lutheranism in America.

The argument says that Lutherans who landed in the New World encountered an opportunity to be free and organize their ecclesiastical system in any way they felt appropriate. Although they had lived and functioned under bishops in the Old World, the freedom, equality, and democracy of the New World demanded fresh forms and new institutions. This has generally been the answer advocated by most historians. There is obviously some truth to the argument, but it is a bit simplistic. If bishops were rejected by New World Lutherans as being too authoritarian for their new context, why were the Lutheran Confessions not also rejected as too conservative or authoritarian for the New World? Some would argue that, indeed, they were rejected by the so-called American Lutherans, but one immediately notes that their opponents, the confessional Lutherans, also rejected the necessity of bishops in the church.

There were a number of reasons why various Lutheran churches in America did not adopt bishops in their church orders when they organized themselves into denominations in the American context. Primary among them was the influence of the American situation itself. A subtle interplay of a variety of American influences helps to explain the absence of bishops. A brief analysis of these influences will help us understand the dynamics of the situation.

DEPENDENCE–INDEPENDENCE

The total American situation shaped the emergence and the organization of all American denominations, from Roman Catholic to Mormon. Perhaps the two most important generalizations concerning the American situation are first, that America was a relatively unsettled space (although there was regular confrontation with Native Americans), and second, that all Europeans who came to America were immigrants. That is, the people who settled in America left their homelands to venture into a wilderness to discover and make a new life. These two factors, broadly interpreted, set the parameters for the discussion of our problem. Further, these early immigrant peoples throughout the Colonial period were overwhelmingly English–speaking and British in background. Not until later did increasing numbers of non–English–speaking immigrants come to the New World.

A number of historians and commentators on the American context have noted that this combination of factors produced a special outlook or psychology in the American people. De Crevecoeur asked,

"What is an American?" His answer emphasized the utter uniqueness of the individual in contrast to his or her European background. His subtle analysis noted a particularly American mentality or outlook that we shall call "dependence–independence," a rather dialectical or perhaps even paradoxical relationship. On the one hand, Americans exhibited—particularly up through the Revolutionary period—a heavy dependence on their English–European background in almost every facet of their lives. On the other hand, from their very first days in America, these colonists exhibited a constant striving for and embodiment of independence from their roots and background.

However, some dependence was unavoidable. Nostalgia, a longing to return home, and the romanticization of their past mark all immigrant groups that came to America. In fact, so strong was the feeling of connection to the homeland that many immigrants returned to their old homes; those who did not still exhibited a high degree of dependence. In a sense, all first–generation immigrants remained in their hearts partially in the old country and partially in the New World; psychologically, they were living on a boundary. Even those immigrants who "shook the dust off their feet" never escaped this mentality.

One obvious symptom of this dependence was the tendency of immigrants to flock together, to establish communities that recapitulated much of their past. Particularly true for foreign–language speaking groups such as the Germans, Swedes, and Poles, it was true as well for the various English–speaking groups. The Irish, Welsh, Scots, Scotch–Irish, and English all tended to settle in their own communities, where they kept their own customs and mores. Such a grouping reinforces the identity that shapes a people through their history. When they are uprooted, they gather together in a new group that sustains itself with the old forms, customs, language, and traditions.

For virtually all immigrant groups, the most important source of continuity and sustenance through familiar language and customs was the church. Moreover, as the individual American colonies were settled, the church was instrumental and central to their founding. All of the New England colonies were founded on the basis of the church itself. Each of the Southern colonies assumed that the established Church of England was the bedrock on which the colony itself was founded. However, not all immigrants were practicing Christians. In fact, the vast majority of the colonists were not. Nevertheless, the church was still a cohesive force. To a greater or lesser degree, these immigrants were "Christian pilgrims" representing various churches within the Christian tradition.

These various churches did not arise in America. They were transplanted from England and Europe. Not bodily, of course, or in their exact form; but every effort was made to organize them as quickly as possible in their new setting. For English–speaking colonists, the political organization of the colonies gave them a tie to their homeland; and in that the church itself was a part of the English political organization, it provided a similar tie. For the non–English speaking, non–British colonists, there was no *political* tie to the Old World; their churches thus provided the primary link to their origins.

For Protestant colonists, their churches and their native language were the major links that sustained their identity. The public worship services of their churches were initially the only public exercise of their native tongue in an English–speaking culture, since the many clubs and organizations founded to promote the language and customs of the homeland were more or less private and, in some cases, even secret. Churches thus became the depository for identity for vast numbers of colonists, even for those not vigorously active in them. The churches were national yet international, connected with the homeland.

It was some length of time before the colonists could prepare a ministry to serve themselves; they had to turn to the old country to secure properly trained and ordained ministers and priests. For example, the early Lutherans remained totally dependent on Swedish and German authorities for ministers in America. Every immigrant group went through the process of moving from complete dependence on their homeland for their ministry to a growing independence, as it found the ways and means to call and prepare candidates for ministry and priesthood. In Halle the Germans had a very missionary–minded center that was profoundly concerned with providing ministers to the New World. The Church of England sought missionaries to the colonies, forming a special organization for this purpose. The Society for the Propagation of the Gospel sent missionaries to all the British colonies, with particular emphasis on the American colonies. In all the colonies the Church of England was legally dependent on the bishop of London, and remained under his jurisdiction until after the Revolutionary War. The Roman Catholic Church in America was a missionary church directly under the control of Rome until the early twentieth century.

The New World churches were dependent on England and Europe not only for their personnel but also for their financing. Only the New

England churches were quick to develop a viable and independent ministry and a financial base of support. The established Anglican churches in the colonies frequently sought and received financial support from England; the Dutch and German Reformed and the Lutheran groups could not have existed long without timely financial help from their home countries—ministerial salaries frequently were paid by authorities in Sweden and Germany. Long after American independence was achieved and independent denominations were created, many churches continued to look to their native lands for support, and they usually received it in the form of missionary aid.

Yet with the exception of the Roman Catholic Church, dependence on the homeland never resulted in the full recapitulation of the original church in the New World. Thus, for neither the Anglicans nor the Lutherans were bishops originally an integral part of their churches. Only after the American Revolution did the Church of England feel free to establish bishops in the American context. Clearly, then, there were countervailing forces in this context that undercut a simple psychology of dependence. Those can best be summarized as a yearning for independence.

Whatever their specific reasons for coming to America, most colonists participated in a common spirit: a search for *renovatio*. Mircea Eliade argued that throughout history, humanity has been driven by the search for a fresh beginning, a new start, a new birth. The New World offered an opportunity for large numbers of people to leave the past behind and begin new lives. The colonists' psychological need for dependence was simultaneously counterbalanced by the urge and opportunity for a new beginning. This was the basis for the push to become an American that De Crevecoeur noted.

The churches, too, experienced this duality. While they retained a sense of identity with the past through their rituals and language, they simultaneously recognized an opportunity for a fresh start. All the foreign-language church groups in America struggled with the need to retain their native languages (to maintain their connection to the old world) and yet adopt English as a way of truly becoming part of the new scene.

However dependent religious groups were on their homelands, they also experienced the need to organize and develop themselves in their immediate context. First and foremost was the increased role and function of the laity in view of the severe shortage of ordained clergy. The laity frequently found themselves overstepping the parameters recognized in their homelands. The New England Congregational churches had organized themselves fully before the

American Revolution; all other denominations found it necessary to establish independent organizations immediately after the Revolution and the subsequent adoption of the federal Constitution.

DISTANCE FROM THE HOMELAND

While distance may make the heart grow fonder, it also fosters forgetfulness. Communication between the Old World and the New was slow and uncertain. It could easily take four or five months to receive advice from the homeland; formal instructions were difficult to transmit and more difficult to enforce, and both political and religious decisions were often ineffective.

Distance also affected the matter of symbolism. Although a number of the colonies had royal governors and displayed the British flag and other reminders of Parliament and the Crown, the absence of both of these severely undermined the continuing power of Great Britain in the colonies. The churches were in a similar situation. Whatever the wish of the bishops might be in the Church of Sweden or the Church of England, the vast distance between them and their American constituents made a profound difference in the way the office itself was perceived and venerated. Churches that possessed bishops in Europe learned that in America, bishops were thoroughly supernumerary; by the time episcopal advice or help reached the New World, new situations had developed, with new questions and new needs. The American churches found it increasingly difficult to feel close to or dependent on bishops who were thousands of miles away and unavailable for consistent communication with their constituents. Logic thus dictated that bishops would be brought to the New World, but it was well over a century before logic prevailed, and by then it was too late for Lutherans.

THE REVOLUTIONARY WAR

The Revolutionary War was the turning point for the question of bishops in a number of churches in the American context. Immediately after the Revolution, both the Church of England and the Roman Catholic Church received their first bishops and completed the full structure of their denominations. The Lutherans neither asked for nor received bishops, and moved ahead with the organization and structure of their churches throughout the eighteenth and nineteenth centuries without them. They were doubtless influenced in this direction by the spirited struggle that occurred throughout the Colonies when members of the Church of England proposed that bishops be brought to America, arguing that the Church of England could not be complete or operationally effective without the establishment of bishoprics. This effort was led primarily by Anglicans in the New England and Middle colonies; it was vigorously resisted by the vast majority of clergy and laity in the Southern colonies, where the Church of England was established. The question of bishops became one of the most publicly disputed issues throughout the Colonies. The question of colonial independence from England thus coincided with the problem of colonial bishops within the Church of England, complicating the ecclesiastical problem.

The establishment of bishops in the New World was seen by many as but one more effort on the part of Britain to solidify its grasp on the Colonies. Bishops were seen as arbitrary, oppressive, and ecclesiastical arms of the political power of Britain: when bishops arrive, tyranny escalates, ran the argument. Numerous tracts were written, a vigorous exchange of letters appeared in the newspapers, and cartoons caricaturing bishops and their role ran rampant throughout the Colonies. In Virginia, the laity, who had seized control of the church through vestries, were appalled at the idea of introducing bishops. New England Puritans viewed the plan as the first step in the repression of both their rights and the whole system they had established upon leaving England. Unfortunately, linking the question of bishops with the question of British political hegemony in the Colonies marked Anglicans as Royalists in the public eye, despite the fact that significant leaders of the Revolution (including Jefferson, Madison, and Washington) were staunch members of the Church of England.

The success of the Revolution did not deter the Church of England from establishing bishops in America, nor did it prevent Roman Catholicism from ordaining Bishop Carroll as its first American bishop. The Revolution undoubtedly had an effect on Lutherans and other Protestant groups as well. Even the Episcopal Church had to be very careful about the way it related to its mother church in England, in order that its true independence be clearly visible to all citizens of the new nation. That the Methodists had bishops was not a problem because they were seen as superintendents who were only *called* bishops. Whether bishops or superintendents, however, they exercised more authority than any of the new Anglican Episcopal bishops in the United States.

The revolutionary reaction against bishops was long gone by the time most Lutheran churches organized in the nineteenth century. It is difficult to say whether the question of the patriotism of bishops had any influence whatsoever on Lutheran reactions in the nineteenth century. Although Roman Catholicism was highly suspect through-out the nineteenth century and experienced violent reactions against its precepts and practices, the new Protestant Episcopal Church in America met no such prejudice; in fact, it was seen as one of the citadels of American democracy. We can only speculate that the episcopal fight over bishops in the Colonial period left a mark on eighteenth– and nineteenth–century Lutherans.

THE INFLUENCE OF NON–EPISCOPALIAN PROTESTANT NEIGHBORS

The Ministerium of Pennsylvania, the first official Lutheran organization in America, founded in 1748 by Henry M. Muhlenberg, was not successful in providing a central or national organization for Lutherans. Rather, Lutherans organized themselves on a geographical or synodical basis throughout both the colonies and the early American Republic. As the various Lutheran national groups—Germans, Swedes, Danes, Norwegians—began to organize, there never seems to have been a serious discussion of adopting the episcopal system.

One of the most important factors in the situation was the over-whelming presence of non–Episcopalian Protestants. Although Lutheran and Episcopalian relations were always good, they did not remain as close in the nineteenth century as they had been in the eighteenth, partly because of the constant stream of fresh immigrants that flowed into the Lutheran churches, keeping them in a constant state of accommodation and reaccommodation to the American scene. The problems of the establishment of the Anglican bishops in America had long since faded from the collective memory, and Episcopalians were regarded as simply one more denomination among all the rest, all working in a condition of religious freedom as voluntary corporations. There was nothing in experience to commend the necessity of episcopal polity to nineteenth–century American Lutherans. Rather, the most successful churches seemed to be the most American and the least dependent an European forms.

Shortly after the turn of the nineteenth century, Lutherans found themselves surrounded by Methodists, Baptists, Presbyterians, Congregationalists, and other groups that did not have bishops. (Again, we are reminded that while the Methodist superintendents were called bishops, they were not generally understood as such in the sense that officeholders in the Protestant Episcopal and Roman Catholic churches carried that title.) This made it very difficult to argue that Protestant bishops provided the best type of organization for the health of the Christian community. Further, German–speaking Lutherans were close to the German Reformed denomination, which also did not have bishops.

When Lutheran churches chose a form of polity under which to live, they did not turn to their homelands for guidance and patterns; rather, they looked to the Protestant groups that surrounded them. As organization took shape, there was some unsuccessful argument for the introduction of bishops, and all Lutheran groups eventually developed forms of polity that were a combination of the Presbyterian and the Congregational forms of government—called by some, "Presbygational."

The movement that most profoundly affected Lutheranism in America was revivalism. This distinctive way of becoming, being, and remaining Christian had a powerful influence during the nineteenth century on most groups of Lutherans, with the exception of those who came out of the anti–union fight in Germany. Already deeply influenced by pietism in their homelands, the Norwegians and Swedes discovered revivalism in the American context as the predominant view. In Pennsylvania, the impact of revivalism was so profound that under the influence of S. S. Schmucker, in particular, a special form of Lutheranism developed that was even willing to alter the Augsburg Confession. The reemergence of confessionalism within Lutheranism in America cannot be understood primarily or simply as a fresh influx of confessionalism from Germany through mid–nineteenth–century immigration; rather, in the case of Pennsylvania and eastern Lutheranism, it must also be seen as a reaction against revivalism.

It is interesting to note that, contrary to what might be expected, in this struggle against revivalism Lutherans did not turn to bishops as an explicit guarantor of theological doctrine and truth. At only one point—during the earliest days of the Saxon Lutherans who were to become the Missouri Synod—did the office of bishop appear momentarily connected with a confessional movement in Lutheranism. The Saxon Lutherans' initial leader, Pastor Stephan, took the title of bishop, with the intention of building his church on that form of polity; however, due to charges of immorality he was removed from office. The eventual polity of the Lutheran Church–Missouri Synod, formulated by C. F. W. Walther, took the most extreme congregational form of any Lutheran group.

Neither the historical office of the episcopate nor the examples of the Anglicans or the Roman Catholics had any influence whatsoever on Lutherans as they developed their polity in the American context. As we have noted, the Presbyterians and the Congregationalists seemed to provide the model for church government, a model further strengthened by the adoption of the presbyterian synodical system by the German Reformed churches.

THE FRONTIER

Many scholars have argued that the frontier was the primary force that shaped the history of all religious groups in America, including Lutherans. Frederick Jackson Turner sketched out the concept of the frontier as the fundamental interpretive motif in every aspect of American history and life. British and European immigrants brought with them a hierarchical, class–differentiated, conservative society, a monarchical political order, and an ecclesiastical establishment. When these values and institutions confronted the frontier, they dissolved or were radically transformed into a new set of values and institutions. Each person who ventured onto the frontier, either as an individual or as a member of a group, was forced to confront the challenges of beginning afresh. The result was that new forms developed. This vast oversimplification of the theory shows how the frontier was understood as a solvent of old forms and a context for the growth of new ideas, concepts, and institutions.

Many historians of Christianity in the United States have made a good deal of this frontier hypothesis. Perhaps William Warren Sweet was the most outspoken proponent of the impact of the frontier on Protestantism in America, arguing that the most successful churches in America—the Methodist and the Baptist—were precisely those that most readily adapted to the frontier and developed forms that enabled them to cope with its challenges. Those churches that adapted least to the frontier, notably the Episcopalian and the Congregationalist, lost the preeminent positions on the American scene that they had established prior to and maintained during the American Revolution. When the nation turned westward, these denominations were left behind.

In my judgment, the impact of the frontier on Christianity in America has been vastly overemphasized. At best, the frontier may have had an indirect, rather than a direct, influence. Turner's hypothesis involves three phases, with only the third being of any real importance for Christianity in America—the point when farm communities began to spring up as woods were cleared, when stable communities were being built, and when farming became the backbone of the American move westward. The frontier did encourage tendencies toward localism and decentralization, and spurred a democratic spirit that was already at work in the American scene. We must remember, however, that the Methodists and the Baptists were the most successful in coping with the frontier, and they were diametrically opposed in their forms of polity: the Methodists were highly centralized, while the Baptists were fluid, flexible, and totally congregational. Each group coped successfully with the new frontier in its own way.

Arriving on the frontier in large numbers somewhat later in the nineteenth century, the Lutherans were involved in its final stages. It is difficult to say whether the frontier worked against the creation of the episcopal form of polity in Lutheranism. The most one can argue is that it was one additional factor that combined with a variety of other factors to move the denomination in that direction.

THE RISE OF THE DEMOCRATIC SPIRIT

Historians have made clear that with the election of Andrew Jackson, a new spirit came over the American scene: the age of the common man had arrived. Jackson was seen as a man of the people, a former frontiersman, a more or less successful entrepreneur, the greatest military hero of the War of 1812, and a person who made no pretense to learning or sophistication.

The beginnings of this Jacksonian period formed the basis for Alexis De Tocqueville's famous treatise, *Democracy in America*. With extraordinary insight, De Tocqueville pointed out that equality had become the basic American principle and that it had, and would continue to have, vast consequences for every facet of American life. No longer was one born to social status or position. A newly emerging wealthy class sought power and position based only on its wealth. One American considered himself as good as any other, and while this concept was not actualized to the degree that society might wish, it was sufficiently prevalent to mark vast numbers of the population.

This new concept of equality could not fail to influence the religious dimension of life. Revivalism had already undercut the basic concept of clerical domination: that which made one Christian was purely the new birth through the Holy Spirit. Anyone who had not experienced that reality was not, in fact, a Christian, and any minister who failed to have such an experience was not in truth a minister. Any layperson was every bit as much a Christian as any ordained person; in fact, one could argue that nineteenth–century America transformed the concept of the ministry from that of a privileged, learned person into one of a truly converted, devout, open, and friendly person.

In such a context, the nature, function, and role of bishops was highly suspect for vast numbers of Protestants, including Lutherans.

The office of bishop was seen as a tradition that granted particular privileges to those who held the office, privileges that separated the bishop from fellow clergy and, even more drastically, from the laity. In an age of rising democratic expectations, such separatism was not appreciated; consequently, the office of bishop was grossly misunderstood and misinterpreted. Moreover, that fact that Roman Catholicism was ruled by its bishops was taken by Protestants as further proof that the office was not to be trusted, because it centralized power in itself rather than in the laity, thus creating a clerically dominated church. Consequently, many Lutherans argued that in a democratic context, the office of bishop did not make sense.

CONCLUSION

We have made an effort to isolate dimensions of the American scene in order to understand the reaction of Lutherans to the role of bishops in their polity. In conclusion, we must add a final factor that was in no way determined by the American context. When all is said and done, there is something in the Lutheran heritage itself that did not (in its past) and does not (in its present) encourage the absolute insistence on the necessity of bishops in order to have the full church and its ministry.

From its very beginnings in Germany and Scandinavia, Lutheranism took a very flexible attitude toward the necessity of bishops. Certainly Lutherans appreciated the significance and role of bishops in organizing and maintaining the church. When the regularly constituted bishops failed to perform their tasks, Lutherans were prepared to turn to the princes as lay–bishops, to do those things in the ordering of the church that the constituted bishops failed to do. One has the distinct impression that had the bishops functioned as they should have, Luther probably would have favored their retention for no other reason than that, at their best, they represented good order and a fine historical tradition. At no point, however, did Luther appear to argue for episcopacy as a constituent mark of the Christian church.

Lutherans agreed with both their Catholic and many of their Protestant brethren that the church was indeed one, holy, catholic, and apostolic. However, for Lutherans, "apostolic" was never defined as the direct succession of bishops from Peter down to the present incumbents. Rather, apostolic meant first, participation throughout history in the true teaching of the church as guaranteed by the creeds, and second, the proper confession of faith. At its center is the living, dynamic Word properly preached and the true sacraments properly administered. These elements embody and preserve the continuity of the Christian church. Its form of government can and does vary from epoch to epoch, from country to country. Normally, but not always, bishops are a part of that government.

While many Lutherans were prepared to argue for bishops strictly in terms of the well–being of the church, they were not ready to argue for the necessity of bishops as constitutive of the life of the church. The office of bishop was not founded by Christ and so is not an absolute necessity for a true church. Because Lutherans tended to define the church more in terms of doctrine than in terms of polity, when their denomination found itself in the American context it did not deem it necessary to argue for bishops even in terms of the well–being of the Christian community. Hence, one can observe that the relation of Lutherans to the question of bishops in the American context was in a profound sense determined before their appearance in America. Once in the American context, Lutherans appeared to find little that argued on behalf of the necessity of bishops for the proper ordering and well–being of the Christian community. Although they could not argue *jure divino*, neither could they argue from the perspective of *bene esse* in the American context. Until recent years, this did not seem to make sense to Lutherans. In the present context, many Lutherans appear ready to reopen the question of bishops in light of a new understanding of what constitutes the true well–being of the church today.

5

THE HISTORIC EPISCOPATE:
FURTHER REFLECTIONS

BY

L. WILLIAM COUNTRYMAN

In the original essay that is returning to our consideration at present, I was seeking to explicate the significance of the historic episcopate for Anglicans in a way that would be acceptable to other Anglicans and also open to ecumenical concerns. The reaction to it thus far suggests to me that I may have been fairly successful with the first goal, but that the second is still uncertain of achievement. To what extent does my discussion of the episcopate shed light on ecumenical issues or make its subject intelligible in an ecumenical context? I hinted at some ecumenical implications of these ideas in the last two paragraphs of the earlier essay. My objective in this addendum is to make these ecumenical implications more explicit, not because I am sure that these reflections will meet with approval, but because I hope they may be useful for discussion and further thinking.

First, with reference to intra–Anglican issues, I was seeking to offer a "high" explanation of the episcopate that avoided some of the quasimagical implications of other such explanations. By suggesting that the historic ministry, the sacraments, the credal tradition, and the canon of scripture were, in effect, independent pillars of church life, I was detaching, in effect, the issue of validity of sacraments from that of the structure of the ministry.[1] The "pipeline" theory of grace—as channeled to the laity through correctly ordained persons by way of the sacraments—is probably neither ancient nor catholic, nor widely accepted by contemporary Episcopalians, even if it remains an important theme for a certain minority. Yet the episcopate is of great importance to us for ordering the life of the Christian community, primarily, I think, because of the way it gives us a sense of being in touch with the great spread of that community in time and space.

The explanation I proffered seems consistent with the Interim Eucharistic Sharing agreement between the ECUSA and the ELCA, which assumes that Anglicans and Lutherans are already broadly at one in matters of faith, Scripture, and the sacraments. It is interesting, in this connection, that Anglican insistence on the historic episcopate crops up, as far as I am aware, at only two points in our most basic formularies. One is our own Ordinal, which establishes the threefold ministry in historic succession as the standard for our own community life. The other is the Chicago–Lambeth Quadrilateral, which indicates that we regard the historic episcopate as vital to the unity of the church catholic in time to come. Neither of these formularies need be read as negating other models of ministry in other Christian communities. Indeed, in our Interim Eucharistic Sharing the ECUSA seems to be affirming one specific existing ministry that does not correspond to the model we hold up for ourselves now and for the reuniting church in time to come. Yet on both sides that affirmation is limited to an arrangement admitted by its very name to be unstable and impermanent. The remaining question is what sort of agreement on ministry would be necessary in order for us to begin thinking of our relationship as fuller and more permanent. Anglicans, I think, would still have to answer that, for the church of the future, the historic episcopate is vital.

Second, with reference to ecumenical issues between Anglicans and Lutherans, I think the argument I presented may offer a different way of looking at some significant points of disagreement. Some Lutherans hear Anglicans as maintaining that the gospel is in some way dependent on the human, churchly institution of a certain ordering of the ministry. Some Anglicans do come close to saying that—they would, indeed, see this as a divine institution and the fountain of other graces. That is not, however, the dominant or official teaching of the Anglican Communion. That some Lutherans persist in hearing our advocacy of the historic episcopate in this way may arise from a misleading equation of this Anglican "distinctive" with something like the *solas* of the Lutheran tradition. The two are not equatable, because the Anglican and Lutheran traditions have approached their understanding and shaping of the Christian community in ways so radically different that they are essentially incommensurable. The goal, if that is true, can never be to fit the existing structures together, like the long–separated continental margins of South America and Africa, for in reality we are not pieces of quite the same puzzle. The goal can only be to conceive a future for the Christian community that will not negate, betray, or falsify any of the streams of history that we hope to see pouring into it.[2]

The question about ministry, then, is, What kind of common ministry might Anglicans and Lutherans evolve that would be faithful to the gospel insights of both traditions, continuous with their past, and expectant of a future in which Christians may, in response to God's gracious love, seek still greater degrees of loving unity among themselves? Certainly we cannot substitute the ministry of either group for that of the other. In both cases there are elements in the other tradition that seem alien or even inimical to what we hold most dear. Perhaps the following lists may help in making comparisons.[3]

Implicit Meanings of Historic Episcopate

for ELCA	*for ECUSA*
pre-Reformation	pre-Reformation
anti-Reformation	reformed
alien to their tradition	native to their tradition
irrelevant to the main business of the gospel and to church life	intrinsic to the life of the church catholic apostolic
authoritarian	pastoral & missionary

Implicit Meanings of Ministry of American Lutherans

for ELCA	*for ECUSA*
Reformation faithfulness	Reformation protest
continuity with church catholic	discontinuity with past
gospel ministry ordering church	gospel ministry in a divided church

The challenge here would be to preserve the positive meanings that each form of ministry embodies in ways that would not have to function as rejections of the other tradition.

One proposal for doing this might be to say, "Let each tradition continue as it is." We are not, after all, talking about a merger of church organizations, but about that somewhat less concrete and specifiable thing called "full communion." Yet I do not think this is a desirable solution, even if it should prove possible. A purely functional, task-oriented understanding of ministry—one that ignores the enormous freight of meaning attached to various ministries over the centuries—might wish to move in this direction; but I doubt that the people of God would move with it. Our ministries are one way of telling the world who we are; it seems clear that we are not ready to abandon that medium of proclamation. And therefore there can be no true state of "full communion" in which ministries are not comparable and even (subject to the due process of each church) interchangeable.[4] What exactly *is* "full communion" without a ministry that is recognizably common?

In any case, the shift to a purely functional understanding of ministry would be an explicit rejection of much of the Anglican stream of tradition that is expected to enter this larger understanding of community, and so would invalidate the whole purpose of these conversations. The question, then, is whether there is some hope of shaping a ministry that would reveal our full communion with one another, as a Christian community genuinely Lutheran and genuinely Anglican, while also taking a step beyond both those identities in the direction of the larger unity of all faithful people in the body of Christ. *The answer, I believe, lies in reunderstanding ordination itself as a kind of gestural language in which our communities announce, for themselves and each other, who they understand themselves, by God's grace, to be.*[5] I offer this specifically as a substitute for other theories of orders, whether metaphysical (such as the pipeline theory) or functional.

Every aspect of the ordination process is relevant language, beginning with whatever process the community has of choosing or assenting to the choice of the ordinand. This choice or assent will be expressed variously in societies of differing political traditions, but it is a critical aspect of the whole process. Too often we focus entirely on the moment of the laying-on-of-hands, as if it were the only thing that mattered. This is analogous to theories of the Eucharistic presence that identify one specific instant at which consecration of the elements takes place. Modern liturgical study has long since replaced such ideas with a conception of the entire rite, from offertory through reception, as consecratory. It is this understanding of the Eucharist that has restored its essentially communal character, so that it becomes unintelligible, even for most Anglo–Catholics, to think of the Eucharist in terms of a priest celebrating entirely by virtue of his or her ordained status. The priest is rather the presiding officer at the community's celebration.

Failure to consider the importance of the community's act of choosing is what led to the absurdity of considering orders bestowed by *episcopi vagantes* as authentic. This works hand in hand with a pipeline theory—which ultimately implies that there can be no church without a priest, while "valid" priests can, in theory at least, be multiplied endlessly without a church.[6] On the other hand, if we take the community's role seriously, we perceive that wherever there is a truly Christian community, one that we can recognize as "church," they cannot fail to have the right to empower an authentic ministry. A difficulty arises only when, as was already the case in Corinth in the nineties of the first century, a community wants to change the existing ministry. Such changes, of course, are fraught with issues, often unspoken ones, about changes in identity and message. These, in turn, raise issues about relationships with other believers with whom we have previously agreed or disagreed, communed or not communed. Accordingly, a certain conservatism arose early on in Christianity that militates against changes in the ordained ministry—which, in fact, uses the ministry as a bond and sign of unity both within the local communities and among them.

It is this, above all, that the ordination rites came to express. To ordain a bishop, three other bishops must lay on hands. Since these will have had to come from neighboring cities, they were, in effect, bringing the new bishop into a larger network and reaffirming the local community's communion with the larger church. The bishop alone laid hands on deacons, to indicate that deacons functioned as extensions of the bishop in serving the church. The intimate connection between the two reemphasized the intimate connection between leadership and servanthood that comes down to us as part of Jesus' teaching. On the other hand, from our earliest records onward, other presbyters share in the laying-on-of-hands when a presbyter is ordained, for the college of presbyters has its own integrity in the local church. While it must function in relation to the larger church, as represented by the bishop, this college also serves as the council of elders whose advice could guide and restrain the bishop on behalf of the local community—in effect, an enlarged voice for that community in the deliberations of its leaders.

Ordination was thus not a single thing, from its very beginning, but a fairly complex set of gestures that wove together into a language through which the identity of each ordained person was defined in relation to the church, both local and universal. Therefore, at the same time, the identity of the church was also being defined in terms of its relationships and allegiances. Now this could become idolatrous (and does become idolatrous) whenever ministry or church is proclaimed for its own sake. The original point of the exercise, however, was to proclaim the Christian community as receiving its identity from the God who made us and gave Jesus for us. Thus, a late second–century ordination would serve to identify a bishop and the community for which the bishop was ordained as belonging to the network of bishops/churches that held to the faith that the Father of Jesus was also the Creator of the world. Ordination thus served as a sign of continuity in faith, hope, and love. It is the gospel, ultimately, that is being proclaimed through identifying the ministry and the church in this particular way.

One of the great hindrances to the task of uniting ministries—perhaps the greatest of them—is our tendency to treat ordinations as if they were governed not by the gospel but by purity laws. Danes, it is said, act as if a Swedish hand in one of their ordinations would invalidate the act. This is peculiar behavior among Christians in communion with one another. Among other things, it suggests a certain fearfulness about the fragility of Danish orders and about the ease with which they might be polluted. Some Anglo-Catholics currently express a similar anxiety, not just about the ordination of women as bishops, but about ordinations by those who participated in or supported such ordinations—as if touching the wrong head might invalidate the ordinations of the ordainers. (I wonder what this would have to say with regard to the old story of the bishop who confirmed a newel post by mistake.) Even more moderate Episcopalians and Lutherans, however, carry some of this purity mentality with them. If a Lutheran bishop participated in an Anglican ordination, would the ordination be less Anglican? If the reverse, would the ordination be less Lutheran? On the purity model, yes; for pollution is seen as intrinsically more powerful than the system it attacks. If our ministries are proclamations of life in the gospel, however, we should be able to find ways of preserving clarity in the "language" of orders without seeking to exclude our cobelievers.

If we can shed the purity model, I believe we can approach a common ministry by ensuring that each tradition retains and contributes to the whole the positive elements it has been expressing in its existing orders. For Anglicans, this must include the historic episcopate; for Lutherans, it must include elements associated in their orders with the Reformation itself and its assertion of the predominance of the gospel over the institutions of the church. Anglicans do not lose the historic episcopate by acknowledging the existing ministry of the ELCA as a true, gospel ministry, as we have already done. But the network of historic episcopate, with its bonds stretching through space and time, has to be an element of the common ministry of the future and must therefore be included in all future ordinations in both the ECUSA and the ELCA.[7] It is the element of physical contact that is vital in perpetuating this order of ministry—not because it replaces the consent of the community of the apostolic faith, but because it imparts to the ordinand a certain relationship to the larger Christian community.

For Lutherans, the preservation of the Reformation heritage is vital. Anglicans have no objection to this; indeed, we see it as embodied in our existing ministry. If Lutherans feel it is insufficiently evident, they should help us see how to make it more so. For Lutherans themselves, the main issue may be how to ensure against any impression that existing orders are being abandoned in favor of something called the "historic episcopate." Such abandonment might raise questions about the integrity of church life in the past, which would be a betrayal of blessings received and must surely be rejected. Accordingly, it is vital that any change in Lutheran rites of ordination should emphasize that continuity with the Reformation successions is not being broken. This could be done partly with a preface to the ordinal, identifying the distinct strands of succession that are being brought together, partly by bringing in the historic episcopate from Lutheran sources rather than or in addition to Anglican ones, and partly by clearly limiting the new ordinal to use for new ordinations.[8] Lutherans have already asserted, in the Augsburg Confession, the right of a gospel ministry of Word and Sacrament to ignore or circumvent those bishops who oppose its work. This, too, would act to preserve a Reformation perspective on the relativity of bishops.

These relatively concrete suggestions go considerably beyond my mandate and stem from purely personal musings—not from conversation with or authorization from the Episcopal participants in this dialogue. I offer them here primarily as a way of adumbrating a possible line of application for my earlier paper on the historic episcopate. It is my hope that they may help us focus our discussion in the relatively short time remaining to the projected life of LED III.

6

EPISCOPACY:
THE LEGACY OF THE
LUTHERAN CONFESSIONS
BY
ERIC W. GRITSCH

CONTEXT

The question of the order and supervision of ministry has been a principal concern to Lutherans since the beginning of the Lutheran reform movement. Although Luther rejected the "indelible character" of priestly orders, he consistently linked ordination to order. Bishops, he declared, should not be abrogated but should function "in the place and stead of the whole community, all of whom have like power"; they should "consecrate...a person and charge him to exercise this power on behalf of the others."[1] Luther went so far as to suggest that, on the basis of their baptism, secular princes should at times function as "emergency bishops." "For whoever comes out of the water of baptism can boast that he is already a consecrated priest, bishop, and pope, although of course it is not seemly that just anybody should exercise such an office."[2]

But at issue was the proper relationship between priest and parish rather than between priest and bishop. Baptism commissions every-one to exercise the ministry of the Word, but only those commissioned by the whole community should do such ministry publicly. "Publicly one may not exercise a right without the consent of the whole body or of the church. In time of emergency each may use it as he deems best."[3]

Since Rome refused to negotiate any change in doctrine or church structure, Luther let the emergency determine ministry of the Word.

In reorganizing Christendom in electoral Saxony, Lutherans reinstituted procedures existing at the time of Emperor Constantine and the Council of Nicaea in 352. "Visitations" initiated this reorganization and supervision. "We would have liked to have seen the true episcopal office and practice of visitation re-established, because of the pressing need" Luther wrote in 1528. "However, since none of us felt a call or a definite command to do this, and St. Peter has not countenanced the creation of anything in the church unless we are convinced that it is willed by God, no one has dared to undertake it."[4] Consequently Luther appealed to "love's office (which is an obligation common to all Christians)" and asked Elector John of Saxony to commission visitors who, on the basis of a thorough assessment of the situation in the Saxon countryside, would recommend reforms. The elector would do what Emperor Constantine had done when he summoned the bishops to Nicaea in order to preserve Christian unity.[5] Thus Luther linked church and state in his proposed reform, being convinced that God had established three essential orders or hierarchies: "the office of priest; the estate of marriage; the civil government." These three orders are grounded in the "common order of Christian love, in which one serves not only the three orders, but also serves every needy person in general with all kinds of benevolent deeds...."[6]

Unlike John Calvin and other sixteenth-century reformers, Luther reinterpreted the existing order of ministry rather than rejecting it. He thought he was in agreement with earlier church leaders, notably Paul and Jerome, in considering bishop (*episcopus*) and pastor (*presbyterus*) to be equals.[7] Luther agreed with Philip Melanchthon's draft of the Augsburg Confession, which made the office of the ministry a principal "article of faith and doctrine" (article 5) while depicting "the power of bishops" as a matter "in dispute, in which an account is given of the abuses which have been corrected." The former is a matter of substance and appears in the first part of the Augsburg Confession, while the latter is a debatable "human tradition" and is contained in the second part.

According to Luther there are, then, only two ways to exercise the ministry of the Word of God; in the vocation of the ordained, and in the vocations of the baptized who are not ordained. Yet Luther was willing to retain the office of bishop as a special assignment of the ordained, as it were, namely to guard the freedom of the gospel. "You could restore the episcopal jurisdiction again, as long as you left us free to preach the gospel" he wrote from Coburg in 1530. Addressing the German princes, he chided them for having used their God-given authority against the gospel—blunting it—instead of using their authority to do what God had ordained: support his Word. [8]

On 21 January 1530, Emperor Charles V issued his summons to convoke an imperial diet. He was aware that the power of Lutheran territories threatened Christian unity, and territorial unity had become as important as doctrinal unity because the Turks had become a major threat to all Christendom. He therefore asked Lutherans to submit their teachings for review by the Diet of Augsburg, which would be willing to hear their complaints about matters of law and ecclesiastical abuse. The Lutherans were required to account for whatever new ordinances they had enacted in their territories, and to show how these were in conformity with Christian tradition.

Elector John asked the Wittenberg reformers (Luther, Justus Jonas, John Bugenhagen, and Melanchthon) to justify their dissension.[9] After meetings in Marburg and Schwabach in 1529 dealing with Lutheran essentials (Schwabach Articles), they met in March in Torgau and drafted the Torgau Articles, with Melanchthon as the principal scribe. The Schwabach and Torgau articles formed the basis for the Augsburg Confession, one draft of which Luther and Melanchthon discussed in Coburg between April 16 and 24, 1530. Melanchthon continued to draft several versions, and the whole Confession—signed by seven princes and the representatives of Nuremberg and Reutlingen—was finally submitted to the diet on 25 June 1530.

The Augsburg Confession was intended to prove that Lutherans had remained catholic and were hoping merely for Rome's toleration of some differences in doctrine and life. Article 28 offered the Lutheran view of episcopacy; it was defended in the Apology of the Augsburg Confession in 1531 and amplified by Luther's Smalcald Articles of 1537; other references to it are contained in the complete edition of the Lutheran confessions, the *Book of Concord* of 1580.[10]

FINDINGS

Recent research into the origins of CA 28 on the question of episcopacy has shown that the text presupposed the continued existence of the medieval hierarchy,

> ...but it makes the recognition of that hierarchy dependent on two conditions: bishops must stop requiring vows of celibacy and renunciation of evangelical doctrine at ordination; and in the same vein, the pope must give the gospel free course. If these two conditions remain unfulfilled, the supply of clergy will decline;

evangelicals will look for other forms of ordination and installa- tion.[11]

The question of "the power of bishops"(*der Bischofen Gewalt*) or "ecclesiastic power" (*potestas ecclesiastica*), as CA 28 put it, was tackled exclusively from the practical side, i.e., from considerations of canon and secular law as experienced in Electoral Saxony and examined during the visitations of 1528. Another decisive factor in questions of jurisdiction and ordination was Elector John's willingness to yield to the church wherever he could do so in good conscience.[12]

Focusing on the proper distinction between temporal and spiritual power, Melanchthon dealt with the doctrinal question of the "power of the keys" (*potestas clavium*) in a preliminary draft to CA.[13] He clearly assigned the power to forgive or withhold forgiveness of sins (Matt. 16:19) to the "office of bishop or priest." At the same time, however, he rejected Rome's "error" of claiming that popes could decide the fate of kings by either denying or offering "confirmation" (*confirma- tio*).[14] The distinction between temporal and spiritual jurisdiction in CA 28 is related to other Lutheran affirmations, such as that of communion in both kinds (CA 22), clerical marriage (CA 23), and a Mass without the notion of "sacrifice" (CA 24).

At issue was the freedom of the gospel in the context of Luther's doctrine of two realms. But CA 28 is not a doctrinal article, for Melanchthon—assuming the doctrine of God's two ways of govern- ing—in CA 28 "laid out a well-prepared strategy for negotiation, approved by Luther; it sets the direction for political and theological discussions at the Augsburg Diet."[15] Thus CA 28 "is not a self-con- tained dogmatic statement; it represents the result of a lively discussion that began long before 1530, continued between Luther and Melanchthon, and still went on during the negotiations at the diet."[16]

CA 28 was intended to overcome the "careless confusion" of spiri- tual and temporal power in the office of bishop.[17] Spiritual power "is exercised only by teaching or preaching the Gospel and by adminis- tering the sacrament either to many or to individuals, depending on one's calling."[18] Temporal power "is concerned with other things than the Gospel," namely protecting law and order by imposing physical penalties.[19] Lutherans distinguish between the two powers, "and they command that both be held in honor and acknowledged as gifts and blessings of God."[20] This distinction is particularly significant with regard to the jurisdiction of bishops.

Hence according to the Gospel (or, as they say, by divine right) no jurisdiction belongs to bishops as bishops (that is, to *those to whom has been committed the ministry of Word and sacraments*) except to forgive sins, to reject doctrine that is contrary to the Gospel, and to exclude from the fellowship of the church ungodly persons whose wickedness is known, doing all this without human power, simply by the Word. Churches are therefore bound by divine law to be obedient to the bishops according to the text [Luke 10:16], "He who hears you hears me."[21]

The only difference between pastors and bishops noted in CA 28 is the borderline area of temporal and spiritual power in matters of matrimonial law and tithing.[22] If bishops neglect these areas, princes may take over these functions "for the sake of maintaining public peace"[23]—a reference to Luther's notion of the prince as "emergency bishop" (*Notbischof*). In all other areas, including the regulation of worship and discipline, "bishops do not have the power to institute anything contrary to the Gospel"—an injunction Lutherans thought grounded in Scripture as well as canon law.[24] Here Christian liberty in matters of law preserves the integrity of the Gospel, which alone justifies before God.[25]

CA 28 clearly upholds the office of bishop, but notes that this office is burdened by abuses: "The bishops might easily retain the lawful obedience of men if they did not insist on the observance of traditions which cannot be kept by a good conscience."[26] The administration of the Eucharist in one kind and clerical celibacy burden consciences committed to the gospel. Nevertheless, the episcopacy is an honorable and dignified tradition in the church.

Our churches do not ask that the bishops restore concord at the expense of their honor (which, however, good pastors ought to do) but ask only that they relax unjust burdens which are new and were introduced contrary to the custom of the church catholic. Perhaps there were acceptable reasons for these ordinances when they were introduced, but they are not adapted to later times. It is also apparent that some were adopted out of misunderstanding. It would therefore befit the clemency of the bishops to mitigate these regulations now, for such a change does not impair the unity of the church inasmuch as changes do not destroy the unity of Christian churches.[27]

CA 28 closes with the reminder that even Peter "forbids the bishops to be domineering" (1 Peter 5:2) and that Lutherans favor episcopal leadership provided bishops "allow the Gospel to be taught purely and that they relax some few ordinances which cannot be kept without sin." If the bishops refuse to do so, the occasion for schism is their own fault, "and they must see how they will answer for it before God."[28]

When Melanchthon became aware that the Catholic opposition was having difficulties with the doctrine of two realms, he drafted a statement on the positive aspects about "human tradition" (*Menschensatzung*) with respect to canon law in particular, sharing his insights with Luther on 14 July 1530. This draft offered three acceptable reasons for "ecclesiastical statutes": (1) they can assure good order; (2) they maintain physical discipline; and (3) they demonstrate publicly that faith is active in love and gratitude. Canon law might be permitted to regulate matters such as matrimonial law, fasting, and works of charity, if it were understood to be by "human law" (*ius humanum*); thus "bishops may rule on the basis of man–made law."[29]

Luther did not agree with Melanchthon, contending that God's two realms are "separate and distinct," especially with regard to the relationship between church and state, and that great alertness was needed to distinguish between them because the pope had confused them. Consequently "the same person cannot be a bishop and a sovereign, nor simultaneously a pastor and a house–father."[30] Moreover, he added, bishops should not impose any statute or ceremony "except with the expressed or silent agreement of the church....The bishops are, after all, merely servants and stewards, and not the lords of the church." Only as citizens should subjects obey whatever statutes are mandated, not as members of the church; and when mandating statutes, bishops should act as temporal rulers. Luther was unhappy about making any changes in his distinction between church and state, and told Melanchthon to stop bringing up such "vain worries."[31] He also expressed his dissatisfaction with the suggested compromise in CA 28.

Melanchthon, however, joined a negotiating committee of fourteen that met daily during the first week of its dialogue on the Augsburg Confession, August 16 to 30, but the committee failed to achieve unity.[32] The Roman Catholic *Confutation* rejected CA 28, claiming that the exercise of ecclesiastical power was by "divine right," and accused Lutherans of confusing Christian liberty with "prodigious license" (*mutwilliger Urlaub, licentia*).[33] Melanchthon wrote a passionate defense of the Lutheran position: "But if our opponents would only listen to the complaints of churches and pious hearts!" The opponents, he declared, defend a position that neglects the actual state of the churches and the reforms that have been accomplished, and, instead of instructing "minds tortured by doubt, they call to arms."[34] The reformers, he added, talk about

> ...a bishop according to the Gospel. We like the old division of power into the power of the order (*potestas ordinis*) and the power of jurisdiction (*potestas jurisdictionis*). Therefore a bishop has the power of the order, namely, the ministry of Word and sacraments. He also has the power of jurisdiction, namely the authority to excommunicate those who are guilty of public offenses or to absolve them if they are converted and ask for absolution. A bishop does not have the power of a tyrant to act without a definite law, nor that of a king to act above the law. But he has a definite command, a definite Word of God, which he ought to teach and according to which he ought to exercise his jurisdiction...when anyone does something contrary to that Word which they have received from Christ.[35]

Yet Melanchthon remained conciliatory, even in the face of the accusation that Lutherans confuse "prodigious license" with Christian liberty. "If all the offenses are put together, still the one doctrine of the forgiveness of sins, that by faith we freely obtain the forgiveness of sins for Christ's sake, brings enough good to hide all the evils."[36] Nevertheless, for the sake of the truth needed in the church, Lutherans would obey God rather than persons (Acts 5:29); they would leave it up to "the judgement of all pious people" whether or not they had been refuted.[37]

The attempt at reconciliation contained in CA 28 and even in AP 28 is based on the Lutheran understanding of the office of ministry stated in CA 5 and CA 14. CA 5 links the Word of God to the office of ministry, which is an "office of preaching" (*Predigtamt*) as well as an "ecclesiastical office" (*ministerium ecclesiasticum*). Word and Sacrament are the "means" (*instrumenta*) used by the Holy Spirit to grant faith, when and where it pleases God, to those who hear the gospel.[38] "Nobody should preach publicly in the church or administer the sacraments without having been 'rightly called' (*rite vocatus*)."[39] "The gift of the Spirit belongs to Christendom as a whole, and only through the church's call does the office-bearer share in that common possession."[40] CA 14 rejects the notion advanced by radical reformers like Thomas Müntzer that the Spirit inhabits one person over against the whole church, and insists that one must be "rightly called" by the church—local, regional, national, or international.

Every assembly nurtured by Word and Sacrament is fully "catholic," thus the office of ministry is by definition public and ecumenical. As Luther put it in his critique of "clandestine preachers": "The Holy Spirit does not come with stealth. He descends in full view from heaven. The serpent glides unnoticed. The doves fly."[41] The public office of the ministry represents the historical record of the apostolic tradition and serves the cause of Christian unity. "For the true unity of the church, it is enough to agree concerning the teaching of the Gospel and the administration of the sacraments."[42]

Since the *Confutation* did not reject the Lutheran insistence on a "regular call" for those ordained, Melanchthon hoped for some compromise on the question of ecclesiastical order. AP 14 therefore speaks of the Lutheran "deep desire to maintain the church polity and various ranks of ecclesiastical hierarchy, *although they were created by human authority.*"[43] But the power of the keys "belongs by divine right to all who preside over the churches, whether they are called pastors, presbyters, or bishops."[44] Melanchthon pushed this point even further when he contended that this divine right is a gift given to the whole church. "So in an emergency, even a layman absolves and becomes the minister and pastor of another."[45] Bishops may not reserve this right for themselves alone, and, if they do, they have become tyrants.[46]

The Smalcald Articles of 1537, Luther's theological testament, are more polemical in tone when dealing with episcopacy, although Luther agreed with Melanchthon that the office of bishop may be a sign of Christian unity. "If the bishops were true bishops and were concerned about the church and the Gospel, they might be permitted (for the sake of love and unity, but not of necessity) to ordain and confirm us and our preachers, provided this could be done without pretense, humbug, or unchristian ostentation."[47] But, since Luther had lost all hope of reform of the existing hierarchy, he suggested that the reform movement instead revive the ancient custom of providing pastors outside the jurisdiction of Rome. "We shall and ought ourselves ordain suitable persons to this office."[48] Melanchthon, more conciliatory than Luther, added a note to his signature on the Smalcald Articles:

I, Philip Melanchthon, regard the above articles as right and Christian. However, concerning the pope, I hold that, if he would allow the Gospel, we, too, may concede to him that superiority over the bishops which he possesses by human right (*iure humano*), making this concession for the sake of peace and general unity among the

Christians who are now under him and who may be so in the future.[49]

IMPACT

Since Roman Catholic bishops opposed the Lutheran reform movement in Germany, the Lutheran territories developed a ministry of supervision by establishing "superintendents" and "consistories" to deal with issues of marriage. The elector of Saxony created one such consistory in Wittenberg. In 1542, Luther, who wanted to establish a truly "evangelical" episcopacy that would exercise and guard the office of Word and Sacrament, installed his friend Nicholas of Amsdorf as bishop of Naumburg. Taking Augustine as his model,[50] he declared that the duties of the bishop should be those of a pastor: "to be holy, preach, baptize, bind and forgive sins, comfort, and help souls to eternal life."

In 1545, Elector John Frederick asked the Wittenberg theologians to offer an "opinion" *(Ratschlag)* concerning the preservation of the Augsburg Confession and the role of a reformed episcopacy. This "opinion," known as "The Wittenberg Reformation" of 14 January 1545, speaks of bishops as part of a tradition that is worth keeping.

> To keep order in the church, one must have bishops, a degree higher than priests *(als ein Grad über andre Priester)* and they must have a designated authority *(müssen bestellte Regiment haben)*; one must have a number of them to ordain, to instruct ordinands, to make visitations, to serve on tribunals, to advise, to write, to represent, and to staff synods and councils, just as Athanasius, Basil, Ambrose, and Augustine had to do all these things in order to preserve correct doctrine in their own and other churches and defend them against heretics. If the existing form of episcopacy were torn apart *(zerrissen)*, barbarism and desolation without end would result, for temporal power and princes are burdened with other matters, and only a few respect the church or reflect on her teaching.[51]

The "Opinion" also charged bishops to use the ban in accordance with Matthew 16 and 1 Timothy 5 in order to preserve right teaching. In addition, they were required to care for universities as "custodians of doctrine" and to hold synods where, for the sake of church unity, pastors should sort out problems and deal with them.[52]

Some territories did have evangelical bishops for a while: Naumburg, 1542–1547; Schleswig–Holstein, 1542–1551; Merseburg, 1544–1550; and Kammin, 1545–1556. Württemberg enacted a "church order" (*Kirchenordnung*) that established a consistory composed of theologians responsible for the examination of ordinands and political councilors responsible for legal and financial affairs. A superintendent was appointed by the duke. Superintendents were soon divided into three ranks: special superintendents, who had local jurisdiction; four regional superintendents to exercise general supervision; and a "dean" to supervise the other superintendents. This form of episcopacy became the model for many German territories, although the titles sometimes changed. In Prussia, for example, superintendents were called "arch–priests"; in Schleswig–Holstein, *Pröpste*, "deans"; in southern Germany, *Dekane*, "deans"; in the Hanseatic cities, *Senioren*, "seniors."

The Peace of Augsburg in 1555 suspended the spiritual jurisdiction in territories adhering to the Augsburg Confession "until a final settlement be reached." But *"cuius regio eius religio"* was soon interpreted to mean that territorial princes, who had already functioned as "emergency bishops," would now exercise episcopal authority; they became known as *"summi episcopi,"* the highest spiritual authority in territories adhering to the Augsburg Confession. This "summa–episcopacy" prevailed in Germany until 1918, when the monarchy gave way to more democratic forms of government.[53]

An attempt to reintroduce the historic episcopate was made in Prussia in 1701, when the first king, Frederick III, was to be crowned according to customary English rites. Since Daniel Ernst Jablonski, the Reformed Court Chaplain in Königsberg, had been consecrated bishop in the Moravian Church in proper apostolic succession through the Hussite connection (*Unitas Fratrum*), he volunteered to function as the bishop required for the occasion. But Fredrick refused to cede his rights as *summus episcopus* and therefore appointed the Lutheran court chaplain Ursinus from Berlin and the Reformed chaplain von Sanden from Königsberg to be his bishops. Though called "bishops," both were eventually recognized only as "chief court chaplains" (*Oberhofprediger*). Jablonski in 1737 consecrated Nicholas von Zinzendorf as bishop of the Moravian community of Herrnhut and thus linked the Hussite tradition to confessional Lutheranism because the Moravian community in Herrnhut accepted the Augsburg Confession. German Lutherans did not consider the consecration of Zinzendorf an expression of apostolic succession, even though German church orders generally retained the title "bishop" for heads of synods and/or geographical territories.[54]

In the wake of the third centennial of the Reformation celebrated in 1817, German Lutherans again debated the nature and function of episcopacy. Wilhelm Löhe and his disciples defended the notion that the office of Word and Sacrament was instituted *iure divino*. The theologian Theodor Kliefoth (1810–1895) succeeded in reorganizing the Mecklenburg territory by distinguishing hierarchically three juridical, divinely instituted offices: (1) the clergy, officers of the means of grace (*Gnadenmittelamt*); (2) the laity (*Gemeindeamt*); and (3) a ruling office identical with the episcopacy (*Kirchenregieramt*). His reorganization lasted until 1918.[55]

The Lutheran king Christian III deposed the existing Danish bishops in 1536 and deprived them of their temporal power. He then appointed new bishops to the seven dioceses, thus exercising what Luther had called the right of princes to be "emergency bishops." In other Scandinavian countries, particularly Sweden, bishops were considered to be in apostolic succession even when kings had appointed them. In its Lambeth Conferences in 1888, 1897, and 1908, the Church of England made it known that the church of Sweden had preserved the episcopal apostolic succession. As a result, the Swedish Bishop's Assembly in 1922 felt obliged to cite CA 5 and declare that Swedish episcopacy was *de iure humano*, not *de iure divino*.[56]

Some Lutheran communities in the Lutheran World Federation have contended that episcopacy represents the well–being of the church (*bene esse*), but there is very little, if any, argument favoring the office of bishop as necessary to the being (*esse*) of the church.[57] There seems to be no consensus among Lutherans regarding episcopal apostolic "well–being" (*bene esse*), and "fullness" (*plene esse*) seems to have given way to more recent assessments of episcopal apostolic succession in terms of "a sign, though not guarantee, of the continuity and unity of the Church."[58]

CONCLUSION

The Lutheran reform movement of the sixteenth century did not succeed in reforming the church catholic in the West. The Peace of Augsburg in 1555 merely confirmed the schism existing between reformers and defenders of the *status quo*; the Council of Trent (1545–1563) erected new walls in Rome's defense against the Reformation churches.

On the other hand, Lutheran territories often ignored the Lutheran Confessions, which cherished not only "the Protestant principle" but also the "Catholic substance."[59] The article of justification became a bland doctrine defended by neo–Aristotelians attacking Trentine Roman Catholicism; it no longer bore any relationship to Lutheran sacramental life, spiritual formation, or any ecclesiastical order distinct from territorial politics.

Although the sixteenth-century call for an evangelical episcopate had been loud and clear, it was ignored by post-Reformation Lutheranism. But more recently, discussion within Lutheranism has focused on the question of whether episcopacy itself can become a threat to the freedom of the gospel, or whether the sixteenth-century Lutheran movement retained an episcopal order with no alternatives.[60] The Lutheran Confessions clearly prefer an episcopate, provided that it is an *evangelical* one, enhancing the ministry of the gospel, through Word and Sacrament, rather than diminishing it. Under those conditions the office of bishop can be understood as part of the office of ministry, instituted by God so that people may gain faith in the God who, through Christ, justifies sinners (CA 5). Debate on the freedom of the gospel must involve everyone engaged in the ministry of that gospel, which assures the world that "the one holy Church is to continue forever" (CA 7). This ministry should not be done without being called to it, for it is to be done in good order (CA 14) and with care for the proper exercise of power on the part of bishops (CA 26).

Both partners in any dialogue with Lutherans must answer the question "What kind of episcopacy enhances the freedom of the gospel?" because Lutherans are bound by their confessional legacy to settle all issues with an eye to Christian unity. The preface to the CA clearly states, "We on our part shall not omit doing anything, in so far as God and conscience allow, that may serve the cause of Christian unity."[61] The Lutheran-Episcopal Dialogue in the U.S. has stated, "If we are faithful, we will *together* discover the forms demanded by the church's new opportunities, so that the church may have an *episcope* which will be an *episcope* of the apostolic gospel."[62] To work for such an episcopacy is the Lutheran Confessions' legacy, even though this legacy has been obscured and distorted in the past and the present.

7

LUTHERAN RECOGNITION OF THE *BOOK OF COMMON PRAYER*
BY
WALTER R. BOUMAN

The assignment emerging out of the discussion at Session 5 of the dialogue was to write, from a Lutheran perspective, a theological review of the 1979 revision of the *Book of Common Prayer* "with a view to eventual recognition."[1] This paper has three sections: first, a brief summary statement; second, commentary on some specific items in the BCP; and third, some attention to the meaning of "recognition."

SUMMARY STATEMENT

The 1979 revision of the BCP is a liturgical and doctrinal expression of the Protestant Reformation of the sixteenth century, with a location in the catholic/conservative end of the spectrum of Reformation concerns. It has a perspective in harmony with the confessional documents of the *Book of Concord*, particularly the Augsburg Confession and its Apology. Some features of the BCP about which Lutherans might have questions need to be understood in the light of historical developments within the Anglican tradition. Some features of the BCP that might surprise Lutherans need to be understood in the light of historical developments within the Lutheran tradition. However, there are no obstacles to doctrinal recognition and liturgical use of the BCP by Lutherans.

COMMENTARY

The Function of the *Book of Common Prayer* in the Episcopal Church

It should be noted at the outset that the BCP is constitutionally required to be used in all dioceses of the ECUSA without "alteration thereof or addition thereto." The provision for such use is to be found in Article X of the Constitution, which reads as follows:

> The Book of Common Prayer and Administration of the Sacraments and other Rites and Ceremonies of the Church, together with the Psalter or Psalms of David, the Form and Manner of Making, Ordaining, and Consecrating Bishops, Priests, and Deacons, the Form of Consecration of a Church or Chapel, the office of Institution of Ministers, and Articles of Religion, as now established or hereafter amended by the authority of this Church, shall be in use in all the Dioceses and Missionary Dioceses, and in the Convocation of the American Churches in Europe, of this church.[2]

Clergy are "subject to the Rubrics of the Book of Common Prayer" in their conduct of worship,[3] and liable to disciplinary proceeding for "violation of the Rubrics of the Book of Common Prayer."[4] Stephen Sykes points to the fact that the Church of England

> has a substantial and quite vigorously enforced discipline, though not so much in the direct area of church doctrine as in the indirect area of canon law and liturgical order.[5]

He quotes the "Declaration of Assent" required of candidates for ordination in the Church of England. "In public prayer and administration of the sacraments, I will use only the forms of service which are authorised or allowed by Canon."[6]

No similar requirement obtains for Lutheran parishes and clergy. Thus, in contrast to that fact that one cannot know whether or in what way *Lutheran Book of Worship* will be used in Lutheran parishes, one can assume that what is to be found in the BCP is actually being said and done in parishes of the Episcopal Church. One must, of course, acknowledge that both the options authorized in the BCP and the traditions/usages of individual parishes will make for considerable variety. However, all such variety will presumably fall within the parameters set by the BCP.

The significance of such liturgical obligation should not escape Lutherans with their confessional concern, ordination promises, and historic commitment to doctrinal orthodoxy.[7] It may well be that the church is *effectively* orthodox in terms of what it does liturgically when it gathers for worship or administers rites of pastoral care, and that the church *teaches* most effectively through liturgy and ritual.[8] This observation is especially important at a time when catechetical instruction has diminished power and duration, when the churches are faced with a new sociological situation (individual mobility and cultural pluralism are but two factors of the new situation), and when the members added to the church from 1950 to 1970 in great numbers may not have been adequately evangelized and/or catechized. Lutherans need to reexamine their neglect of the liturgy as a locus for teaching, spiritual formation, confession, and mission.

Formal Comparison between the *Book of Common Prayer* and *Lutheran Book of Worship*

The BCP contains all the rubrics, rites, and alternatives necessary for its use. For Lutherans, comparable materials are scattered throughout three different editions of *Lutheran Book of Worship*: the pew edition, the *Ministers Desk Edition* (only liturgical materials), and *Occasional Services*. The consequence of this is that some materials that are needed for parish use (e.g., the special congregational liturgical materials for Ash Wednesday and for Holy Week) are not available in the pew edition. Nor are materials necessary for pastoral care (e.g., Holy Communion for those in special circumstances). The publication of the more detailed rubrics, proper prefaces, and alternative eucharistic prayers in the Ministers Desk Edition means not only that these materials are not available to the congregation, but they also receive less attention and use from the clergy.

The completeness of the BCP in this regard testifies to the differences in historical development between Lutherans and Anglicans. Lutherans have, for several centuries, combined hymn collections with liturgical materials. That has necessitated a space limitation for liturgical materials. LBW has actually expanded the liturgical materials available to the entire congregation, but it is still not enough, as any reading of the BCP indicates.

The BCP is a *revision* of an existing book with its roots deep in the Anglican reformation. That accounts for some of the features of the 1979 BCP, e.g., the inclusion of rites and collects in traditional language beside the rites and collects in contemporary language. Revision may ensure greater continuity, but it may also be a limitation. The inclusion of rites in both traditional and contemporary idiom will mean some (perhaps much) loss of shared expression and common

115

tradition. Revision also makes it more difficult to move creatively in new directions under the impact of new theological, historical, and liturgical insights. Nevertheless, there are significant additions and improvements evident in the 1979 revision.

The Reformation Perspective of the BCP

The basic historical/theological premise that underlies the BCP is that there was serious distortion of the Christian tradition in the (late?) medieval church, that this distortion particularly affected worship and pastoral care, and that the significant reforms made necessary by this distortion should be "an attempt to return to the pattern of the early church."[9] This is surely a historical/theological premise shared by the Lutheran reformers.

The opening statement of the BCP that the Holy Eucharist is "the principle act of Christian worship on the Lord's Day and other major feasts"[10] echoes the position of the Augsburg Confession and its Apology. The Augsburg Confession states:

> Inasmuch as the mass is such a giving of the sacrament, one common Mass is observed among us on every holy day, and on other days, if any desire the sacrament, it is also administered to those who ask for it.[11]

The opening paragraph of Article XXIV of the Apology reaffirms this.

> To begin with, we must repeat the prefatory statement that we do not abolish the Mass but religiously keep and defend it. In our churches Mass is celebrated every Sunday and on other festivals, when the sacrament is offered to those who wish for it after they have been examined and absolved. We keep traditional liturgical forms, such as the order of the lessons, prayers, vestments, etc.[12]

There is thus genuine congruity in intent and perspective between the BCP and the BC.

The Calendars

The liturgical calendars of the two traditions are nearly identical. The Feast of the Transfiguration comes on August 6 in the Anglican tradition, and it comes on the last Sunday after Epiphany in the Lutheran tradition. The commemoration of St. Joseph on March 19 is accorded lower status in LBW than in the BCP. LBW makes no provision for observing American Independence Day on July 4. The inclusion of such a national day in the BCP may reflect the fact that the Episcopal Church is much more part of the "establishment" in the United States than are the Lutheran churches.

Significant differences occur in the commemoration of those persons not mentioned in the Scriptures. LBW is the first liturgical book of a Lutheran church in the U.S. to include the names of persons not mentioned in the Scriptures, although parishes have been named in honor of St. Lawrence, St. Olaf, St. Ansgar, St. Martin of Tours, St. Elizabeth of Thuringia, St. Francis, and Martin Luther (all of whom are commemorated), as well as St. Anthony, St. George, St. Sebald, Gustavus Adolphus, Erik Pontoppidan, and even the French revolutionary general Jean Bernadotte, who ruled Norway and Sweden as King Charles XIV (none of whom are commemorated).

The list of commemorations in LBW is more "catholic" than that of the BCP, at least from the sixteenth century onward. LBW commemorates Anglicans George Herbert, John and Charles Wesley, John Donne, John Mason Neale, and William Tyndale. The only Lutheran name in the BCP list is Muhlenberg, but, alas, it is nineteenth-century Episcopal clergyman William Augustus Muhlenberg rather than American Lutheran patriarch Henry Melchior Muhlenberg. One ecumenical gesture for both churches might be dutiful attention to the other's commemorations in addition to one's own. A Lutheran cannot help but be the richer for having read the brief biographies of the persons commemorated in the BCP.[13] Reading the biographies of persons commemorated in LBW[14] can be commended with equal enthusiasm to members of the Episcopal church.

The Psalter and Other Matters

The BCP is to be commended for printing the entire Psalter. One wishes LBW had done likewise. LBW is to be commended for consistently printing the ICET text of the Lord's Prayer first and making the "traditional" text an alternative. One wishes the BCP had done likewise. We need to cultivate a common text for the Lord's Prayer among English–speaking Christians. Another ecumenical discipline to which we could commit ourselves would be the regular congregational use of the ICET translations.

The Eucharist

The rite for the Eucharist is central for both the BCP and LBW. The text for the liturgy of the Eucharist in the BCP raises several significant questions for Lutherans.

1. The penitential emphasis in the rite of the BCP seems to determine how the Eucharist itself is understood. While the BC states that forgiveness of sins is imparted in the sacrament, that the sacrament is

thus a source of consolation and comfort, that communicants should be penitent, and that "worthiness" consists wholly in a communicant's penitent awareness of need, this does not mean that the Lutheran Confessions view the Eucharist as basically a penitential rite. Nor does a penitential emphasis dominate the eucharistic rite of LBW.

By way of contrast, note the following aspects of the BCP rite:

a. The exhortation (BCP, pp. 316–317) is based on a questionable interpretation of 1 Cor. 11:28, "Examine yourselves, and only then eat of the bread and drink of the cup." St. Paul was referring to the way in which the poor were excluded and individual selfishness had come to characterize the celebration of the Eucharist at Corinth (1 Cor. 11:21–22). Such behavior meant that the meal of the Corinthians was no longer the Lord's Supper, the eschatological Eucharist of the church (1 Cor. 11:20). St. Paul's exhortation, "Examine yourselves," meant that the more affluent Corinthians were to remember that in *this* meal they were proclaiming the self–giving death of the Lord; and therefore they were to share what they had brought with the less affluent members of the congregation. But the Exhortation in the BCP urges, on the basis of 1 Cor. 11:28, that preparation for the Eucharist means penitent self-examination on the basis of the Decalog, followed by confession, intention to amend one's life, and "restitution for all injuries and wrongs." This is hardly what St. Paul had in mind.

b. The printing of penitential orders, though they may be used as separate services, directly before the Eucharist leads inescapably to understanding confession/absolution in the context of Eucharist rather than in the context of Baptism. The latter is Martin Luther's important insight in the Large Catechism.

> Here you see that Baptism, both by its power and by its significa-tion, comprehends also the third sacrament, formerly called Penance, which is really nothing else than Baptism....If you live in repentance, therefore, you are walking in Baptism...Repentance, therefore, is nothing else than a return and approach to Baptism, to resume and practice what had earlier been begun but aban-doned.[15]

When penitential discipleship is understood in this way it allows Baptism to be a lifelong *experience,* and it frees the celebration of the Eucharist to be the rite that gives identity and mission to the eschato-logical community.[16] The pietist linkage between the Eucharist and penitence frustrates authenticity and integrity for both. It is disap-pointing to see this still done in this revision of the BCP.

c. Rite One then prefaces the Kyrie with the Decalog or a summary of the Decalog, so that the Kyrie, too, is understood within a penitential context (BCP, p. 324). This is a misunderstanding of the Kyrie, both liturgically and theologically, but one that can be traced to Calvinist influence on the 1552 revision of the BCP.[17]

d. Both Rites One and Two then prescribe a confession before the sharing of the Peace (BCP, pp. 330, 359), "if it has not been said earlier." The rubrics thus seem to ensure that a penitential dimension will under no circumstances be omitted from the eucharistic rite. To be sure, "on occasion, the Confession may be omitted." But Hatchett makes clear that it is to be omitted only "on great festal days of the church year."[18] Just prior to the distribution the "Prayer of Humble Access" may be said (BCP, p. 337), emphasizing once again the penitential perspective of the entire Eucharist.

While Rite Two modifies this accent somewhat, both rites seem to be limited by the fact that they are *revisions*, that there is a strong emphasis on continuity with a traditional (pietist?) interpretation of the Eucharist, rather than an attempt to provide a rite that is more reflective of the perspective that has informed, for example, the Lima text for the Eucharist.[19] To be sure, Lutherans, whose sacramental piety has also experienced a strong pietist influence, cannot raise fundamental objections to this penitential interpretation of the Eucharist in the BCP, especially since there are traces of it also in LBW. But it is to be hoped that both traditions can move together toward greater liturgical expression of the eschatological and eucharistic character of this sacrament.

2. One distribution formula retains the "Zwinglian form" from the 1552 revision of the BCP.[20] Following the "Prayer of Humble Access" the celebrant (*sic*), "facing the people" (has he or she not been doing so all along?), may say the following Invitation:

The Gifts of God for the People of God.

and may then add Take them in remembrance that Christ died for you, and feed on him in your hearts by faith, with thanksgiving (BCP, p. 338).

The first administration form repeats this. Rite Two allows the celebrant to say the identical invitation, but it does not offer the option of using the first administration form from Rite One.

The question for Lutherans is whether the Invitation and the subsequent administration form from Rite One are an implicit denial of the real presence of the Body and Blood of Christ "in, with, and under" the forms of bread and wine. Article XXVIII of the Articles of Religion states:

> The Body of Christ is given, taken and eaten, in the Supper *only* after an heavenly and spiritual manner. And the mean whereby the Body of Christ is received and eaten in the Supper, is Faith (BCP, p. 873).

Several factors combine to indicate that the "Zwinglian form" is not intended to be understood in a Zwinglian manner. First, the Articles of Religion are identified as one of the "Historical Documents of the Church," along with the Chicago–Lambeth Quadrilateral, and these documents are not ultimately normative for the ECUSA. The "Zwinglian form" is thus *not* to be understood in the light of Article XXVIII.

Second, both Rite One and Rite Two have a number of references to the presence of the body and blood of Christ. The Great Thanksgiving of Rite One prays that we "may be partakers of his most blessed Body and Blood" (BCP, p. 335), and that we "may worthily receive the most precious Body and Blood of the Son, Jesus Christ" (BCP, p. 336). The "Prayer of Humble Access" speaks of eating "the flesh" and drinking "his blood" (BCP, p. 337). The alternative administration forms refer simply to the "Body" and the "Blood" (BCP, p. 338). In the Great Thanksgiving of Rite Two the prayer is that the bread and wine "be for your people the Body and Blood of your Son" (BCP, p. 363). The "Zwinglian form" is not an option for administration. Such language is consistently employed in all the options available for the Great Thanksgiving, as well as for the forms for administration and the post-communion prayers.

Third, the language of "remembrance" and feeding "on him in your hearts by faith, with thanksgiving" may have a valid and profound content never understood or intended by Zwingli. According to the Lima document of the WCC Faith and Order Commission, *anamnesis*, or remembrance, is "not only a calling to mind of what is past and of its significance." Through such remembering Christ himself is present in terms of his unique and redeeming sacrifice, with the effective promise of his benefits and the "foretaste of his parousia." *Anamnesis* and real presence are not alternatives; they are interdependent. The Lima text links them—and also records an ecumenical consensus on the appropriate place of "faith."

> The words and acts of Christ at the institution of the eucharist stand at the heart of the celebration; the eucharistic meal is the sacrament of the body and blood of Christ, the sacrament of his real presence.

Christ fulfills in a variety of ways his promise to be always with his own even to the end of the world. But Christ's mode of presence in the eucharist is unique. Jesus said over the bread and wine of the eucharist: "This is my body...this is my blood..." What Christ declared is true, and this truth is fulfilled every time the eucharist is celebrated. The Church confesses Christ's real, living and active presence in the eucharist. While Christ's real presence in the eucharist does not depend on the faith of the individual, all agree that to discern the body and blood of Christ, faith is required.[21]

While Lutherans would therefore prefer that the first administration form of Rite One not be used and the "may" rubric with regard to the Invitation not be exercised in order to avoid misunderstanding, the form itself does not necessarily imply a denial of the real presence of the body and blood of Christ in the Eucharist.

3. Lutherans are concerned that the concept of "sacrifice" with regard to the Eucharist not call into question the finality of Christ's saving death. Lutherans are also concerned that references to sacrifice within the eucharistic rite not negate the gift character of the gospel in the sacrament by transforming the Eucharist into a pious work designed to manipulate or propitiate God.[22] At the same time, Lutherans recognize the validity of offering our sacrifice of praise and thanksgiving, through which we both remember and receive Christ's benefits and are united with Christ's mission for the world.

> There are two, and only two, basic types of sacrifice. One is the propitiatory sacrifice....The other type is the eucharistic sacrifice; this does not merit the forgiveness of sins or reconciliation, but by it those who have been reconciled give thanks or show their gratitude for the forgiveness of sins and other blessings received....We are perfectly willing for the Mass to be understood as a daily sacrifice, provided this means the whole Mass, the ceremony and also the proclamation of the Gospel, faith, prayer, and thanksgiving.[23]

The LBW rite expresses *our* offering in the offertory prayers, identifies Christ's unique and unrepeatable offering with the words, "we remember the life our Lord offered for us," and gives thanks with the words, "that we who receive the Lord's body and blood may live to the praise of your glory."

A careful examination of the prayers for Rite One and Rite Two in the BCP indicate that these Lutheran concerns with regard to sacrifice are shared in the ECUSA celebration of the Eucharist. The once–for–

all–time sacrifice of Christ is made more explicit than it is in the rite of LBW.

> All glory be to thee, Almighty God, our heavenly Father, for that thou, of thy tender mercy, didst give thine only Son Jesus Christ to suffer death upon the cross for our redemption; who made there by his one oblation of himself once offered, a full, perfect, and sufficient sacrifice, oblation, and satisfaction, for the sins of the whole world; and did institute, and in his holy Gospel command us to continue, a perpetual memory of that his precious death and sacrifice, until his coming again (BCP, p. 334).

> He stretched out his arms upon the cross, and offered himself, in obedience to your will, a perfect sacrifice for the whole world (BCP, p. 362).

When our offering is mentioned, the reference is either to gifts of bread and wine (BCP, p. 335) or to ourselves (BCP, p. 336). That "holy gifts" means bread and wine is evident from the fact that the offertory statement precedes the prayer that these "gifts and creatures of bread and wine" be blessed and sanctified by the Word and the Holy Spirit so that we may be partakers of his body and blood.

That "sacrifice" refers to our praise and thanksgiving is also explicit. This has been the intention and the language of the BCP since Thomas Cranmer. Lutherans cannot, therefore, object in any way to the language and the intentions of the BCP Eucharistic rites with regard to the concept of sacrifice.

4. A question, perhaps minor, arises because of the constant use of the term "celebrant" instead of "presiding minister" for the person with leadership responsibility in the Eucharist. Is this another example of the basic conservatism of the BCP? Surely there is a consensus among the Christian traditions today that supports J. G. Davies' 1965 definition of "celebrant":

> Celebrant: The one who officiates at the eucharist. The renewed understanding of the corporate nature both of the Church and of worship has tended to issue in the emphasis that the celebrant at the eucharist is the congregation and that the function of the priest or minister is not to celebrate on behalf of or apart from the faithful but to preside.[24]

Or does this usage reflect negatively on the commitment of the BCP to the corporate priesthood of the eschatological people of God? Just a question, of course. But it does seem as if the BCP has missed an opportunity for teaching because it perpetuates a designation that other liturgical books have abandoned.

The Ordinal

It is impossible to comment on the BCP and its possible recognition by the Lutheran churches involved in this dialogue without reference to the ordination rites. Since the issues involved in the mutual recognition of our respective ordained ministries are still under consideration by this dialogue, attention to the ordination rites of the BCP in this context cannot replace our discussion and our task. There is much that Lutherans can learn from these ordination rites. Here it seems necessary to comment briefly on two matters.

1. It is clear from the section entitled "Episcopal Services" that the ECUSA understands ordained ministry to take place in three orders: bishops, priests, and deacons. It is also clear that discreet duties and responsibilities are assigned to each of the orders. Lutherans do not at this time understand ordained ministry to take place in three orders. What is of special significance is that Lutherans do not understand bishops to constitute a separate order of ministry in the church. Lutherans understand bishops to be pastors (presbyters) with regional rather than parochial responsibility for the ministry of gospel and sacraments. Lutherans therefore do not ordain to any office other than that of pastor (presbyter).

2. However, these differences in understanding the ordained ministry and especially the ministry of bishops are no obstacle to Lutheran recognition of the orthodoxy of the BCP. Indeed, the Lutheran commitment to the BC as the normative confession of the Lutheran churches requires Lutherans to recognize the legitimacy and authenticity of the traditions preserved in the orders of ministry and the ordination rites of the ECUSA. The CA states:

> It is not our intention that the bishops give up their power to govern, but we ask for this one thing, that they allow the Gospel to be taught purely and that they relax some few observances which cannot be kept without sin.[25]

Similarly, the AP states:

> Those who are now bishops do not perform the duties of bishops according to the Gospel, though they may well be bishops according to canonical polity, *to which we do not object.* But we are talking about a bishop according to the Gospel. We like the old division of

power into the *power of the order* and the power of jurisdiction. There a bishop has the *power of the order*, namely, the ministry of Word and sacraments. He also has the power of jurisdiction, namely, the authority to excommunicate those who are guilty of public offenses or to absolve them if they are converted and ask for absolution. A bishop does not have the power of a tyrant to act without a definite law....But he has a definite command, a definite Word of God, which he ought to teach and according to which he ought to exercise his jurisdiction.[26]

This means that Lutherans can at least recognize as orthodox the rites for the ordination of bishops, priests, and deacons as they are found in the BCP, even though they do not have identical rites for their own bishops. It is the task and challenge of Lutherans to be attentive to their confessional heritage and commitment, to ask how we can most faithfully understand both polity and order so that we can participate with the utmost integrity in the unity and mission of the eschatological community that is the church.

RECOGNITION

We must now ask what Lutheran recognition of the BCP might mean. I would propose that there are three dimensions to such recognition. The first is a negative dimension. Recognition does not mean that Lutherans must somehow adopt the BCP as a replacement for the three editions of LBW now being used by the Lutheran churches.

The second dimension is positive. Lutheran recognition of the BCP means recognition that the doctrine implied in the rites prescribed for use in the ECUSA is orthodox. This is no small matter, for what is at stake in these rites is the gospel itself. In his discussion of the sacraments, Lutheran theologian Robert Jenson says that "Every liturgy is a communication event."

> Since a liturgy speaks, we must ask what it says. Every liturgy in the church is to be the gospel to us and right prayer to God....A *liturgical hermeneutics* must be practiced in the church, an examination of actual and proposed rubrics, both for continuing orders and for single liturgies, by the same norms that hold for all teaching and preaching. We must always ask, Is what by these rubrics would get said indeed the gospel?[27]

To say that the rites of the BCP are orthodox is to say that through the rubrical language and action of these rites the gospel is being addressed to the community and right prayer is being offered by the community to God.

Thirdly, Lutheran recognition of the BCP means that Lutherans acknowledge the liturgy of the ECUSA to be the equivalent of its own confessions as a standard of orthodoxy. This is not a simple or self–evident move for Lutherans to make. The CA states

> For the true unity of the church it is enough to agree concerning the teaching of the Gospel and the administration of the sacraments. It is not necessary that human traditions or rites and ceremonies, instituted by men, should be alike everywhere.[28]

On the basis of these sentences Lutherans have traditionally said that rites for worship are *adiaphora,* that they ought not be prescribed. What is required instead, Lutherans have said, is a doctrinal standard that evaluates the content of preaching and the content of teaching about the sacraments.

However, the CA itself is speaking about the actual communication that is taking place, the actual teaching of the gospel and the actual administration of the sacraments. If Jenson is correct, that liturgies are actual communication events, then the orthodoxy of a church *can* be located in its rites, in its worship book. That is just what Stephen Sykes has claimed in citing the "declaration of assent" required of Anglican ordinands. Someone, usually the bishop, begins with the "preface."

> The Church of England is part of the One, Holy, Catholic and Apostolic Church worshipping the one true God, Father, Son and Holy Spirit. It professes the faith uniquely revealed in the Holy Scriptures and set forth in the catholic creeds, which faith the Church is called upon to proclaim afresh in each generation. Led by the Holy Spirit, it has borne witness to Christian truth in its historic formularies, the Thirty–nine Articles of Religion, the Book of Common Prayer and the ordering of Bishops, Priests and Deacons. In the declaration you are about to make will you affirm your loyalty to this inheritance of faith as your inspiration and guidance under God in bringing the grace and truth of Christ to this generation and making Him known to those in your care?

The ordinand replies,

> I, A.B., do so affirm and accordingly declare my belief in the faith which is revealed in the Holy Scriptures and set forth in the catholic creeds and to which the historic formularies of the Church of England bear witness; and in public prayer and administration of

the sacraments, I will use only the forms of service which are authorised or allowed by Canon.[29]

"The *performance* of liturgy expresses doctrine," Sykes writes.[30]

Recognition of the BCP is therefore an action of considerable existential significance for Lutherans. It is not just the recognition of the orthodoxy of a book, a collection of rites and documents. It is not even just the recognition of the orthodoxy of the ECUSA which binds itself to the concrete use of this book in worship, ordinations, and the administration of the sacraments. It is finally the recognition that Lutherans may be in for some questioning, some examination of themselves.

8

ANGLICAN RECOGNITION OF THE AUGSBURG CONFESSION: AN ACTUAL POSSIBILITY?

BY

J. ROBERT WRIGHT

The officially appointed representatives of the ELCA have claimed, in their dialogue with the ECUSA, that they and their church are committed to the Augsburg Confession, which for them is a "binding document," and that some sort of recognition or agreement on the points of faith that it contains is a major prerequisite, even a necessary "condition," so to speak, for ecumenical unity, for full communion, of their church with any other. Would it be possible for the ECUSA to meet such a condition, to give such a recognition, to reach such an agreement? This essay will seek to answer this question.

We shall proceed by six steps, each of which has its own related question, which I shall seek to answer with a tentative conclusion before reaching my final conclusion in the sixth step.

Step one: How is the Augsburg Confession presented and described in contemporary popular American Lutheran apologetic? Here I choose three examples of this genre of literature:

First, from E. W. Gritsch and R. W. Jenson:

> At the Diet of Augsburg and elsewhere, the Lutheran reformers and their followers proposed further dogma to the church. Many, including groups that the reformers could not simply regard as not-church, did not accept the offer. Thus the Lutheran confessions remain *proposals* of dogma. If the Lutheran proposals had been ecumenically accepted, there would be no Lutheranism. As it is, Lutheranism is a *confessional movement* within the church catholic

that continues to offer to the whole church that proposal of dogma which received definitive documentary form in the Augsburg Confession and the other writings collected in the Book of Concord.[1]

And from the same work,

"Even the Augsburg Confession can be revised in the name of Christian unity....The whole effort of the Augsburg Confession was to reestablish the threatened unity of the Western church."[2]

Second, from A. C. Piepkorn:

The Augsburg Confession has served as the most widely accepted statement of the evangelical understanding of the catholic faith. Although it affirms the catholic heritage, it clearly interprets that heritage from an evangelical perspective. The doctrine of justification by grace through faith stands at the center, and all other doctrines are explicated with that center in mind.

The Augsburg Confession was formulated as a summary statement and apology of the faith confessed by the Lutherans.[3]

And again, from Piepkorn:

In the first twenty–one articles the Lutheran reformers presented their confession of the ancient faith of the catholic church; condemned the heresies, ancient and modern, which the Catholic Church condemned; and were at pains to prove that on no doctrinal point did they vary from the teaching of the sacred Scriptures, the catholic church, or, as far as its approved literary representatives are concerned, the historic church of the West. Subsequently Lutherans, by the very act of subscribing their signatures to the Augsburg Confession or by invoking its authority in synodical or congregational constitutions, have affirmed that these articles are the Lutheran witness to an evangelical catholicity and thus are a call to the church to be what she had been for the first eleven centuries and to reaffirm her intention of being what she was then (and always is) in peril of ceasing to be.[4]

Third, from D. W. H. Arnold and C. G. Fry:

The Lutheran confessions are a product of the sixteenth–century soteriological debates surrounding justification. They represent the consensus of the evangelical church as to the proper doctrines.

In that sense they are received as a faithful response to the sacred Scriptures in the matters that had previously been disputed.[5]

The confessions normally received within the Lutheran churches are bound together in *The Book of Concord*. Within that book are creeds of three kinds.

First are the ecumenical, catholic, or universal creeds. These are the Apostles', the Nicene, and the Athanasian creeds. They come to us from the ancient church. While Lutherans realize that there never has been (and probably never will be) a truly ecumenical creed, accepted by all Christians, these statements of faith have been widely used within the Christian churches. By endorsing them, the Lutherans manifest their unity with the church of the Greek and Latin fathers.

Next are the evangelical confessions. These include the Augsburg Confession and its Apology, as well as Luther's Small and Large Catechisms. While these were written by Lutherans to articulate their stand on justification over against the position of the Roman Catholic Church, the truths of these documents commended themselves to other evangelicals. Reformers in Switzerland and England employed these confessions in part in the construction of their own statements of faith. Both authors know of churches that are not formally members of a Lutheran denomination but use the Small Catechism and adhere to the Augsburg Confession.

Last are the distinctively Lutheran confessions. These include the Formula of Concord, which states the consensus of Lutherans concerning controversies that divided them from one another and from other Protestants during the late sixteenth century. To our knowledge, while the ecumenical creeds are received by most Catholic Christians and the evangelical confessions are acknowledged by many Protestant believers, no group outside the Lutheran family has given assent to these documents.

Normally a Lutheran congregation contains in its constitution some reference to *The Book of Concord*, or, at the very least, to the ecumenical creeds and the Augsburg Confession. Theoretically a church could be impeccably Lutheran without any mention of these creeds. It would be quite possible for a gathering of believers to compose a new statement of faith, *ex corde, ex tempore, ex nihilo*, and still be recognized as Lutheran. If the affirmations made in that congregational testimony were harmonious with biblical truth and, therefore, compatible with the existing Lutheran confessions, such a community could be acknowledged as Lutheran, no matter what its name or creed.

Such a situation arose when the Batak churches, indigenous evangelical communities in Indonesia, sought membership in the Lutheran World Federation. After examination of their statement of faith, they were accepted, even though the creed of the Batak churches makes no reference to the historic creeds of Lutheranism.[6]

And now I reach a conclusion to my first question: The CA is accorded high status as a confessional document in contemporary popular American Lutheran apologetic, but such authors do not fully agree among themselves, and none of them describe it as "binding," but rather present it in more modest terms.

Step two: How is the Augsburg Confession officially presented in the Constitution, Ecumenical Position Statement, Ordination Vows, and Installation Rites of the ELCA?

The ELCA Constitution presents it as follows: "This church accepts the Unaltered Augsburg Confession as a true witness to the Gospel, acknowledging as one with it in faith and doctrine all churches that likewise accept the teachings of the Unaltered Augsburg Confession" (Chapter 2.05).[7]

The official statement entitled, "Ecumenism: The Vision of the Evangelical Lutheran Church in America," begins by admitting that "The Lutheran Confessions were the products of an effort at evangelical reform, which, contrary to its intention, resulted in divisions within the Western church." Later in the text we read the following:

> The primary Lutheran confessional document, the Augsburg Confession of 1530, claims to be a fully catholic as well as an evangelical expression of Christian faith. Part I, which lists the chief articles of faith, states that the Confession is grounded clearly in Scripture and does not depart from the universal Christian Church. The confessors at Augsburg asked only for freedom to preach and worship in accordance with the Gospel. They were willing, upon recognition of the legitimacy of these reforms, to remain in fellowship with those who did not share every theological formulation or reforming practice, e.g., Augsburg Confession, Preface, Article XV, Article XXVIII and Conclusion. It is in this historical context that Article VII is to be understood: "for the true unity of the church it is enough (*satis est*) to agree concerning the teaching of the Gospel and the administration of the sacraments."

The historical situation is now different. Today the western church is divided into hundreds of denominations; moreover, in the nineteenth century the urgency of missionary proclamation underscored the scandal of a divided church. Such developments challenge the Evangelical Lutheran Church in America to strive toward fuller expressions of unity with as many denominations as possible.

Lutherans may differ in evaluating the difference between the sixteenth century and the present. Some Lutherans in the Evangelical Lutheran Church in America hold that unity was already broken when the confessors presented the Augsburg Confession in 1530; others hold that the confessors were attempting to maintain a unity that still existed. But all agree that the *"satis est"* of Augsburg Confession VII established an ecumenical principle as valid today as it was in 1530. Augsburg Confession VII continues to be ecumenically liberating because of its claim that the truth of the Gospel is the catholic faith and is sufficient for the true unity of the Church.

In today's denominationalism the *satis est* provides an ecumenical resource and basis to move to growing levels of fellowship [i.e., communion] among divided churches. Article VII remains fundamental for Lutheran ecumenical activity; its primary meaning is that only those things that convey salvation, justification by grace through faith, are allowed to be signs and constitutive elements of the Church. Yet, for all its cohesiveness and precision, Article VII does not present a complete doctrine of the Church. It is not in the first instance an expression of a falsely understood ecumenical openness and freedom from church order, customs, and usages in the Church. What it says is essential for understanding the unity of the Church, but does not exhaust what must be said. The primary meaning of Article VII is that only those things that convey salvation, justification by grace through faith, are allowed to be signs and constitutive elements of the Church. It is also necessary to recognize the evangelical and ecclesiological implications of the missionary situation of the global church in our time, which did not exist in the 16th century.

Article VII of the Augsburg Confession continues to be ecumenically freeing because of its insistence that agreement in the Gospel suffices for Christian unity.[8]

The (semi–official) Lutheran *Occasional Services*, in its rite of ordination, makes the following distinction between (1) "confess," (2) "accept, teach, and confess," and (3) "acknowledge," reserving the last and weakest of these verbal formularies for the CA (and the other Lutheran confessions), as follows: "The Church in which you are to be ordained confesses that the Holy Scriptures are the Word of God and are the norm of its faith and life. We accept, teach, and confess the Apostles', the Nicene, and the Athanasian Creeds. We also acknowledge the Lutheran Confessions as true witnesses and faithful expositions of the Holy Scriptures." It goes on to ask: "Will you therefore preach and teach in accordance with the Holy Scriptures and these creeds and confessions?" The rite for the Installation of a Pastor asks: "Will you preach and teach in accordance with the Holy Scriptures and the Confessions of the Lutheran Church?" interestingly omitting the reference to the creeds that was asked at the time of ordination. And the rite for the Installation of a bishop asks, "Will you discharge your duties in accordance with the Holy Scriptures and the Confessions of the Lutheran Church...?" again omitting any reference to the creeds.[9]

Conclusion to the second question: The CA is not officially described by the ELCA as "binding" in either its Constitution or its ecumenism statement, nor does the latter even hold out the prospect of unity on the basis of the CA that is proposed in the Constitution. The Constitution itself, one must add, does not propose acceptance of the text of the CA as the basis for church unity, but rather acceptance of its "teachings." Thus, a verbal agreement with it is not constitutionally required for unity with the ELCA, but a conceptual one, an agreement in principle.

An important and related problem must also be noted, namely that the official ELCA ecumenism statement does not itself seem to be consistent with the CA when it interprets (above) Article VII as insisting that "agreement in the Gospel suffices for Christian unity." Any Anglican/Episcopalian reading the same Article VII, however, would not fail to note that it calls for agreement concerning "the teaching of the Gospel and the administration of the sacraments." Episcopalians, for whom an emphasis on worship and its right ordering is extremely important, would therefore be more likely to welcome the original content of Article VII of the CA, rather than any ecumenical dilution of it that would omit or downplay its concern for the administration of the sacraments.

Also, in the contents of the (semi–official) ordination and installation rites, the CA is not described as "binding," nor even explicitly mentioned by name.

Step three: Who then does say that the Augsburg Confession is "binding" for Lutherans, and how do they describe its binding nature?

Here a catena of eight representative statements and authors may be surveyed and compared as evidence:

(1) "A binding foundation of doctrine for the Lutheran churches."[10]

(2) "Still the doctrinal basis of the Lutheran churches and still has binding authority for them even today."[11]

(3) "Binding for the Lutheran Christian family today."[12]

(4) "The churches which belong to the Lutheran World Federation have accepted the Confessio Augustana as an authoritative doctrinal basis."[13]

(5) "After the Reformation, the Confessio Augustana or (and) other Lutheran confessions were made binding on every Lutheran pastor at ordination."[14]

(6) "The Lutheran churches...consider [the Augsburg Confession] as being of binding significance for their teaching and work."[15]

(7) "The role played by the Augsburg Confession in the pledge taken on ordination. Here, commitment to the Confessio Augustana is, at the same time, a commitment to the early church and, in the final analysis, to Holy Scripture."[16]

(8) "The promise of loyalty to the Augsburg Confession at ordination."[17]

Conclusion to the third question: Some very significant authorities, both Lutheran and Roman Catholic (the above is only a sampling) regard the CA as "binding," much as it has been represented to Episcopalians by Lutherans in the third round of the official Lutheran–Episcopal Dialogue, but this is in contrast to the much weaker statements about the CA written and published in the ELCA Constitution, Ecumenism Statement, and Ordination and Installation rites, as well as in popular American Lutheran apologetic. Also, by contrast, Anglicans themselves no longer tend to describe their own Thirty–Nine Articles with such "binding" terminology.

Step four: What hard questions might Anglicans/Episcopalians raise about any proposal for a direct recognition of the Augsburg Confession by the General Convention of the Episcopal Church? If a theologically literate Episcopalian were reading this document for the first time, and without Lutheran preconceptions, and in its English translations, what reactions might be generated?

Here I shall proceed on such a basis, moving through each of the twenty–eight articles of this document, recording "No problem" where I (at least initially) see none. It should be noted and emphasized at the outset, though, that the following comments are intended as a critique, not an appreciation, and that if I had time and space for the latter I would have much more to say by way of praise.[18]

Article 1: No problem.

Article 2: I doubt that Anglicans would want to say today that original sin "condemns to the eternal wrath of God all those who are not born again through Baptism and the Holy Spirit." The damnation of the unbaptized, explicit here and implicit in articles 7–9, would not be a belief we would readily endorse.

Article 3: No problem.

Article 4: No problem.

Article 5: Many Anglicans today would hold, contrary to the second paragraph of this article, that the Holy Spirit can come to human beings, as to the followers of many non–Christian religions, "without the external word of the Gospel."

Article 6: No problem.

Article 7: In its ecclesiology, this article seems to define the church as the assembly of believers rather than as the assembly of the baptized, and to this Anglicans would generally object.

As for this article's second major assertion, that "for the true unity of the church it is sufficient to agree concerning the teaching of the Gospel and the administration of the sacraments," its famous *satis est* clause, I think we would tend to agree with its literal statement but to emphasize, as I have noted above, that it demands agreement *both* on the teaching of the gospel *and* on the administration of the sacraments. Sometimes one gets the impression that Lutherans only read the first half of this assertion, and even then give no thought as to the need for a ministry of oversight (*episkope*) so that the gospel may indeed be preached in its purity.

We would also want to raise a major question, as to whether the true unity of the church is really possible without some clear agreement on polity, on ministerial structure, in order that the sacraments may indeed be administered "in accordance with the divine Word," as the article puts it. This does, therefore, raise a major question for us about any church that, no longer living in the "emergency situation" of the Reformation, continues to decline to adopt or return to the historic episcopate, on behalf of which it claims to have made a temporary protest in the sixteenth century. For the ECUSA, by action of its General Convention of 1982, the historic episcopate is considered to be "central to the apostolic ministry and essential to the reunion of the Church." We do not condemn or un–church those churches not possessing it, but we would humbly urge that there is no better or more time–tested way to implement the *satis est* clause of CA 7 than by adoption of the historic episcopate. If Lutherans have some better proposal for seeking "agreement on how the sacraments are to be administered," we urge them to speak now or hold their peace!

Article 8: Here again, as in CA 2, 7, and 9, an Anglican would question the ecclesiological implications of defining the church as "the assembly of believers and saints." Our own catechetical tradition leads us to say that "The Church is the Body of which Jesus Christ is the Head and all baptized persons are members," and we would tend to question any church teaching that belief, or even sainthood, rather than Baptism, is the initiatory mark of church entrance.

Article 9: No problem.

Article 10: No problem.

Article 11: No problem.

Article 12: No problem.

Article 13: There is a problem with the addition to the Latin text of this article of the CA in the so–called *editio princeps*, which reads, "Our churches therefore condemn those who teach that the sacraments justify by the outward act," which is interpreted by note 5 in BC 36 as being a condemnation of the *ex opere operato* doctrine of the sacraments. The *ex opere operato* doctrine is again condemned in AP 4:63 (BC 115), to which the same note makes reference. If Lutherans condemn this doctrine, then Anglicans would find themselves at variance because of our own classical position on this question, set forth in article 26 of the Thirty–Nine Articles: "The unworthiness of the minister hinders not the effect of the sacraments." Anglicans do *not* believe, and this is the point of the *ex opere operato* doctrine (even though we would not be inclined to use the scholastic Latin terminology today), that the efficacy of the Eucharist is dependent on the particular moral rectitude of the celebrant or upon the subjective psychological feeling of the recipient. Anglicans thus have generally held to the classical catholic *ex opere operato* doctrine on this point, rather than the classically Protestant *ex opere operantis* doctrine, which is the reverse, implied here in the CA and in AP 4:63. Is it possible, though, that CA 8 could be interpreted as negating CA 13 at this point?

Article 14: No problem.

Article 15: Here and in CA 27 it is taught that monastic vows, as well as distinctions of foods and of days, "are useless and contrary to the Gospel." This is a position that Anglicans cannot accept. Since the time of their revival and renewal in the later nineteenth century, the religious orders, living under monastic vows in the Church of England and other parts of the Anglican Communion, have become far too widespread and positively appreciated for Anglicans to allow them to be condemned in this way. And the traditional Christian distinctions of foods and of days are clearly endorsed and written into the 1979 BCP, pp. 15–33. We might well agree with these articles of CA if they were intended to condemn *only* those monastic vows and distinctions of foods and days "by which it is intended to earn grace and make satisfaction for sin," but the wording of these two articles clearly holds categorically that all monastic vows and distinctions of foods and days are so intended; otherwise the wording would have been different. These two articles are condemning *use* and not merely *abuse*, and this is an extreme position of the Reformation that Anglicans have generally managed to avoid. It may well be that such human institutions *seemed* to be totally corrupt to most sixteenth-century reformers, but they were clearly not "instituted" (the wording of CA 15) for such purposes ("to propitiate God, merit grace, and make satisfaction") in the patristic and early medieval periods. Many Lutherans today might well prefer the Anglican position on this subject, but that *all* such institutions, and not merely their abuse, are condemned by these two articles of the CA has recently been confirmed by Leif Grane.[19] No Lutheran has been able to show me any standard commentary on the CA that says otherwise.

Article 16: Here it is taught, and further in CA 28, that "*all* government in the world and *all* established rule and laws were instituted and ordained by God for the sake of good order," and that the gospel *requires* that civil authority and the state "be kept as true orders of God" (emphases added). The principle of such subservience to every command and decision of civil government is, however, contrary to the social policies of the ECUSA and would, for example, contradict the Christian critiques made by our presiding bishops of some policies of the national governmental administrations, as well as many of the stockholder actions of the ECUSA's Executive Council, as regards South Africa, for example.[20]

As in the case of CA 15 and 27, on monastic vows and distinctions of foods and days, some contemporary Lutherans might well wish to soften these positions by claiming that they are historically and culturally conditioned and should not today be taken literally. This is precisely the way Anglicans today (at least most Episcopalians in the U.S.A) take the Thirty–nine Articles, but, then, Anglicans do not claim that the Thirty–Nine Articles are "binding," nor that agreement on them is a condition for full communion—as many Lutherans *do* say about the CA.

I do see one way, however, by which this CA 16 could be found acceptable to Anglicans, and that is contained in its last sentence, which reads: "When commands of the civil authority cannot be obeyed without sin, we must obey God rather than men." Prescinding from its sexist language, which few Episcopalians today would accept, I do wonder if this last sentence could be accepted as governing the rest of the article, and as therefore rendering its principle void for the many persons who today find such subservience to every whim of the secular government to be sinful indeed?

Article 17: No problem.

Article 18: No problem.

Article 19: No problem.

Article 20: Anglicans would not agree that "rosaries, the cult of saints, monasticism, pilgrimages, appointed fasts, holy days, brotherhoods [or sisterhoods], services in honor of saints, etc." are "useless," even though we would differ widely as to our estimates of the relative value of these various devotional practices.

Anglican scholars would also probably have some factual/historical disagreement as to whether, as this article's second paragraph states, the teaching about (justification by) faith had, by the time of the sixteenth century, been long neglected. What are we to make, for example, of the substantial introduction and the selections from such later medieval theologians as Holcot, Bradwardine, Biel, and Staupitz within chapter 3 of Heiko Oberman's book *Forerunners of the Reformation*?[21] Or, if this article really refers only to *Martin Luther's* teaching about justification by faith as being long neglected, I still do not think all Anglicans would agree.

Finally, I am sure that Anglicans would have serious reservations about this article's claim that justification by faith is "the chief article in the Christian life" (German text) or "the chief teaching in the church" (Latin text), reinforced by the claim in CA 28:52 (BC 89) that justification is "the chief article of the Gospel." Anglicans would be quite reluctant to claim that any one particular article of the Christian faith stands out above all the others. Stephen Sykes has already well expressed this reservation for Anglicans.[22] In fact, one may well ask whether this claim of CA 20:8 and 28:52 does not stand in direct contradiction to St. Paul's announcement in 1 Cor. 15:1-5,11: "I would remind you...of the good news that I proclaimed to you, which you in turn received, in which also you stand, through which also you are being saved....For I handed on to you as of first importance what I in turn had received: that Christ died for our sins in accordance with the scriptures, and that he was buried, and that he was raised on the third day in accordance with the scriptures, and that he appeared to Cephas, then to the Twelve....so we proclaim and so you have come to believe."

Article 21: No problem.

Article 22: No problem.

Article 23: No problem.

Article 24: No problem, except that Anglicans today would prefer to describe the Eucharist in more contemporary ways.

Article 25: To insist on "not administering the sacrament to those who have not previously been examined and absolved" is a practice upon which Anglicans would not insist, and hence this article would be unacceptable to us. The general Anglican rule about confession, examination, and absolution is, "all may, some should, none must," and thus we would not wish to be so rigid about this matter. I wonder, though, once again, whether all Lutherans really regard this article as "binding," or whether they tend to treat it more as Anglicans tend to understand the Thirty–Nine Articles? On the question at hand, the ECUSA's position is stated in the BCP: "The Reconciliation of a Penitent is available for all who desire it. It is not restricted to times of sickness. Confessions may be heard anytime and anywhere" (p. 446).

There are still two other problems with this article from an Anglican viewpoint. One problem lies in such statements as, "Our people are taught to esteem absolution highly," and "confession is to be retained for the sake of absolution (which is its chief and most important part)." To place the major emphasis on absolution, as this article does, is to opt exclusively for only one of the three major positions current in the late medieval church, as Thomas Tentler has so well shown,[23] and most Anglicans who have considered the matter would want to allow at least for all three equally, even perhaps giving some greater weight to confession or to counsel, and perhaps less to absolution.

The final problem, however, concerns this article's assertions that "no one should be compelled to recount sins in detail," and that "there is no need to compel people to give a detailed account of their sins." Generally Anglicans would agree that people should not be *compelled* (to do anything!), but those higher traditions of Anglicanism that place much emphasis on confession and absolution would be unanimously opposed to *selective* confession and would thus disagree with at least the Latin edition of this article (BC 62) which states that "an enumeration of sins is not necessary."

Article 26: No problem, because here, unlike in CA 15, "fasting in itself is not rejected, but what is rejected is making a necessary service of fasts on prescribed days and with specified foods" (BC 69).

Article 27: Here again we find the problem of monastic vows, as has already been discussed under CA 15. Anglicans would readily agree that all the corruptions mentioned in this article should be condemned, but to conclude (as in the last sentence, BC 80) that therefore all monastic vows are null and void is impossible for us today, for the reasons I have already stated. We would not agree that *all* monastic vows are "chosen and instituted by men to obtain righteousness and God's grace" (BC 76). If the last sentence of CA 27 could only read *"To the extent that* all these things are false, useless, and invented, monastic vows are null and void," rather than "Inasmuch as," it might be acceptable. But as the article stands, it would be unacceptable.

Article 28: The Anglican position on the historic episcopate, as it relates to the CA I have already tried to summarize in my comments under CA 7. But there are still other problems that I believe Anglicans would have with this article.

As in CA 16, there is a denial of "the power of the church or of bishops" to "interfere at all with government or temporal authority," to "undermine obedience to government," or to "make or prescribe to the temporal power laws concerning worldly matters." The Anglican Communion as a whole would have serious reservations about subscribing to any such article as this for, if taken literally and as binding, it would be in opposition to the archbishop of Canterbury's status as the chief religious advisor to the crown, as well as to any pastoral letters of our American House of Bishops in criticism of our government's positions on war, the economy, or still other matters.

Nor am I sure that all Anglicans would want to claim today (although at one time we did) that the office of the episcopate is by "divine right" (BC 84) unless we were to nuance this term in the way it was nuanced by the Anglican–Roman Catholic International Commission (*Final Report*, pp. 85–87) as really meaning "divine providence." Otherwise it is too pretentious a claim for us to make in this modern world.

The call in this article (BC 84-85) not to obey the bishops if they err, teach, command, introduce or institute anything contrary to the gospel, is one that would need careful discussion. Certainly Anglicans would not agree with the official Roman Catholic position, written in canon 273 of the new Roman Catholic Code of Canon Law, which demands virtually unqualified obedience to the supreme pontiff. And certainly we would agree in principle that the episcopate must be subordinate to the gospel; many Episcopalians would even say there is need for some better mechanism in order to accomplish this. But would we be ready to allow, as CA 28 might be interpreted (and indeed is by some Lutherans today), that every individual Christian has the right to decide whether every teaching of every bishop is contrary to, or consonant with, the gospel? This article, like so many others in the CA can easily die of overkill! Who is to decide when something that the bishop says is contrary to the gospel, or to Scripture? Anglicans are sufficiently Protestant not to want to give the bishops themselves (or the pope) the last word in such matters, but this article sanctions rank individualism. Some reasonable process would be absolutely necessary for determination of disputed questions, which this article does not provide.

Finally, the bold claim of this article (BC 89) to have identified "the chief article of the Gospel,"..."that we obtain the grace of God through faith in Christ without our merits," is a claim already discussed earlier under CA 20, and one that has already been questioned by the Anglican theologian Stephen Sykes. As he remarks (pp. 30, 34, 39), this claim is the essential assumption of the CA as a whole, and although the influence of this doctrine is everywhere present in the official Anglican documents from the Reformation period, nowhere do the Anglican documents state that justification by faith alone, or even the atonement or the incarnation or anything else, is *the* chief article of the gospel. We would have the gravest difficulty in agreeing to this, Sykes remarks (p. 41), and might even question whether to do so is in fact *contrary* to the gospel.[24]

Step five: In view of all the foregoing, if the Episcopal Church were to move in the direction of some sort of official "recognition" of the CA as an attempt to meet this Lutheran condition for unity, in spite of the ambiguity about how or in what sense it is "binding" for ELCA Lutherans, what are some possible "recognition" formulas that have already been proposed in previous ecumenical discussions or elsewhere?

(1) "A particular expression of the common Christian faith."[25]

(2) "An expression of the Catholic faith."[26]

(3) "A particular but authentic expression of the common Christian faith."[27]

(4) "A basis for the common confession of central doctrinal truths."[28]

(5) "A legitimate form of the apostolic faith."[29]

(6) "An expression of the Catholic faith acceptable as such."[30]

(7) "One possible and legitimate expression of a common Christian faith." (See note 30).

(8) "A legitimate interpretation of the faith, [bearing] witness, in its own way and in its own language, to the same content of faith as that to which the Catholic church bears witness....a legitimate expression of Christian truth."[31]

(9) "The most widely accepted statement of the evangelical understanding of the catholic faith. Although it affirms the catholic heritage, it clearly interprets that heritage from an evangelical perspective."[32]

(10) "The Lutheran witness to an evangelical catholicity."[33]

(11) "Intended to be a Catholic and ecumenical confession."[34]

(12) "A product of the sixteenth–century soteriological debates surrounding justification, representing the consensus of the evangelical church as to the proper doctrines, received as a faithful response to the sacred Scriptures in the matters previously disputed."[35]

(13) "The CA's claim that its confessional affirmations are catholic need not prevent us from acknowledging the time–conditioned character of its formulations and emphases....Thus only an interpretation which takes account of the one–sidedness and time-conditionedness of the CA can at the same time properly appreciate its catholicity."[36]

(14) "Is the projected recognition, reception, or acceptance to be by the Catholic Church, as catholic, as a Roman confession, as a legitimate expression of Christian truth, as an independent expression of catholic belief, or as a testimony to the faith which the churches have in common?"[37]

(15) "We also acknowledge the Lutheran Confessions [including the Augsburg Confession] as true witnesses and faithful expositions of the Holy Scriptures."[38]

Conclusion to the fifth question: None of this voluminous ecumenical discussion and argumentation has yet persuaded the Roman Catholic Church officially to make such a recognition, but this of course does not prohibit the ECUSA from doing so, if it chooses. Such a recognition remains, in my opinion (and to borrow the subtitle from a book by Heinrich Fries and Karl Rahner), "an actual possibility."[39]

Many varieties of wording have been proposed for such a recognition, of which the foregoing are only a sampling, and obviously a common, agreed formulation is needed if there is to be a direct recognition. Agreement would be needed, especially on the verb used and the descriptive clause employed. For example, the operative sentence might well begin with something like the following: "The Episcopal Church hereby (choose one:) recognizes, or receives, or accepts, or acknowledges, or affirms, or approves...the Unaltered Augsburg Confession (or, the faith expressed in the Unaltered Augsburg Confession, or, the teaching of the Unaltered Augsburg Confession) as..." (complete this sentence with some recognition clause, crafted probably from one or more of the above formulae). Still another possibility, borrowing terminology from the international Anglican–Roman Catholic conversations, would be to recognize, acknowledge, or affirm that the Unaltered Augsburg Confession is "sufficiently consonant in substance with the faith of this church" to (for example) afford a basis of faith for the establishment of full communion between the Episcopal Church and the Evangelical Lutheran Church in America.

Step six: Is an Anglican/Episcopal recognition of the CA an actual possibility, and if so then how best might it be done?

Here we must distinguish between a direct recognition, about which I shall have more to say in a moment, and an indirect one. An indirect recognition, which may actually be the more prudent and responsible path to take, could be developed along the following lines: The two churches could produce, as a result of ecumenical dialogue, something like a concordat or agreement establishing full communion between them on the basis of the key documents held in highest regard (after the Bible) by each church, namely the CA and the BCP. I think that LED III needs to consider this approach very seriously.

If there is to be a direct recognition, however, of the sort that has already been much discussed in Lutheran–Roman Catholic ecumenical dialogue, how might it be done? I believe that the following wording might be a viable formula: "Resolved, that the Episcopal Church recognizes the Augsburg Confession to be an authentic evangelical expression of the catholic Christian faith we hold in common with the Lutheran Churches." Such a direct recognition, however, would have to explain that we were in no way taking the Lutheran side over against the Roman Catholic side in the great controversies of the sixteenth century, and that we were not taking the Augsburg Confession to be "binding" in whatever sense some Lutherans may still believe it to be. And I think there would have to be, finally, some satisfactory explanation for Episcopalians as to how Lutherans today understand the following points contained within its particular articles:

1. Damnation of the unbaptized (articles 2 and 8).

2. Denial of the presence of the Holy Spirit outside the gospel (article 5).

3. Entry to church membership on the basis of belief rather than on the basis of baptism (article 7).

4. The relationship of the historic episcopate to the *satis est* clause in article 7.

5. The apparent denial of the *ex opere operato* doctrine of the sacraments (articles 8 and 13).

6. The condemnations of monastic vows and of distinctions of foods and days (articles 15, 20, and 27).

7. The denial of the church's mission to the temporal order (articles 16 and 28).

8. Insistence on compulsory examination, confession, and absolution (article 25).

9. The question of how agreement can be reached as to when bishops are teaching things contrary to the gospel (article 28).

10. The question of whether justification by faith alone is *the* chief article of the gospel (articles 20 and 28).

In conclusion, my only question is to ask whether the cause of church unity might better be served by some sort of *indirect* recognition, as I have hinted at the beginning of this final step, rather than by a direct one. Would the ELCA really want a direct recognition of the CA that had to make so many qualifications and reservations as the ten that I have listed above? And, given these problems, would the ECUSA, or, for that matter would any other non–Lutheran church, be likely to give a *direct* recognition to the CA today? *Some* sort of recognition, I am convinced, is an actual possibility, but *what* sort of recognition is a matter for careful consideration.

9

BISHOPS AND THE MUTUAL RECOGNITION AND RECONCILIATION OF MINISTRIES

BY

RICHARD NORRIS

It is a well–known fact, which I need only submit as it were by title, that ecumenical discussions between Anglicans and other churches in the tradition of the sixteenth–century Reformation have tended in the past to founder upon the question, bristling as it does with thorns, of bishops and of episcopal succession. In the dialogue between Lutherans and Anglicans in the U.S., this question now looms before us not as a theoretical issue to be encountered down the road a ways, but as an immediate practical problem to be dealt with. Our exchanges, arguments, and agreements have brought us to the point where the next step toward full communion can only be a process through which the official ministries of our churches are mutually recognized and reconciled; the question is, how. How can justice be done on the one hand to the experience of communities that have maintained a Christian and catholic faith for some centuries without much ado about bishops—and on the other hand to communities that have discovered in the episcopal office and its continuity one of the basic institutional bonds that sustains believers in the apostolic faith and life?

In taking up these issues today, I do not intend to attempt any "final solution" of them; and in any case I am not sure that there is any single, uniformly applicable solution. When, in the past, these problems have been dealt with—in practice or in principle—more or less successfully, it has been by methods that have differed according to time and place. What we have to look for is a course of action suited to the circumstances of our particular churches, to the particular goal—that of full communion between autonomous denominations—that we have set before ourselves, and to the particular agreements we have already achieved. To that end, I want to begin by looking very briefly at *The Niagara Report* and calling attention to a fundamental principle it provides to guide our approach to these questions. Only then will I try to develop some implications of this principle and—finally— make some tentative observations about the proposals for mutual recognition and reconciliation of ministries now before us.

The most striking part of Niagara, at least to my eyes, lies not in its treatment of the mission of the church, precise and helpful though that may be, but in its recording and reflection of the path that, over many years, has brought our two communions to the point they have now reached. It would be tempting to describe this path simply in terms of evolving or progressing doctrinal agreement, and there would be some truth in such a description. Nevertheless, a glance at the text of Niagara suggests that this is not a full account of the matter. Its section entitled "The Truths We Share" alludes to basic formulations of the Rule of Faith, not to mention confessional and liturgical documents. However, it does not attempt to set out a formal theological consensus as the basis for a closer relation between the two bodies. Rather it records shared practices and the shared beliefs and confessional stances that these embody and attest; and it alludes to them, not as evidence that we all have the same theology, but as evidence that when we argue theologically, within and across our denominational boundaries, we do so as people who share a commitment to the same apostolic faith. The truths we share turn out to be the realities testified to in the Scriptures, confessed in the creeds, brought home to us in preaching and in sacrament, and appropriated in faith.

Agreement of this sort is, and must be acknowledged to be, of a rather peculiar order. It is not simply agreement about things to be said or assented to, though it is that. It is agreement in a common way of life and in the relationships, attitudes, and values which that way of life, as shared among many persons, embodies and diffuses. In fact, when you come right down to it, what is being said in that section of Niagara is that, despite our differing idioms, histories, and subcultural peculiarities, we recognize each other—even though reluctantly at times and with lifted eyebrows—as communities that share the same roots, in which the same essential sorts of things go on and the same hopes are generated and lived out. And all this is summed up in the rather solemn statement that "We acknowledge each other as true Churches of Christ."[1]

Now no doubt it is the case that behind such a statement as this, and behind the brisk summary of "The Truths We Share" in the text of Niagara there lies a good deal of mutual inspection, testing, conference, and debate. Yet it is important to notice that what we have here is not simply, or even primarily, a series of agreed statements on matters of moment, nor a theological platform that provides a new basis for church unity, but simply a record of what one might call a recognition scene. Not everything has been cleared up, all the details are not in order, every conceivable point has not been dealt with; but for all that it is clear to both parties, beyond the shadow of a doubt, that this bunch of "others" is—of all things—church. And the question I want to raise here is what this recognition, taken as the basis and starting-point of our process, signifies for the question of the mutual recognition and reconciliation of ministries.

In the history of Anglican thought and argument over the matter of episcopacy and its relation to the church, one can, I think, discern three "moments," which can, with due caution and qualification, be described as roughly successive; and I want to characterize these briefly in order to lay a foundation for our consideration of the implications of Niagara.

The first of these is best represented in the writings of Richard Hooker, who saw episcopacy as the proper and normative form of church government—or "regiment," as he would have preferred to say—but refused to acknowledge it as an element in the definition of "church." What defined the church or marked it out was its faith or doctrine, not its mode of government: though of course Hooker's notion of "government" had more to do with moral and doctrinal admonition on the basis of the Word of God than it did with what we like to call "administration."

The second of my "moments" had its inception, perhaps, in the days of Charles II, but came into its own only in the eighteenth and nineteenth centuries: an era in which Hooker's happy myth of "the godly prince" no longer enjoyed as much credit as it once had, and it seemed important to call attention to an identity and authority that the church possessed over against crown and state. For people like William Law and the Tractarians later on, bishops, even when their views proved disappointing, had an almost numinous quality about them: they were the personal symbols of the church's apostolic character, and thus of its self–identity through the centuries, and their jurisdictions therefore defined the realm of covenanted grace. On this view—reminiscent in many ways of that taken centuries earlier by Cyprian of Carthage—there was no church where there was no bishop in succession from the apostles: episcopacy was, one might say, a precondition of the reality of the church. It is this view—defended in our century in a work titled *The Apostolic Ministry* and edited by the late Bishop of Oxford, Dr. Kirk—which many, inside and outside the Anglican Communion, have taken as the norm for Anglican practice.

But for every Cyprian there is an Augustine; and starting in the later nineteenth century—and not oddly, in the United States, where the Christian movement was represented not by a dominant establishment but by a multifarious variety of "denominations" and sects—there arose a movement of thought that in a sense relativized episcopacy by envisaging it in a way that was different both from Hooker's and from that of the Tractarians. On this view, episcopacy, or "the historic ministry," was not, so to speak an issue separable from that of the identity of the church, a matter of mere government rather than of faith; nor was it, in the order of things human and creaturely, the church's one foundation. Rather it was conceived as one of a concatenated set of institutions that, even though they were, in each case, contingent products of the historical evolution of the Christian movement, had nevertheless functioned, in their totality, as the regular bearers and signs of the church's continuing identity as church of Christ. In the formulation of the so-called Lambeth Quadrilateral, these institutions were specified as the canonical Scriptures, the two gospel sacraments, the ecumenical creeds, and the historical threefold ministry; though why these items were taken as adding up to precisely four, I cannot imagine.

Now it is important, for our purposes here, to examine this view— of which the Lambeth Quadrilateral may stand as a relatively authoritative representative—fairly closely, for the difficulties it involves as well as for the affirmations it makes; for it is, as I shall suggest later, rather closely related to the position espoused in Niagara.

The most important thing to note—and one that I have already alluded to—is the fact that each of these institutions or sets of institutions is envisaged as emerging or growing up with, and out of, the life of the family of Christian assemblies. Tradition, to be sure, has, in different ways, assigned to each of them a certain priority to the life of the church. The Scriptures have been described as the inspired Word of God, which addresses the church from beyond itself. The sacraments, in an Augustinian view, are not human works but visible signs of God's active presence in Christ. The ministry of the church is described, in Niagara, as "a gift of God to his Church and therefore an office of divine institution." The confession of faith embodied in the ecumenical creeds is, as employed in baptism, a precondition of the existence of the church. Each of these institutions, then, is somehow constitutive of the church. Nevertheless it remains true that they are institutions whose human and historical origins we can, within limits, trace; and therefore the priority they are assigned is not a given, but a reflection of the function they perform and have performed in the life of the church. If in their different ways they signify or mediate the transcendent source of the church's life and calling, they do so precisely because they are immanent and historically contingent products of that life.

Just because this is the case, however, none of these institutions in the forms in which we know them can be described as absolutely necessary to the life and identity of the church. It is not merely that we can imagine—not captiously, but seriously and reasonably—a course of historical development that would have produced, for example, a different canon of the Scriptures or different forms of ministry; we can observe that as a matter of fact the church's history has produced such variations. Furthermore, we can observe congregations of believing Christians in which the Scriptures are not publicly read or accorded any normative status; congregations in which the sacraments are either neglected or deprecated; congregations in which the creeds are officially repudiated. One is free of course to wonder whether such groups do not so limit their experience and cripple their understanding of the life of faith as, in the end, to risk departing from what is central to it; but one cannot maintain that any one of these institutions is absolutely necessary, in a given time and place, to the stimulation and sustenance of living faith. Indeed there is no one here, I venture, who would not, by casting about in his or her mind for a moment, think of a time and place when each of these institutions has been so corrupted in its use and functions that reasonable and faithful persons might well be willing to consider dispensing with it.

Here, then, we find ourselves in a paradoxical position. On the one hand, we see the continuing identity of the church as the community of apostolic faith rest on the continuity of certain distinctive and typical institutions—each of which, traditionally, has been valued for its role in opening us to the gospel, to the self–communication of God in Christ. On the other hand, these institutions are very human affairs, to which we can ascribe no abstract necessity. What necessity they have rests on the fact that they "happened" in the way they did to function, on the whole, as they function. We do not deduce them, we observe them as enduringly focal or nodal points in the life of the churches.

It may be, though, that part of the solution of this paradox lies in the fact that these institutions are closely interrelated: that what we have in such a formula as the Lambeth Quadrilateral is not so much a list of items as it is a description of a system of communication whose several parts presuppose and depend on each other. If these institutions are in fact constitutive for the life of the church, and can thus lay claim at any rate to a diminished and hypothetical sort of necessity, that is because of the way they function together. The gospel set forth in the Scriptures is answered in the confession of faith represented by the creeds, sealed and enacted in the sacraments, and ministered and safeguarded by persons officially set apart for just that purpose—that is, for the purpose of keeping this system of communication, of *koinonia* between God and humanity in Christ, alive. That the system can become diseased or dysfunctional, through the failure or neglect of one of its constituent elements, we know; but we also know that, no doubt within limits, it can compensate for and correct its own weaknesses, because each of the constituent elements symbolizes and carries, in its own special way, the same gospel. The Scriptures can reiterate what the ministry forgets; the creeds assert what disuse or overly ingenious interpretation loses in the Scriptures; the ministry proclaims what the sacraments are no longer seen to enact.

Here, then, one can discern the logic of the outlook embodied in such a document as the Lambeth Quadrilateral. It does indeed relativize "the historic ministry"; and it does so by envisaging that ministry as real and essential only *in* and *through* its relation to certain other institutions from which it is inseparable; and second, by acknowledging that this whole system of institutions is relative to, because it is dependent on, the community or communities that are its matrix. It commends none of them in and for itself, but all of them in their interrelation. If it is true, as it surely is, that continuity in episcopal succession cannot of itself guarantee the identity or faithfulness of the church, neither is it true that—to use the words of one Anglican divine—"the Bible and the Bible alone is the religion of Protestants." What defines and constitutes the church for practical purposes is a historically emergent system of communication. As someone has remarked, the church is "a congregation....in which the pure Word of God is preached, and the sacraments be duly administered...."

Now it seems to me that if, in the light of this interpretation of the Lambeth Quadrilateral, we return to Niagara, it is possible both to discern a genuine convergence between them and to identify a problem that is common to both.

The convergence in question lies, it seems to me, in an acknowledgment that the phenomenon "church" and the set of institutions that carries and maintains its identity are in the strictest sense *correlative*. That is to say, it is true at one and the same time *both* that the institutions in question are an ultimate precondition of the existence of "church," *and* that the same institutions exist—and *can* exist—only in a community that already *is* "church." Hence when Niagara attempts to substantiate its assertion that Lutheran and Anglican bodies see each other as "church of Christ," it does so in effect by alluding to their common valuation of sacraments, Scriptures, confessions of faith, and ministry. And when the Lambeth fathers set out their convenient checklist of institutions, it is clear that they were telling us how to recognize a church when we see one. Everyone understands, of course, that the institutions in question are not identical in all respects from Christian body to Christian body. Wicked westerners insert *filioque* in the text of the Nicene Creed; wicked Roman Catholics read *The Wisdom of Solomon* as Scripture. Still, the institutions are identifiable, in their slightly variant forms, as being of a piece; and by their means the church is discerned. Yet clearly *these* institutions can only exist where "church" itself is also a given.

So much for the convergence: but what of the problem? That, it seems to me, grows directly out of the acknowledgment that the community—church—and its characteristic institutions are correlative. Ecumenical dialogue is possible only because one recognizes in another group of people the lineaments of the church; ecumenical dialogue is necessary only because, to one degree or another, one observes in the same group some neglect or blurring of, some departure from, the faith and practice sustained by the church's characteristic institutions. The problem of unity thus becomes, quite literally, a chicken–and–egg proposition. Shall we treat institutional fulness as the precondition of the acknowledgment of a particular body as church? Or shall we admit that acknowledgment of its ecclesial character through wholehearted fellowship is the only likely condition under which a particular body will ever come spontaneously closer to institutional fulness?

Now it might reasonably be argued that this problem marks the position at which we have arrived in this dialogue: the position, that is, of arguing the relative priority of chickens and eggs. And of course there is some truth in such a suggestion. Nevertheless circumstances, we are taught, alter cases, and this case is marked by certain peculiarities of circumstance. I spoke above of recognizing in another group of people "the lineaments of the church." That phrase was chosen with some care, as representing an experience I have enjoyed. It does not, however, represent the situation in which we stand in this dialogue. For we have gone further and acknowledged in each other's bodies *true churches of Christ*: which can only mean that at one and the same time we see both sets of preconditions present in recognizable form—the community in which alone this characteristic set of institutions can exist, and the institutions that, in their interrelation, mark and sustain the identity of that community. And there is the further peculiar circumstance that we are seeking not merger but "full communion."

Under these circumstances, it seems to me right and reasonable to suggest that the chicken–egg dilemma can be overcome: or rather, that it *has* been overcome. Both the community of faith that characteristically maintains itself through these institutions, and an authentic form of the institutions themselves, are present in both bodies; and this, we might say, is the fundamental *a priori*. With this given, it becomes possible to adjust and correct the *forms* of these institutions in each body, and to do so in increasing fellowship. And this leads me to some concluding remarks about how such adjustment and correction might occur.

In the first place it is important to stress the principle already embodied in the proposed report of this group: the principle, that is, of simultaneous and cooperative action. We are not in the business of creating, or recreating, each other's churches. Rather, we are in the business of mutually adapting the forms of certain institutions that exist in both bodies with a view to their closer correspondence and—ultimately—exchangeability. Furthermore, we are committed to doing so in a fashion that embodies what might be called the grace of ecumenical tact—a certain loving sensitivity to the eccentric but engaging prepossessions of the other party. And what this entails, as I see it, is precisely a willingness to engage in simultaneous, step–by–step change on both sides.

Furthermore, the agenda for this cooperative enterprise is fairly clear. Most of it has to do with the forms of ministry that presently exist in our churches.

We want first of all to assure that the episcopate shall not in the future run the risk of being conceived, or of functioning, in separation from the message of the gospel as that is borne by Scriptures, creeds, and sacraments. This has happened in the past history of the churches, and it is arguable that Anglicans have been guilty of it, frequently in theory and not infrequently in practice.

The second item on our agenda has to do with the establishment of episcopacy as a sign of the churches' diachronic and synchronic continuity and unity. This implies a concern both for the collegiality of bishops in their pastoral calling (synchronic), and a concern for the traditional manner in which, by election and ordination, the college of bishops has been maintained in continuity over time (diachronic).

Finally, we are mutually concerned for the pastoral character of the episcopal office; and the import of this item on our agenda is not exhausted by commitment to the bishop's role as preacher and teacher of the gospel and minister of the sacraments. It has to do rather, one might say, with the bishop's collegial relation, on the local level, with presbyters, deacons, and laity: i.e., the bishop's presence with and among them as both a colleague and a leader (as distinct from the bishop's presence *over* them as an administrator or manager).

These agenda items, if pursued intentionally and cooperatively, will involve changes in both of our denominations; and in thus taking them up and dealing with them, we will not so much contrive full communion among our churches as wake up one day and find ourselves in it.

10
MUTUAL RECOGNITION OF MINISTRIES
BY
WILLIAM G. RUSCH

INTRODUCTION

The assigned topic is to discuss mutual recognition of ministries to allow for full communion, which means where two church traditions allow communicant members freely to communicate at the altars of each other and where there is freedom of ministries to officiate sacramentally in either church tradition.[1] In spite of some misunderstanding about the *Lutheran Episcopal Agreement*, full communion has not yet been achieved between us. We have taken one significant but small step in that direction. In this essay I wish to describe where Lutheran–Anglican discussions have come on this matter and where ecumenical theology has led, and then suggest two models that the dialogue may wish to consider as a way out of this apparent ecumenical cul–de–sac.

A few preliminary observations will be useful in order to place this topic in its proper context.

(1) The Lambeth Quadrilateral of 1888 is often quoted in the Lutheran–Episcopal Dialogue as a description of the essentials for a reunited Christian church. In Lutheran–Anglican discussions the fourth point is often raised as a problem. "The Historic Episcopate, locally adopted in the methods of its administration to the varying needs of the nations and peoples called of God into the Unity of His Church."[2] Is the distinction between "a reunited Christian Church" and "full communion" of any importance here? In other words, could greater differences be allowed between churches in living out full communion, as opposed to "a reunited christian church," which could imply organic merger?

155

(2) Our topic is, in a sense, artificial. Mutual recognition of ministries cannot be treated in isolation from other concerns. There is a question behind the question, and it is of ecclesiology. Lutherans and Anglicans have different models of church, but if they have agreed that these are viable paradigms of the church, then their patterns of ministry should be viable. What more is needed for full communion?

(3) In many ways Lutherans in the U.S. have at least a twofold pattern of ministry: pastors exercising *episkope* over churches, and pastors exercising *episkope* within a parish. Thus Lutherans do have offices of *episkope* in the church. Since Anglicans have no official theology of the episcopate, perhaps Lutherans should press Episcopalians as to what more in terms of order must be clarified prior to full communion.

(4) Because mutual recognition of ministries is to be seen in the context of ecclesiology, there will not only be Episcopal questions about church order, but Lutheran questions about the gospel.

(5) The patristic church may provide models to be examined in regard to the ordering of the church. A rehearsal of much traditional Lutheran and Anglican scholarship about the New Testament and patristic churches will supply little new knowledge, but may offer some helpful insights.[3]

LUTHERAN-ANGLICAN DISCUSSIONS AND ECUMENICAL THEOLOGY IN REGARD TO RECOGNITION OF MINISTRIES

The first series of Lutheran–Episcopal Dialogue in the U.S. in its fourth meeting dealing with apostolicity, took up the question of ministry. The participants in that dialogue believed both communions should affirm the ordained ministries of both communions as true ministries of the one church of Christ. They observed that mutual recognition of ministries could create conditions for a new relationship. Succession was viewed as a succession of the gospel by means of Scripture, creeds, and confessions, as well as the institution of an ordered ministry and succession of ministries. The dialogue members saw, within the one church, both Anglican continuity of the episcopal order and Lutheran concentration on doctrine as means of preserving the apostolicity of the one church. In any future ordering in the one church there will be a ministry, and within that ministry an *episkope*.[4]

The second series of Lutheran–Episcopal Dialogue in the U.S. also addressed the ordained ministry in the context of apostolicity. The dialogue noted the great measure of agreements between Lutherans and Episcopalians on the understanding of the pastoral office, including the necessity of oversight *(episkope)*, which is embodied in an ordained office. Episcopalians in the dialogue recognized Lutheran affirmation of the full dignity of the pastoral office and that Lutherans are open to the historic episcopate as a valid and proper form of that office. The preference of the Lutheran Confessions for the historic episcopate was acknowledged, although it was recognized that Lutherans do not hold the historic episcopate to be the only legitimate form of *episkope*. Basic and extensive elements of agreement on all aspects of apostolic succession, including ordained ministry, were recognized.[5] Most of these ideas were picked up and restated in "A Statement by Lutherans to Lutherans."[6]

Many of these observations and conclusions were already expressed in the International Anglican–Lutheran Conversation, which issued its final report in 1972. Section D of the Pullach Report on apostolic ministry is especially relevant here. Apostolicity of the church is God's gift in Christ to the church. Apostolicity pertains first to the gospel and then to the ministry of Word and Sacrament. The succession of apostolicity is guarded and given expression in and through a wide variety of means, activities, and institutions. Ordained ministry is essentially one, though it assumes a diversity of forms. Ordination to ministry gives authority to preach the gospel and administer the sacraments according to Christ's command and promise, for the purpose of the continuance of the apostolic life and mission of the church.

In regard to episcopacy, the Pullach Report declared that *episkope* is inherent in the apostolic character of the church's life, mission, and ministry. It has been embodied and exercised in the church in a wide variety of forms, episcopal and non–episcopal. The Anglican participants stated that they do not believe the episcopate in historic succession alone constitutes the apostolic succession of the church or its ministry. They see in the Lutheran communion true proclamation of the Word and celebration of the sacraments. While the Anglican participants could not foresee full integration of ministries (full communion) apart from the historic episcopate, they did envision increasing intercommunion between Anglicans and Lutherans. The Lutheran participants stated that the particular form of the episcopate is not for them a confessional question. Lutherans should not accept the historic episcopate as a necessary condition for interchurch relations or church union. On the other hand, Lutheran churches that have not retained the historic episcopate are free to accept it where it serves the growing unity of the church in obedience to the gospel.[7]

The Anglican–Lutheran European Regional Commission met between 1980 and 1982. It issued its report in September 1982 in Helsinki. In part III of the report, "Doctrinal Issues: Agreements and Convergences," a section was devoted to ordained ministry and episcopacy. This work is placed in the context of broad ecumenical discussion of the topic. Anglicans and Lutherans increasingly note much agreement and similarity in their understanding and practice of ministry. Considerable common ground has been discovered in multilateral and bilateral conversations. This understanding was shaped by the Reformation tradition and by a continuity with biblical witness and the tradition of the early church. Obvious differences in the ordering of Anglican and some Lutheran ministries do not imply a deeper ecclesiological difference. Agreement and convergence on the level of doctrine is complemented by common pastoral and liturgical experience. The importance of the ministry of the whole people of God has been rediscovered. Anglicans and Lutherans hold the ordained ministry to be a gift of God and of divine institution. Through the act of ordination, God, through the church, calls, blesses, and sends ministers. There is agreement about the interrelation between general priesthood and the ordained ministry.

This dialogue report identifies with the growing ecumenical agreement on the apostolicity of the church and the acknowledgement that apostolic succession cannot be limited to the succession in episcopal consecration and ordinations. However, orderly transmission of ordained ministry is one element in the process because it is a sign of apostolic continuity of the church and serves it.

There is also agreement about the service of *episkope* as essential to ordained ministry and necessary for the life, unity, and mission of the church. The dialogue participants agreed on a description of the function and responsibilities of bishops to preach, to preside, and to administer discipline. They are to serve the apostolicity and unity of the church's teaching.

This section of the report of the European Commission concludes, building on the work of the Faith and Order document *Baptism, Eucharist and Ministry,* that the remaining difference on the question of the historical succession cannot be regarded as a hindrance to closer fellowship between Anglican and Lutheran churches. The members of the commission were convinced that there exists sufficient agreement for mutual recognition of Anglican and Lutheran ministries.[8]

This conviction found expression in the recommendations of the report that, subject to the tradition and law of the respective churches, and where local conditions make it desirable, occasional mutual participation in presbyterial and episcopal ordinations was encouraged.[9]

The Niagara Report, the report of the Anglican–Lutheran Consultation on Episcope, built on the earlier work of Anglican–Lutheran dialogues and the studies of Faith and Order, especially BEM. It anchors its work in the nature of the church and its mission. This provides an extremely helpful context in which to discuss the question of ministry. Among the requirements for the church's mission is the development of structure. In this discussion Niagara points out that oversight is the heart of the episcopal office, but oversight is never viewed apart from the continuity of apostolic faith. Bishops do not guarantee the continuity of apostolic faith. Because of the comprehensive doctrinal agreement between Lutherans and Anglicans, neither tradition can reject the apostolic nature of the other. Thus the ordained ministry is no longer an issue that need divide Lutheran and Anglican churches. In view of the symbolic position of the bishop as reflecting both the universal and local *koinonia,* the continued isolation of those who exercise this office of *episkope* in the two churches is no longer tolerable and must be overcome.[10]

On the basis of the consensus in the faith and in light of the common mission shared by Anglicans and Lutherans, the question was raised as to what needs to be reformed in the Anglican and Lutheran expressions of *episkope.* Lutheran churches were asked to make four changes in current practice: (1) all persons who exercise an ordained ministry of *episkope* should receive the title of bishop or suffragan bishop, (2) constitutions should be revised so bishops are elected to the same tenure as other pastoral ministers, (3) there should be a laying-on-of-hands by at least three bishops in the rites of installation for bishops, and (4) only bishops or suffragan bishops should preside at all ordinations.

Anglican churches were asked to make three changes: (1) they should make the necessary canonical revisions to acknowledge and recognize the full authenticity of existing ministries of Lutheran churches, (2) Anglican churches and bishops should establish and welcome structures for collegial and periodic review, and (3) Anglican churches should regularly invite Lutheran bishops to participate in the laying-on-of-hands at the consecration and installation of Anglican bishops.[11]

This brief review of Lutheran–Anglican dialogue indicates clearly that the third series of Lutheran–Episcopal Dialogue in the U.S. is not without resources when it takes up the second half of its mandate in the fifth point of the Lutheran–Episcopal Agreement of 1982. At many places there has been identified between Episcopalians and Lutherans considerable agreements and convergences about the apostolic gospel and many aspects of the pastoral office. Based on this common teaching of the gospel, joint ordinations have been proposed in a manner that respects the doctrine and practice of Lutherans and Anglicans. The problem is not the lack of resources, but the challenge of adopting these resources to the particular situation of the ECUSA and the ELCA.

All these reports from Lutheran–Anglican dialogues were not drafted in a vacuum. They are all influenced by the bilateral discussions on ministry that have occurred. There are implicit and explicit references to this general ecumenical discussion in the literature of Lutheran–Anglican dialogue. This influence can be seen in many ways. For example, ministry is usually taken up only after a discussion of broader or related topics, e.g., the gospel, Scripture, the sacraments. Also, the historical character of the church and ministry is accepted. Specific conditions, particular situations in history, and openness to further change and development are employed to interpret past decisions or documents. The broadening of the concept of apostolicity has been developed in the wider ecumenical conversation and is taken up in Lutheran–Anglican reports.

A larger ecumenical reconception has taken place. The individual traditions continue to stress what they regard as necessary, but no longer in absolutistic terms. These are now tempered by the reappropriation of signs of apostolicity emphasized by the other. There is an ever-larger ecumenical convergence that is accepted by most episcopal and non–episcopal churches. This includes the recognition of the need for personal *episkope*, along with a recognition by churches possessing the historic episcopate that non–episcopal churches have the gifts of the Spirit in other modes of succession and oversight. On the other hand, there is evidence that some non–episcopal churches are open to considering the historic episcopate as a useful sign of continuity and unity, if a particular interpretation is not required.

Such a wider ecumenical background has had its effects on Lutheran–Episcopal dialogue in several places. It will no doubt make a contribution to the final report of Lutheran–Episcopal Dialogue III in the U.S. The documents from the larger context clearly state that the recommendations of several Lutheran–Anglican dialogues are not idiosyncratic, but fit into a larger, emerging ecumenical consensus.[12]

TWO POSSIBLE MODELS

In this section I want to take up two possible models from the wider ecumenical background that this dialogue could explore, to address the recognition of ministries. Both come from recent ecumenical endeavors, one multilateral and the other bilateral. Both share a common characteristic. They look to the early church as a resource for overcoming present divisions. This is not surprising. Edmund Schlink, speaking of apostolic succession, noted the following:

> We must never separate the succession of ministries from the succession of the church; they have always to be considered together. But it is absolutely decisive for the future of ecumenical encounter that we should go beyond the particular theme of succession to a new understanding of the unity of the church, in taking hold once more of the type of fellowship prevalent in the Primitive Church. This is important not only for solving the problems of the Church order, but also for tackling the question of dogma. For, in both these areas, the Primitive Church shows a much greater diversity of thought and definition than is shown in the later history of dogma and canon law, and greater than most would feel to be reconcilable with the future unity of the Church in the midst of the divisions of the churches.[13]

The first example is BEM.[14] Much has been written and will continue to be written about this convergence document. Many churches, including the churches in this dialogue, have made a response to it and have become engaged in the process of reception.[15]

The final section of BEM directly addresses mutual recognition of ordained ministries. Its position is deliberate. Based on the convergences on baptism, Eucharist, and ministry, what can churches do to recognize each other's ministries? See section VI regarding ministry, ¶¶51–55.[16] The following comments, based on these paragraphs, may offer insights to the present dialogue as it reflects on mutual recognition of ministries.

51. The churches must be ready to renew their understanding and practice of ministry and take deliberate steps.

52. Recognition is a process. Apostolic succession is of special importance. Can churches recognize their respective ordained ministers as transmitting the ministry of Word and Sacrament in continuity with apostolic times?

53. Different steps by different churches:

    a. Churches with episcopal succession recognize apostolic content of ordained ministry in churches without such succession and also existence of a ministry of *episkope*.

    b. Churches without succession, with ministry of Word and Sacrament, realize that continuity with the church of the apostles finds profound expression in successive laying-on-of-hands by bishops and recover the sign of episcopal succession.

54. Does not apply to Lutheran–Episcopal relations in the U.S., apart from the practice of the Lutheran Church–Missouri Synod.

55. Mutual recognition implies the decision of authorities and some liturgical act.

Generally speaking, the essays in *Ecumenical Perspectives on Baptism, Eucharist and Ministry* on convergence and reconciliation of ministry are not that helpful to this assignment.[17] The essay by Geoffrey Wainwright, "Reconciliation in Ministry," does suggest a method employed in the international Lutheran–Roman Catholic dialogue and elsewhere. It is a *"lex orandi"* method to recognize and promote convergence in liturgical practice as the most effective factor in the process toward mutual reconciliation of ministries. This dialogue may well wish to examine the pertinent liturgical texts used in the Episcopal and Lutheran traditions as one way to address the subject of mutual recognition of ministries.[18]

The second model comes from the international Lutheran–Roman Catholic dialogue. It is common today for various bilaterals to employ the results of other bilaterals. This is a sign of the growing maturity of ecumenical theology. The report and recommendations from the second series of Lutheran–Episcopal Dialogue in the U.S. used materials from both the U.S. and international Lutheran–Roman Catholic dialogue. *Facing Unity: Models, Forms and Phases of Catholic–Lutheran Church Fellowship* is a product of the Roman Catholic–Lutheran Joint Commission, sponsored by the then Secretariat for Promoting Christian Unity of the Vatican and the Lutheran World Federation.[19] Its value for Lutheran–Episcopal dialogue is that it provides a model for growing into church fellowship through mutual recognition and reception. The proposals of *Facing Unity* should be more easily attainable for Lutherans and Anglicans than for Lutherans and Roman Catholics.

After a discussion of the concept of unity and models of union, *Facing Unity* turns to forms and phases of Catholic–Lutheran church fellowship. It envisions a growth of church communion with three elements, taken together as part of a process including the interlocking accomplishments of recognition and reception.

The first includes a communion of faith with a common witness to the apostolic faith, a unity of faith in a diversity of forms, and a removal of doctrinal condemnations. Lutheran–Anglican dialogue has shown repeatedly that Anglicans and Lutherans can claim together such a communion of faith.

The second element includes a communion of sacraments, with a growth of sacramental life in the churches, an increasing agreement in the understanding and practice of the sacraments, and an acknowledgment of remaining diversities along with basic agreements. Here, too, Lutheran–Anglican dialogue has demonstrated a basic agreement that Anglicans and Lutherans can share.

The third element includes a communion of ministry (service). If churches confess the same apostolic faith and share a common understanding of the sacraments, they should be committed to a structured fellowship together. Thus *Facing Unity* provides the description of a process that would lead to a common ecclesiastical office for the common practice of *episkope*. The early church offers some useful models. The process need not be identical everywhere, at the same time. First there would be preliminary forms of a common exercise of *episkope*. From this would develop an initial act of recognition. This act would be based on a consensus of faith, sacramental life, and ordained office. Diversity would continue, but it would no longer be church dividing; mutual condemnations of teaching would become invalid. Both churches would recognize each other as churches of Jesus Christ. Sacramental sharing would occur. In time this relationship would lead to a transition from a commonly exercised *episkope* to one common ecclesiastical office. The commonly exercised office of *episkope*, including ordinations in common, leads gradually to the realization of one common ecclesiastical office. Each of the common ordinations is seen as confessional, epicletic, and confessional. Each is a gift of God with the total community involved. It is not a question of what one partner gives to the other. This model of common new ordinations to fill vacancies avoids problems that have hampered other ecumenical suggestions, vis-à-vis reordinations, supplementary ordinations, acts of reconciliation of offices, and mutual commissionings. A period of transition would occur. The exercise of the common ordained ministry would need not be uniform for each place. Finally, the churches would be united into a single church.

Facing Unity devotes some attention to the implications of a Lutheran church in full communion with the Roman Catholic Church.

The report closes with the word that while these efforts have their goal in Catholic–Lutheran church fellowship, the task and aim of wider Christian unity should not be lost. Each individual step toward unity must be understood as a step taken toward the unity of all churches.

The conclusion of this essay is simple and direct. Lutheran–Episcopal dialogue in the United States has ample resources from earlier Lutheran–Anglican dialogue and other ecumenical theological conversations to suggest a responsible way, building on the consensus on the gospel between Lutheran and Episcopal Christians, for the ECUSA and the ELCA to recognize mutually each other's ordained ministries, and thus to move closer to full communion.

11

FULL COMMUNION BETWEEN EPISCOPALIANS AND LUTHERANS IN THE UNITED STATES: WHAT WOULD IT LOOK LIKE?

BY

MICHAEL ROOT

The question in the title of this essay can appear deceptively simple. One is tempted to answer: Full communion would be a relation between the Lutheran[1] and Episcopal churches in the U.S. that would evince certain institutional characteristics widely agreed to be constitutive of full communion or fellowship.[2] List the characteristics and one has a description. Such an answer is true as far as it goes, and this essay for the most part will focus on the institutional elements of full communion. Nevertheless, some qualifications need immediately to be added.

First, we must not forget that full communion as an intrahistorical reality always exists in some tension with the perfection of communion that will exist only eschatologically.[3] Full communion as a set of relations among churches exists as a sign, foretaste, and instrument of that eschatological communion which is present to us now in the Spirit but the full realization of which we still yearn for. Full communion must have within it a dynamism and discomfort, a sense that it is only a pilgrim reality on its way to the heavenly Jerusalem.

Second, full communion must not be reduced to a set of institutional elements, finished once the enumerated elements are in place. As has been stated repeatedly (see below, "What Sort of Common Life Is Implied by Full Communion?"), communion between churches must be the structure in which a common life is lived. Since this life is a life in Christ, under the living Word, it has a free and open–ended character. At all levels, the structures of unity must be free to develop in ways that conform to the true life of the church. As that life progresses, grows, and meets crises, so the shape that communion takes must be open to adjustments and innovations. The constant features of full communion create the context for a life together and are not a substitute for it.

Third, recent discussions among and between Anglicans and Lutherans have made it clear that if full communion is a way of describing the ecumenical goal, then it must describe nothing less than the full visible unity of the church. In the present situation, the question, "What would full communion look like?" is a more precise form of a more sweeping question, "If full visible unity need not mean denominational merger, then what *does* it mean?" If the exploration of possible forms of communion between Episcopalians and Lutherans in the U.S. is to be fruitful not only for themselves but also for the wider church, then this larger question needs to be kept in mind.

THE STATUS OF THE QUESTION AMONG ANGLICANS AND LUTHERANS

Lutherans and Anglicans have discussed the nature of full communion in varying contexts: within their own tradition, in ecumenical discussions with each other, and in the wider ecumenical movement. The appendix to this essay is meant to indicate the outline of that discussion and provide background. I will not here repeat what can be easily followed there, but only note the general shape the discussion has taken.

Among both Lutherans and Anglicans, the discussion of the nature of communion or fellowship has proceeded in relation to two groups of questions: concerning the internal unity of the Anglican or Lutheran communions and concerning the structures that could rightly embody the ecumenical unity we seek.

The former question has taken slightly different shapes in the two communions. The Anglican Communion started with the reality that the Anglican churches or provinces were in communion, and has then reflected on what that relation is and should be. Increasing diversity and new tensions have impelled this reflection, but this diversity and tension have developed within established relations of fellowship. The Lutheran churches began with no such certainty that they were already in communion with each other. Even if most Lutherans at the first Lutheran World Convention in 1923 understood themselves to be in fellowship with most other Lutherans, this judgment was not universal. Not until 1984 did the LWF amend its constitution to state that its member churches were in pulpit and altar fellowship with one another. Discussions of the nature of the LWF often centered on whether the member churches were in fact in fellowship, and what that might mean for the world family of Lutheran churches. Thus, while Anglican discussion in the twentieth century has focused on *what it means to be* in communion, the parallel Lutheran discussion has focused on *whether we are* in communion.[4]

These internal discussions are not irrelevant to the subject at hand. For both Episcopalians and Lutherans in North America, our most extensive experience of living in communion is with other churches of our own tradition. If the Anglican and Lutheran communions are in fellowship among themselves, then the reality of those relations can provide a touchstone for our thinking on Anglican–Lutheran fellowship. One should not assume, however, that the present shape of the Anglican or Lutheran communions form perfect or even good examples of what life in communion should be. Unease exists in each communion over whether its present forms are institutionally or theologically adequate. This unease must also inform reflection on the possible shape of Anglican–Lutheran relations.[5]

As participants in the wider ecumenical movement, both Anglicans and Lutherans have faced a second question: "What is the unity we seek?" What sort of communion among the churches can be called "full"? Within the past ten years, Lutheran-Anglican discussions seem to have come to an agreement on this question. On the one hand, the ecumenical unity we seek must be more than mere mutual tolerance; it must involve a truly common life. On the other hand, when fellowship involves such a common life, it can be a form of the visible unity of the church for which we are striving. This consensus will be looked at in detail below ("Is Full Communion Too Much, Too Little, or Just Right?").

WHAT ARE THE ESSENTIAL ELEMENTS OF FULL COMMUNION?

If we limit our survey to descriptions of the nature of full communion in Anglican–Lutheran dialogues (Appendix, nos. 2, 3), in bilateral or multilateral discussions in which at least one of our churches participates (nos. 6, 8, 10, 15), and in documents of Anglican or Lutheran churches (nos. 13, 15, 23, 26), a consensus on the elements of full communion is visible.[6] In summary, the descriptions agree that full communion is:

I. a relation between distinct church bodies

II. which agree that all are:

    A. confessing the one Christian faith,

    B. rightly celebrating the true Christian sacraments, and

    C. rightly ordering their ministry,

III. and thus the churches

    A. admit each other's members to their sacramental life

    B. admit the clergy of the other church (priests/pastors and bishops), within normal disciplinary limits, to exercise aspects of their ministry within the other church,

    C. live a truly common life of witness and service, involving

    D. a true interdependence, with mutual consultation and decision making on issues of common concern.

This picture can be filled in, with particular reference to the possible communion between the ELCA and the ECUSA.

I. The relation of full communion assumes the continuing existence of distinct church bodies. These bodies may be simply distinct dioceses within a larger church or distinct denominations in the typical American sense. Full communion thus does not necessarily foresee the disappearance of distinct Lutheran or Anglican church organizations.

The Cold Ash Report (see App., no. 2) and the 1981 study for the ACC (no. 23) both add that the involved churches are not only distinct but autonomous. While there is a sense in which this term is appropriate, one can wonder whether "autonomous" is a good term to describe any church that understands itself to be but a part of the wider church, or is even a good term to describe the entire church, since no church is a law unto itself, but all are under Christ. Whatever the juridical autonomy of churches in communion is, it need be seen in conjunction with the interdependence that should typify such churches.

II. Foundational for a relation of communion or fellowship must be the mutual recognition that the churches are true to the apostolic heritage of faith and order. For Lutherans and Anglicans, this recognition must include three elements:

A. There must be recognition that each church is confessing the one Christian faith. Such a recognition need not imply that the churches agree on details of doctrine or even on how best to state major themes of the Christian gospel. It does imply that each can affirm that the other teaches and proclaims the apostolic message. In light of the interpenetration and common life envisaged by full communion, there must be sufficient consensus on the gospel to make possible a common witness to all essential aspects of Christian faith.

B. Lutherans and Anglicans have tied fellowship to the right celebration of the divinely instituted sacraments of baptism and the Lord's Supper. Again, agreement need not extend to details of interpretation or liturgy, but there must be mutual affirmation that the churches are celebrating the sacraments in such a way that the other can conscientiously participate in that celebration. Agreement must be sufficient to allow joint celebrations that do not violate the conscience of either side, even if a joint celebration will not fully meet the liturgical and even theological preferences of either.

C. Neither Lutherans nor Anglicans can enter into fellowship without recognition that the divinely instituted office of ministry is present and being exercised in the other church. A recognition of ordained ministries is thus the third essential element.[7]

Any relation of full communion would have to begin with a declaration of these recognitions, and would need some means whereby the churches can be assured that they continue to hold. The Leuenberg Agreement in Europe has led to the creation of structures whereby continuing conversations and consultation can go on. In at least one case, a signatory church revised a proposed change in its ordination practices when questions from other churches arose in the Leuenberg Executive Committee.[8] A relation between only two churches would probably not require structures of the same complexity, but there would need to be the recognition that questions about the continued validity of the necessary recognitions are an appropriate part of life in communion and should be raised and discussed in a spirit that serves both truth and unity.

III. At the center of a relation of full communion between Anglican and Lutherans must be pulpit and altar fellowship/*communio in sacris*. For both Anglicans and Lutherans, the oneness of the church is realized and decisively manifested in the common preaching of the one gospel and especially in the unity at the table of the Lord.

A. For the most part, our churches already unquestioningly receive each other's members at the Eucharist. The 1982 agreement extended a "special welcome" from each church to communicants from the other(s). While individual conscience would be respected, a relation of full communion would constitute an official acceptance of this welcome on the part of each church, something not included in the 1982 agreement. While this official acceptance would probably make little immediate difference for most lay persons, it must be seen as part of a larger network of new relations.

B. A more obvious change would come in the openness of each church to the clergy of the other. We would move from standing together at the altar to standing in each other's place. Full communion is not fully realized until a Lutheran pastor filling in for an Anglican priest (and vice versa) ceases to be seen as an unusual affair or a special ecumenical event.

Of course, the normal disciplinary structures of both churches will need to be respected. The openness of each church to the preaching and liturgical leadership of clergy from the other must not destroy the normal oversight that each church exercises over its own life. Nevertheless, such oversight will need to be so organized that the occasional substitution of clergy from one church within the other is not an overly complicated matter.

The continuing distinct character of the churches will need to be respected when one considers the possibility of clergy from one church permanently exercising their ministry in the other. It is not unreasonable to ask persons transferring from one church to the other to do special work to become more acquainted with the education or confirmation materials, polity, liturgy, or theology of their new church. Even an internship, serving perhaps as an associate in a parish in order to become more acquainted with the ethos of the new church, may not be an unreasonable demand in some cases. In addition, a permanently transferring priest or pastor would come under the discipline of the new church and would be expected to make the commitments expected from the clergy within the new church (e.g., in terms of confessional subscription). Some special rite of acceptance for such a permanent transfer may be appropriate. Such matters, however, should not be so onerous as to block the transfer of ministers from one church to the other, nor be such as to call into question the validity of ministry in the other church.

While judgments about the availability of clergy in one church for service in the other, either temporarily or permanently, would need to take into account the individuals involved, full communion means that no discrimination can be systematically made among entire groups in the other church, e.g., between men and women or between persons ordained before or after some date (see App., no. 25). If a church judges that it must make some such discrimination, then that judgment should be squarely faced and the admission made that full communion is not yet possible.[9]

Between churches with a ministry of oversight focused in a bishop or other similar official, this openness to the ministry of clergy from the other church should take an additional form. This mutual openness is a recognition of the single apostolic mission that is carried out by the involved churches. We can stand together and in place of each other because we see ourselves as one in mission. This oneness in mission should mean that along with all churches we share a common responsibility for this mission. The gifts of the Spirit are given to individuals but for the good of the body as a whole. The body as a whole has a legitimate interest and oversight in relation to the exercise of these gifts. Most notably, oversight must address whether the gifts are serving the one gospel and thus serving the unity of the church. Because oversight must be exercised in the interests of the body as a whole and for the sake of its unity in the gospel, those who are most directly involved in oversight (in our churches, bishops) should carry out this oversight in a collegial way. If the church is to be one in mission, then the bishops need to be one in their oversight. The collegial unity of the bishops in their ministry of oversight is thus not simply a sign of the unity of the church, but a means by which unity is maintained.[10]

This collegiality is signified and, to a degree, realized in the participation of other bishops in the installation or consecration of a new bishop. The collegial unity of the two churches in mission is brought into sharp focus in such a celebration (see App., no. 19).[11]

The churches will need to ask themselves whether such a mutual participation in the laying-on-of-hands should signify a more extensive cooperation in the ministry of oversight. This question is addressed below.

WHAT SORT OF COMMON LIFE IS IMPLIED BY FULL COMMUNION?

The aspects of full communion discussed so far are relatively straightforward, even if the churches have found it hard to realize them in their life together. The last two aspects (III.D & E) have received increased recognition in recent years, and are much harder to define in the abstract or in advance.

D. That full communion implies some form of common life is obvious once reflected upon, even if sometimes left unmentioned. Communion is not just a juridical relation between two church organizations. It must be a true community of life and mission. Communion has its center and focus in altar and pulpit fellowship/*communio in sacris*. Nevertheless, community at the Lord's Supper cannot be separated from community in wider life. Here, 1 Corinthians 11 is unambiguous: unity in the proclamation of the gospel and celebration of the sacraments is oriented toward community in the wider Christian life. Peter Brunner stated this connection with particular clarity from a Lutheran perspective:

> We dare not console ourselves merely with an arrangement of mutual admission to Holy Communion and see in it alone the overcoming of the divisions.... Rather, we must realize that the unification of the churches [*Kirchenvereinigung*] manifests itself through an abundance of actually lived, concrete, historical, and of course, legally formulated relationships and forms of expression. I suggest the word "church fellowship" [*Kirchengemeinschaft*] as incorporating all of these elements.[12]

That fellowship must be not only established but also lived was the insight of the Leuenberg Agreement in its distinction between the declaration and the realization of fellowship. The same insight can be found throughout Lutheran–Anglican dialogues, nationally and internationally. The 1982 agreement in the U.S. called on the churches to "encourage the development of common Christian life," especially through "mutual prayer and mutual support," "common study," "joint programs of religious education, theological discussion, mission, evangelism, and social action," and "joint use of physical facilities." The European *Helsinki Report* of the same year called for "a visible sharing in the *common life* of the Body of Christ (see App., no. 1, emphasis in original). It is difficult to find any dialogue that recommends actions to the participating churches that does not recommend the development of some forms of common life.

One cannot specify in advance or nationwide what forms such common life should take. They will obviously vary from place to place both in content and intensity. The sort of common life realized by Lutheran and Episcopal mission congregations sharing physical facilities in the North Carolina mountains, far from other Lutherans or Episcopalians, will be different from the common life shared by large, established parishes in St. Louis. One can say, however, that such a common life should have certain general characteristics.

First, it should be realized at all levels of church life: national, synodical/diocesan, and parochial/congregational. No level of church life should remain untouched. The reality of life in many of our congregations, parishes, dioceses, and synods, however, is that they carry on their lives with very little living relation to the other such units within their own church. We should not set our expectations for such a common life overly high. Nevertheless, ways need to be found whereby, at the local and regional level, people can find the interpenetration of Lutheran and Episcopal life enriching. Only then will the common life take on a self–sustaining quality.

Second, such a common life must be open to other churches. Lutheran–Episcopal communion must not create a front *against* rapprochement with other traditions, but should be seen as one step in a larger process of reconciliation. Care should be taken to avoid the impression that either church is pursuing this fellowship as a form of opposition to some other ecumenical development. Various activities on the local and regional level can include other churches, even if such churches are in fellowship with neither the ELCA nor the ECUSA. There is no general reason why a joint Episcopal–Lutheran Vacation Church School could not expand to include a Presbyterian congregation or Roman Catholic parish.

E. Common life as so far described represents no threat to the churches, even if some might look upon it as a burden. Matters are different in relation to common decision making. Here the juridical autonomy of the churches seems to be threatened. Here one must reflect and act with particular care. On the one hand, one must not design structures for which sufficient trust has not developed and which seem to violate the existing and valid structures of power and authority within the churches. On the other hand, one should not give up the fight for what should be an important part of a unified church, even a church unified in reconciled, yet organizationally distinct, diversity.

I will not here try to lay out possible structures of common decision making. At first (and maybe at last) they should be modest. To the degree that there are truly common actions, there will need to be structures whereby common decisions are made about those common actions (e.g., who does what with the sixth- graders in the Vacation Church School). Little more than such structures that are inherent within common actions need be instituted when the churches first enter into a relation of full communion. More important is a spirit of consultation on important matters that affect the foundations of fellowship, e.g., the standards of doctrinal discipline or the revision of eucharistic liturgies or ordinals. The development of such a spirit of consultation must precede the creation of more far–reaching and authoritative structures of common decision making. Precisely in this area there will need to be growth into deeper unity *after* the establishment of a relation of full communion.

One area where such growth may be particularly appropriate is in the ministry of oversight, as carried out both by bishops and by synodical structures. As noted above, the decisive task of such a ministry is to safeguard that the one faith is being witnessed to in the life of the church and the activities of its ministers. This ministry is thus directly related to unity, and is appropriately a matter of ecumenical cooperation. The churches need to think how such a ministry increasingly can be carried out jointly.[13]

One area in which such a spirit of mutual consultation would need to develop would be in ecumenical relations. That each church will be in fellowship with churches with which the other is not in fellowship is inevitable. Communion between the ELCA and the ECUSA would not imply that each immediately enters into full fellowship with all churches of the world communion of which the other is a member. Nevertheless, if a true common life develops between the two churches, then a certain "fellowship at one remove" will inevitably exist between, say, the ELCA and churches with which the ECUSA is in communion. This "remove" would be all the smaller if the "third church" is not another Anglican church overseas but a church within the U.S. The continuing juridical autonomy of each church means that each church must finally make its own ecumenical judgments. Ecumenical progress is probably impossible without the creation of some "unclosed ecumenical circles," in which church A is in fellowship with B, B with C, but C not in fellowship with A. Such situations require open and honest consultation, in which the judgments of the other are respected, even if not agreed with.[14]

If such a modest form of common decision making seems inadequate to the reality of full communion, it is worth remembering that little more presently exists within either the Lutheran or Anglican communions. Whatever moral authority they may carry, neither an LWF Assembly, a Lambeth Conference, nor the ACC can make decisions that are binding on the constituent churches. Some lament this nonetheless true fact; yet the world communions understand themselves to be made up of churches in full communion or fellowship with each other. Both communions seem to be granting the larger fellowship more authority, at least informally and in some circles. If such a process of gradual growth in common decision making, without an assurance of where it will lead, is sufficient for the worldwide communions, more cannot be initially required of a possible relation between Lutherans and Episcopalians in North America, where the level of acquaintance and trust is in many ways less developed than within the world communions.

IS FULL COMMUNION TOO MUCH, TOO LITTLE, OR JUST RIGHT?

What has been described when one has described full communion? Has one described the ecumenical goal for which we should be striving? The assumption here has been that this question should be answered "Yes," and such an answer seems now to be shared by international Lutheranism and Anglicanism. Nevertheless, this agreement is not of long standing, and there are still dissenting voices.

The Lutheran affirmation that full communion as here described is the ecumenical goal can be seen nationally in the appendix, nos. 12 and 13, and internationally in nos. 14 and 15. Lutherans have consistently said that the true unity *requires* only agreement in the gospel and the sacraments, and is adequately realized in relations of fellowship. "Organic union" is a possible result, when mission dictates, but Lutherans have proven reluctant to judge that mission ever in fact *does* dictate union with non–Lutherans.

Despite this congruence between contemporary descriptions of full communion and what Lutherans have traditionally argued ecumenically, a Lutheran still might contend that CA 7 finds the unity of the church only in agreement on the pure preaching of the gospel and the evangelical celebration of the sacraments. Where such agreement exists, then nothing more is needed: no common life, no mutual availability of clergy, not even openness to each other's members at the Lord's Supper, since neither is this mentioned in CA 7.

This objection derives from a truth: it is unity in Word and Sacrament (and the office that enacts them) that unites us as church. This truth, however, has been noted above and does not contradict full communion as the ecumenical goal. A full discussion of CA 7 in its relation to full communion is not possible here. Three comments must suffice.[15] First, CA 7 already presupposes a degree of common life and common decision making in asserting that unity is found when churches *agree* on preaching and sacraments. Second, CA 7 must not be isolated from the broader ecclesiology of the reformers, where one finds it constantly reiterated that unity is to be lived out in a life of mutual love and concrete fellowship. For example, in the Smalcald Articles (2:4.9), Luther wrote that the bishops should be "diligently joined together in unity of doctrine, faith, sacraments, prayer, works of love, etc." Third, Lutheran churches have uniformly stated that fellowship is to be lived out in a common life of love and witness. For example, the American Lutheran Conference's 1952 *United Testimony on Faith and Life* states: "Christian faith *seeks* fellowship, that is, the discovery and the practice of this spiritual fellowship with other Christians. It laments isolation; it yearns for communion. Christian faith seeks fellowship in prayer, in corporate worship, in Communion, in doing the Lord's work, and even in suffering for the faith."[16] In full communion, churches live out the unity described in CA 7.

The Anglican affirmation that full communion as here described is a form of the ecumenical goal can be seen nationally in the appendix, no. 16 and especially 17, and internationally in no. 27. A glance at nos. 21, 22, and 23, however, shows that this affirmation is recent, and there are still dissenting voices, particularly, it seems to me, among British Anglicans.[17] Anglicans (and the WCC) have in the past tended to insist that only when the distinct churches give up their identities within a united church have we reached the unity for which we should be striving. Only on the Indian subcontinent, however, have Anglicans in fact agreed to enter such a union.

Again, a full discussion here is not possible. A few comments must suffice. The criticisms of full communion as ecumenical goal seem to equate it with "mere intercommunion" or "federation alone" (see App., nos. 21 and 22). The more recent Anglican acceptance of full communion as an appropriate realization of visible unity seems tied to an emphasis on full communion as more than a mere federation. Full communion implies a truly common life, even if denominational identity is preserved. If full communion is a mere mutual acceptance, indiscernible from mutual tolerance, then it is not an adequate realization of fellowship in Christ. Those (such as Lutherans) who insist that fellowship or communion between distinct churches is an adequate realization of the visible unity of the church need to make clear that fellowship means more than mere mutual tolerance (see App., nos. 14 and 15).

The argument also needs to be made that the continued existence of distinct denominations serves a diversity that enriches the church. In India, the United Churches of North and South India and the Mar Thoma Syrian Church, which geographically overlap, are in full communion and cooperate through a Joint Council. The churches contend that this is a relation of "organic oneness," even though they maintain their distinct identities and juridical autonomy. The judgment is that the continued existence of a distinct Mar Thoma church serves the wider church and is thus justified.[18] The question to be asked within the pluralistic situation of the U.S. is, when does the continued existence of reconciled yet distinct denominations serve the church and when is a more united structure called for.

We thus return to a concern raised at the very beginning of this essay. To describe full communion at the present moment is a task in contextual ecclesiology. Details can only be lived into, not spelled out in advance. But such a life must have as its central concern that we live out and live toward the unity we are given in Christ, so that "joined and knit together by every ligament with which it is equipped, as each part is working properly, promotes the body's growth in building itself up in love" (Eph. 4:16).

APPENDIX: FULL COMMUNION BETWEEN ANGLICAN AND LUTHERAN CHURCHES: SOME RELEVANT TEXTS

ECUMENICAL DOCUMENTS

ANGLICAN-LUTHERAN

(1) Anglican–Lutheran European Commission. *Anglican–Lutheran Dialogue: Helsinki Report 1982*. London: SPCK, 1983.

Paragraph 64 stated:

We therefore propose the following interim steps towards the full communion which we believe is now ultimately possible and which must also necessarily involve not only the complete inter-changeability of our ministries but also a visible sharing together in the *common life* of the Body of Christ" [emphasis in original].

(2) Anglican–Lutheran Joint Working Group (International). *Anglican–Lutheran Relations: The Cold Ash Report*. London: ACC; Geneva: LWF, 1983.

By far the most complete statement from a Lutheran–Anglican dialogue of the nature of full communion:

§24. We look forward to the day when full communion is established between Anglican and Lutheran churches.

§25. By full communion we here understand a relationship between two distinct churches or communions. Each maintains its own autonomy and recognizes the catholicity and apostolicity of the other, and each believes the other to hold the essentials of the Christian faith:

(a) subject to such safeguards as ecclesial discipline may properly require, members of one body may receive the sacraments of the other;

177

(b) subject to local invitation, bishops of one church may take part in the consecration of the bishops of the other, thus acknowledging the duty of mutual care and concern;

(c) subject to church regulation, a bishop, pastor/priest or deacon of one ecclesial body may exercise liturgical functions in a congregation of the other body if invited to do so and also, when requested, pastoral care of the other's members;

(d) it is also a necessary addition and complement that there should be recognized organs of regular consultation and communication, including episcopal collegiality, to express and strengthen the fellowship and enable common witness, life and service.

§27. Full communion carries implications which go beyond sharing the same Eucharist....To be in full communion implies a community of life, an exchange and a commitment to one another in respect of major decisions on questions of faith, order, and morals.

(3) *Auf dem Weg zu sichtbarer Einheit: eine gemeinsame Feststellung.* Kirche von England, Bund der Evangelischen Kirchen in der Deutschen Demokratischen Republik, Evangelische Kirche in Deutschland. Berlin and Hannover, 1988.

Usually referred to as the *Meißen Statement*, this document is not strictly a Lutheran–Anglican text, since it includes Reformed and United churches within the structures of the EKD and the (former) BEK/DDR. Nevertheless, it bears a closer resemblance to the Lutheran–Anglican than to the Reformed–Anglican discussions. It refers to the hoped-for goal as "full visible unity." Its description of what this unity must include, however, is much like other descriptions of full communion:

§8.... We can already claim together that full, visible unity must include:

—a common confession of the apostolic faith in word and life....

—the sharing of one baptism, the celebrating of one Eucharist, and the service of a reconciled, common ministry....

—bonds of communion which enable the church at every level to guard and interpret the apostolic faith, to take decisions, to teach authoritatively, to share goods and to bear effective witness in the world

STATEMENTS FROM THE FAITH AND ORDER COMMISSION, WCC

(4) Third World Conference on Faith and Order, Lund, 1952. V. *Intercommunion.* In *A Documentary History of the Faith and Order Movement 1927–1963.* Edited by Lukas Vischer. Pp. 115–125. St. Louis: Bethany, 1963.

An attempt was made to define ecumenical terms. *"Full communion* (though the adjective need rarely be used)" was defined as: "where Churches in doctrinal agreement, or of the same confessional family, allow communicant members freely to communicate at the altars of each, and where there is freedom of ministers to officiate sacramentally in either Church (i.e., *Intercelebration*) e.g., the Orthodox, Anglican, Lutheran, and Reformed (Presbyterian) 'families' of Churches, respectively." It was explicitly noted that full communion in this sense cannot "be regarded as the fulfillment of that complete unity which we believe to be God's will for His Church."

(5) Faith and Order Commission, WCC. *Bangalore 1978, Sharing in One Hope.* Reports and Documents from the Meeting of the Faith and Order Commission, 15–30 August, 1978, Bangalore, India. Geneva: WCC, 1978.

At this meeting, a definition of full communion as the ecumenical goal was put forward that reflects the discussions of church unity at the WCC Assemblies in New Delhi, 1961, and Nairobi, 1975. The Commission concluded (p. 237):

> It is its [the Faith and Order Commission's] constitutional task to contribute to the creation of conditions which will make it possible for the churches to enter into full communion. They will then recognize each other's ministries; they will share the bread and the cup of their Lord; they will acknowledge each other as belonging to the body of Christ in all places and at all times; they will proclaim together the Gospel to the world; they will serve the needs of humankind in mutual trust and dedication; and for these ends they will plan and take decisions together in assemblies constituted by authorized representatives wherever this is required.

BILATERAL DIALOGUES WITH ANGLICAN PARTICIPATION

(6) Anglican–Roman Catholic Commission in the U.S., *ARC–VII Statement* (1969). In *Called to Full Unity: Documents on Anglican–Roman Catholic Relations 1966–1983.* Washington: United States Catholic Conference, 1986.

Full communion must not be interpreted as an agreement to disagree while sharing in the Eucharistic gifts, nor may organic unity be understood as a juridical concept implying a particular form of Church government. Such a unity is hard to visualize, but would include a common profession of faith and would mean a sufficient compatibility of polity to make possible a united mission to the human family. Whatever structural forms emerge, it is hoped that cultural and liturgical variety will remain so that the values of both the Roman and the Anglican ethos will survive and develop (p. 40).

(7) Anglican–Reformed International Commission. *God's Reign and Our Unity*. The Report of the Anglican–Reformed International Commission 1981–1984. London: SPCK; Edinburgh: St. Andrew Press, 1984.

This dialogue seems to insist on local organic union as the ecumenical goal. It states (§110):

We are not simply seeking a *modus vivendi* between two globally organized denominations which would continue their separate though reconciled existence....We are agreed that Christian unity must in the last resort be discovered and actualized at the local level. Hence we seek the emergence of reconciled local communities, each of which is recognizable as 'church' in the proper sense: i.e., communities which exhibit in each place the fullness of ministerial order, eucharistic fellowship, pastoral care, and missionary commitment and which through mutual communion and cooperation, bear witness on the regional, national and even international levels.

In its next paragraph, however, the dialogue notes (§111):

In order to be effective in missionary outreach the Church may have to encourage the formation of distinct forms of ministry and eucharistic fellowship for different groups in the same area.

(8) Second Anglican–Roman Catholic International Commission. *Church as Communion: An Agreed Statement*. London: Church House; Catholic Truth Society, 1991.

[§45.] In the light of all that we have said about communion it is now possible to describe what constitutes ecclesial communion. It is rooted in the confession of the one apostolic faith....It is founded upon one baptism. The one celebration of the Eucharist is its pre–eminent expression and focus. It necessarily finds expression in shared commitment to the mission entrusted by Christ to his Church. It is a life of shared concern for one another....Also constitutive of life in communion is acceptance of the same moral values, the sharing of the same vision of humanity created in the image of God and recreated in Christ and the common confession of the one hope in the final consummation of the Kingdom of God. For the nurture and growth of this communion, Christ the Lord has provided a ministry of oversight, the fullness of which is entrusted to the episcopate....This ministry of oversight has both collegial and primatial dimensions....In the context of the communion of all the churches the episcopal ministry of a universal primate finds its role as the visible focus of unity.

BILATERAL DIALOGUES WITH LUTHERAN PARTICIPATION

(9) *Leuenberg Accord* (Lutheran/Reformed in Continental Europe, 1973). In *An Invitation to Action: A Study of Ministry, Sacraments, and Recognition. The Lutheran–Reformed Dialogue Series III, 1981–1983*, edited by James E. Andrews and Joseph A. Burgess, pp. 61–73. Philadelphia: Fortress, 1984.

The relation between the churches is called one of *Kirchengemeinschaft* (which can be translated either as fellowship or communion). This relation (§29) "means that, on the basis of the consensus they have reached in their understanding of the gospel, churches with different confessional positions accord each other fellowship in word and sacrament, and strive for the fullest possible cooperation *(Gemeinsamkeit)* in witness and service to the world."

This relation involves first a declaration *(Erklärung)* of fellowship, in which the churches state that they are "one in the understanding of the gospel" (§31), that earlier doctrinal condemnations "no longer apply to the contemporary doctrinal position of the assenting churches" (§32), and that "they accord each other table and pulpit fellowship; this includes the mutual recognition of ordination and the freedom to provide for intercelebration" (§33). This declaration of fellowship is to be followed by an ongoing realization (Verwirklichung) of fellowship, involving common witness and service (§36) and ongoing theological discussion (§37).

(10) Lutheran–Reformed Joint Commission (International). *Toward Church Fellowship*. Geneva: LWF and World Alliance of Reformed Churches, 1989.

The ecumenical goal is here said to be full communion, which is then said to have the following elements:

§80: Acknowledging that the condemnations pronounced upon one another in former times are no longer to be regarded as applicable in today's situation.

§81: Establishing full pulpit and alter/table fellowship, with the necessary mutual recognition of ministers ordained for word and sacrament.

§82: Committing themselves to growth in unity through new steps in church life and mission together.

§83: We have come to this recommendation on the basis of our belief that both Lutheran and Reformed churches agree on those matters which are necessary and sufficient for the true unity of the church: the right preaching of the gospel and the administration of the sacraments in accordance with the word of God.

The new steps referred to in §82 are said to include continuing theological discussion (§88) and common witness and service in the world (§89).

(11) Roman Catholic/Lutheran Joint Commission (International). *The Ministry in the Church* (1981). In *Growth in Agreement.*

Paragraph 82 states:

The precondition for such acceptance of full church communion (*volle Kirchengemeinschaft*) is agreement in the confession of faith—which must also include a common understanding of the church's ministry—a common understanding of the sacraments, and fraternal fellowship in Christian and church life.

CHURCH STATEMENTS AND DOCUMENTS

LUTHERAN

(12) ELCA *Constitution*:

(4.02) To participate in God's mission, this church shall:

f. Manifest the unity given to the people of God by living together in the love of Christ and by joining with other Christians in prayer and action to express and preserve the unity which the Spirit gives.

(4.03) To fulfill these purposes, this church shall:

e. Foster Christian unity by participating in ecumenical activities, contributing its witness and work and cooperating with other churches which confess God the Father, Son, and Holy Spirit.

(13) ELCA. *Ecumenism: The Vision of the ELCA.* Chicago: ELCA, 1991.

The ecumenical goal is defined as "full communion, i.e., the fullest or complete actualization of unity possible before the parousia with all those churches that confess the Triune God....Full communion, a gift from God, is founded on faith in Jesus Christ. It is a commitment to truth in love and a witness to God's liberation and reconciliation. Full communion is visible and sacramental. It includes all that Lutherans have meant by 'pulpit and altar fellowship,' but goes beyond that historical formulation because of the obligatory mission given by the Gospel....It points to the complete communion and unity of all Christians that will come with the arrival of the kingdom of God at the parousia of Christ, the Lord. It is also a goal in need of continuing definition. It is rooted in agreements on essentials and allows diversity in nonessentials" (section II.D, p. 13).

Full communion is said to

include at least the following, some of which exist at earlier stages:

1. a common confessing of the Christian faith;

2. a mutual recognition of Baptism and a sharing of the Lord's Supper, allowing for joint worship and an exchangeability of members;

3. a mutual recognition and availability of ordained ministers to the service of all members of churches in full communion, subject only but always to the disciplinary regulations of the other churches;

4. a common commitment to evangelism, witness, and service;

5. a means of common decision making on critical common issues of faith and life;

6. a mutual lifting of any condemnations that exist between churches.

(14) Lutheran World Federation. *In Christ—A New Community.* Proceedings of the Sixth Assembly of the Lutheran World Federation, Dar es Salaam, Tanzania, June 13–25, 1977. Edited by Arne Sovik. Geneva: LWF, 1977.

At this Assembly, the LWF adopted a statement on "Models of Unity." Rejecting "organic union," i.e., denominational merger, as the required ecumenical goal, it stated:

Unity and reconciliation do not mean mere coexistence. They mean genuine church fellowship, including as essential elements the recognition of baptism, the establishment of eucharistic fellowship, the mutual recognition of church ministries [*Ämter*], and a binding common purpose [*Gemeinsamkeit*] of witness and service (p. 174).

(15) *Budapest 1984, "In Christ—Hope for the World."* Official Proceedings of the Seventh Assembly of the Lutheran World Federation. LWF Report 19/20 (1985).

This Assembly adopted two statements relevant to our concerns. "The Unity We Seek" further developed the Dar es Salaam statement on unity. It stated:

> The true unity of the church, which is the unity of the body of Christ and participates in the unity of the Father, Son, and Holy Spirit, is given in and through proclamation of the gospel in Word and sacrament. This unity is expressed as a communion in the common and, at the same time, multiform confession of one and the same apostolic faith. It is a communion in holy baptism and in the eucharistic meal, a communion in which the ministries exercised are recognized by all as expressions of the ministry instituted by Christ in his church. It is a communion where diversities contribute to fullness and are no longer barriers to unity. It is a committed fellowship, able to make common decisions and to act in common [p. 175].

A second statement, "The Self–Understanding and Task of the Lutheran World Federation," explored the nature of the communion that binds the LWF churches together:

> This Lutheran communion of churches finds its visible expression in pulpit and altar fellowship, in common witness and service, in the joint fulfillment of the missionary task, and in openness to ecumenical cooperation, dialog, and community [p. 176].

ANGLICAN

(A full collection of Anglican statements can be found in: *A Communion of Communions: One Eucharistic Fellowship.* The Detroit Report and Papers of the Triennial Ecumenical Study of the Episcopal Church 1976–1979. Edited by J. Robert Wright. Pp. 216–295. New York: Seabury, 1979.)

(16) ECUSA, *Declaration on Unity* (1979). Reproduced in *Handbook for Ecumenism* (see below, no. 17)

This convention resolution stated:

The visible unity we seek will be one eucharistic fellowship. As an expression of and a means toward this goal, the uniting Church will recognize itself as a communion of Communions, based upon acknowledgement of catholicity and apostolicity. In this organic relationship all will recognize each other's members and ministries. All will share the bread and the cup of the Lord. All will acknowledge each other as belonging to the Body of Christ at all places and at all times. All will proclaim the Gospel to the world with one mind and purpose. All will serve the needs of humankind with mutual trust and dedication. And for these ends all will plan and decide together in assemblies constituted by authorized representatives whenever and wherever there is need.

We do not yet see the shape of that collegiality, conciliarity, authority and primacy which need to be present and active in the diocese with its Parishes as well as nationally, regionally, universally; but we recognize that some ecclesial structure will be necessary to bring about the expressions of our unity in the body of Christ described above.

(17) Episcopal Diocesan Ecumenical Officers (ECUSA). *Handbook for Ecumenism* (1989). In *Ecumenical Bulletin* 95 (May/June and July/August, 1989).

The description of full communion from the study for the ACC (see below, no. 23) is reproduced in full, but without explicit endorsement. Two statements in the handbook are particularly relevant to our concerns:

Currently there is less certainty that union in church organization is the goal. The model of full communion without absorption, with which the Episcopal Church and the Anglican Communion have growing experience, is another approach [p. A–3].

Though we cannot immediately realize the model of unity which the Council of Chalcedon and the tradition as a whole once regarded as essential, that there be one bishop in a single place, it is of capital importance to achieve the unity of *episcopoi*. If such unity cannot be personal, at least it can be collegial [p. B–6].

(18) Lambeth Conference 1958. *The Encyclical Letter from the Bishops together with the Resolutions and Reports*. London: SPCK; New York: Seabury, 1958.

The Conference adopted (p. I.35) the suggestion that the term "full communion" be used to described "all cases where a Province of the Anglican communion by agreement enters into a relation of unrestricted *communio in sacris*, including the mutual recognition of ministries, with a Church outside our Communion" (p. II.24). The Committee Report on "Church Unity and the Church Universal" stated: "The unity between Christian Churches ought to be a living unity in the love of Christ which is shown in full Christian fellowship and in mutual service, while also, subject to sufficient agreement in faith and order, expressing itself in free interchange of ministries, and fullness of sacramental Communion. Such unity, while marked by the bond of the historic episcopate, should always include congregational fellowship, active participation both of clergy and laity in the mission and government of the Church, and zeal for evangelism."

(19) *Intercommunion Today.* Report of the Archbishop's Commission on Intercommunion [Church of England]. London: Church Information Office, 1968.

A comprehensive study of intercommunion, the following remark is typical and worth noting:

> Full communion involves not only mutual recognition of members, but also of ministers, so that the clergy of one church can act in and for the other. It also means that the bishops of one church can take part in the consecration of the bishops of another, thus solemnly acknowledging the duty of mutual care and concern which exists between sister churches within the body of Christ [pp. 17f].

(20) Anglican Consultative Council. *The Time Is Now.* Anglican Consultative Council, First Meeting, Limuru, Kenya, 23 February—5 March 1971. London: SPCK, 1971.

On the first page of its first report, the ACC states:

> Anglican Churches and Provinces are in full communion with one another. This means that there is mutual recognition of members and ministers, so that the clergy of one Church can act in and for another Church and the bishops of one Church can take part in the consecration of bishops of another. Our Churches share a common way of thinking and acting, though this is very hard to define....The heart of full communion is sacramental fellowship, but there are new depths of fellowship in Christ ever to be explored and new ways of working together....Full communion thus commits us to

"mutual responsibility and interdependence in the Body of Christ" [pp. 1f].

(21) Anglican Consultative Council. *Partners in Mission.* Anglican Consultative Council Second Meeting, Dublin, Ireland, 17–27 July 1973. London: SPCK, 1973.

In reaffirming its ecumenical commitment after failed union efforts in various countries, the Council states: "While avoiding any quest for uniformity or for centralization, we reaffirm the conviction that organic union in the sense of united Churches is a goal for which intercommunion alone or federation alone is no substitute" (p. 2).

At its fourth meeting in 1979, the council requested a study be made of "the implications of full communion between the Churches of the Anglican Communion and other episcopal Churches." The study began with the commissioning of an essay:

(22) Chadwick, Henry. "Full Communion with Other Episcopal Churches." *Churchman* 95 (1981):218–226.

This essay was circulated both within the Anglican communion and among other church bodies (including the LWF). The description of full communion in this essay was taken up almost verbatim into the study's report to the fifth meeting of the ACC in 1981. Chadwick also stated:

It [mere intercommunion] runs the major risk of implying that the Lord's intention for his church is to have a large number of diverse ecclesial bodies, all of which are equally valid or invalid expressions of his will for his people, with the consequence that the painful realities of division and group rivalry are ignored or condoned [p. 220].

(23) "Full Communion, A Study Paper for the Anglican Consultative Council." Paper presented at Fifth Meeting of the Anglican Consultative Council, Newcastle upon Tyne, September, 1981.

Full Communion normally means a relationship between two distinct and autonomous Churches or ecclesial communities, often but not always located in different geographical areas, of such a nature that each recognizes the catholicity and autonomy of the other and maintains its own and each believes the other to hold the essentials of the Christian faith:

(a) subject to letters of recommendation or such other safeguards as ecclesial discipline may properly require, members of the one body may receive the sacraments of the other;

(b) subject to local invitation, bishops of one Church may take part in the consecration of the bishops of the other, thus acknowledging the duty of mutual care and concern;

(c) subject to canon law and episcopal license, a bishop, presbyter/priest or deacon of one ecclesial body may exercise liturgical functions in a congregation of the other body if invited to do so. In such cases commendatory letters from the home diocese and metropolitan would be expected as customary, and visiting clergy are not understood to possess rights in respect of liturgical functions. On the other hand it is also normal for such an invitation to be given;

(d) if the Full Communion established on these understandings is to be fruitful for the churches concerned, and not only for individuals on their travels, then it is also a necessary addition and complement that there should be recognized organs of regular consultation and communication, including episcopal collegiality, to express and strengthen the fellowship and enable common witness.

To be in Full Communion with others is necessarily both an enhancing of the corporate strength of the churches in love and also a restraining of individualism or subjectivism. But it inheres in the relationship of Full Communion that:

(a) the two bodies remain both autonomous and interdependent without elevation of the one to be judge of the other and without insensitivity;

(b) the two bodies remain themselves without either being committed to every secondary feature of the traditions of the other;

(c) Organic Union [discussed but not precisely defined earlier in the study] is appropriate and ultimately necessary if the ecclesial bodies in Full Communion are, or come to be, immediately adjacent in the same geographical area. A single visible fellowship of this sort need not, however, imply the suppressing of ethnic, cultural or ecclesial characteristics or traditions (which may in fact be preserved by different units of episcopal jurisdiction within the one Organic Union.

(24) Anglican Consultative Council. *ACC–5.* Fifth meeting, Newcastle upon Tyne, England, 8–18 September 1981. London: ACC, 1981.

The Council "took note of the Study Paper, but felt that its concentration on terminology excluded sufficient attention to the *implications* of full communion" (p. 45). It went on to state: "Communion must be understood as involving more than *liturgical* celebration: it surely implies a visible sharing together in the common *life* of the Body of Christ" (p. 46).

(25) Anglican Consultative Council. *Bonds of Affection.* Proceedings of ACC–6. Badagry, Nigeria, 1984. London: Anglican Consultative Council, 1984.

The Council noted that intercommunion is an appropriate stage on the way to visible unity, but added: "Inter–communion is not enough unless it is the sacramental expression of a wider sharing in the whole life of the churches concerned and in their joint mission. There must necessarily be elements of common life, worship, and mission at all stages of the ecumenical pilgrimage" (p. 89).

While not offering a new explication of "full communion," the Council noted two of its aspects: "The term surely implies at least that the ministry of one church or Province is in fact accepted by another, except in individual cases on individual and personal grounds—thus excluding the unacceptability of whole categories within the ministry of a particular church" (p. 91). Explicit reference is then made to "the few remaining non–episcopally ordained presbyters of the church of South India" and ordained women.

"Full communion surely also at least implies that there is some organ of regular mutual consultation between churches if the communion between them is indeed to be a fellowship in life and mission as well as worship....Where either of these two implication of full communion—the mutual acceptability of ministry and regular organs of consultation—is in fact rejected we believe the relationship of full communion is to that extent impaired" (p. 92).

(26) *The Emmaus Report.* A Report of the Anglican Ecumenical Consultation which took place at The Emmaus Retreat Centre, West Wickham, Kent, England, 27 January–2 February 1987 in preparation for ACC-7, Singapore, 1987 and The Lambeth Conference 1988. London: Church House Publishing, 1987.

This meeting of Anglican bishops and ecumenical officers stated:

The phrase "full communion"...appears to have different emphases in the various international theological dialogues with different denominations. All seem to be agreed that it means:

(a) sharing a common essential faith;

(b) full interchangeability of ministry and membership, including the participation of bishops of one Church in the consecration of bishops in the other.

Most agree:

(c) that it should include regular organs of consultation and common action [p. 33].

(27) Lambeth Conference 1988. *The Truth Shall Make You Free: The Lambeth Conference 1988.* The Reports, Resolutions and Pastoral Letters from the Bishops. London: ACC, 1988.

Of great importance was the Conference's new vision of the relation between organic unity and full communion:

We have mentioned three pictures which have been used to describe the visible unity of Christ's Church: organic unity, conciliar fellowship, and full communion between autonomous Churches. These are not the only pictures used. Each tends to give a different emphasis. However, they should be regarded as complementary and not contradictory....The pictures supplement and correct one another as we try to glimpse the goal ever more clearly....Throughout history Christian divisions have developed gradually and untidily. We should not expect the healing of these divisions to happen tidily or all at once [p. 143f].

The Conference went on to say:

If the goal of unity is one Church in each place, full communion should at least imply that Churches in the same country and area should have means of regular consultation and of sharing in one another's life, with a view to growth into closer unity. Were such consultations and sharing totally absent, "full communion" would not have been the correct description of the relationship [p. 147].

12
TOWARD FULL COMMUNION
BY
WILLIAM G. RUSCH

The first draft of this essay was written in 1986. Since that date the ELCA was formed and "Ecumenism: The Vision of the ELCA" was adopted in 1991 by its Second Churchwide Assembly. Although in some regards I have attempted to update the essay, generally I have allowed it to stand as originally written. In this way it is possible to show how it played a role in the work of the dialogue as it completed its last reports, *Toward Full Communion* and *Concordat of Agreement*.

In this century a consensus has developed within the ecumenical movement about its goal. This consensus is not precise in all of its details, but much of its shape and content is now clear. The ecumenical movement is concerned with the unity of divided churches. Whether this unity is to be sought as a gift of God for its own sake or whether it is desired only to facilitate mission is a question of continuing debate in some circles. What is not disputed is that the churches are being called to express their unity. While there is no single model of unity presented to the churches, there is a general agreement that this unity is given in Christ, rooted in the triune God, realized in the proclaimed Word and Sacraments, and lived out in witness and service to the world. There is also a consensus that such unity requires a visible outward form. This position rejects the view that "spiritual unity," which deliberately dispenses with common structures and visible organization, can be the final goal of the ecumenical movement.

In this quest for visible unity, ecumenical theology has developed several models. Some are models of partial union; others of comprehensive union. None of these models will by itself lead all the churches everywhere to an expression of visible unity. Some models will work better in some settings than in others.[1]

The purpose of this essay is to examine one model of unity, full communion, as it relates specifically to Episcopalians and Lutherans in the U.S. As one begins this task, it is quickly realized that considerable ecumenical thinking has been done on the topic. There are numerous resources available. Much, although not all, of the challenge is to assemble and evaluate what has been produced to determine whether the dialogue is prepared to call the churches to receive this earlier work.

The last point of the Lutheran–Episcopal Agreement approved in 1982 by the conventions of the Episcopal Church, U.S.A., the American Lutheran Church, the Association of Evangelical Lutheran Churches, and the Lutheran Church in America, defined the goal of the third series of Lutheran-Episcopal Dialogue and at least implied a definition of full communion.

> 5. Authorize and establish now a third series of Lutheran–Episcopal Dialogues for the discussion of any other questions that must be resolved before full communion (communio in sacris/altar and pulpit fellowship) can be established between the respective churches, e.g. implications of the Gospel, historic episcopate, and the ordering of ministry (bishops, priests, and deacons) in the total context of apostolicity.[2]

This text would seem to suggest that "full communion" means at least that the Episcopal and Lutheran traditions would allow communicant members of each to communicate at altars of the other and that there would be the freedom of ministries of both traditions to officiate sacramentally in the two churches. This would be a significant step beyond the agreement of 1982, but it would not be the equivalent of the "reunited Christian Church" spoken of in the fourth point of the Lambeth Quadrilateral. "Full communion," then, is not synonymous with "organic church union," and presupposes *no final model of unity*.

Such an interpretation of point 5 appears to be in conformity with the report of the Anglican–Lutheran Joint Working Group, which was drafted in December 1983. That document declared:

> By full communion we here understand a relationship between two distinct churches or communions. Each maintains its own autonomy and recognizes the catholicity and apostolicity of the other, and each believes the other to hold the essentials of the Christian faith:

a. subject to such safeguards as ecclesial discipline may properly require, members of one body may receive the sacraments of the other;

b. subject to local invitation, bishops of one church may take part in the consecration of the bishops of the other, thus acknowledging the duty of mutual care and concern;

c. subject to church regulation, a bishop, pastor/priest or deacon of one ecclesial body may exercise liturgical functions in a congregation of the other body if invited to do so and also, when requested, pastoral care of the other members;

d. it is also a necessary addition and complement that there should be recognized organs of regular consultation and communication, including episcopal collegiality, to express and strengthen the fellowship and enable common witness, life and service.

To be in full communion means that churches become interdependent while remaining autonomous. One is not elevated to be the judge of the other, nor can it remain insensitive to the other; neither is each body committed to every secondary feature of the tradition of the other. Thus the corporate strength of the churches is enhanced in love, and isolated independence is restrained....To be in full communion implies a community of life, and exchange and a commitment to one another in respect of major decisions on questions of faith, order, and morals. It implies, where churches are in the same geographical area, common worship, study, witness, evangelism, and promotion of justice, peace and love.[3]

The third series of Lutheran–Episcopal Dialogue in the U.S. may well be able to give clarity to its work by the acceptance of this material from the Joint Working Group as its interpretation of what the churches are asking of it in point 5.

If there is agreement as to what is being requested by "full communion," then the pressing question becomes how that goal is to be reached. Here again the Joint Working Group report is of value, for what it says and the support that it gives to the practice of the U.S. churches. The report recognizes the concept of unity by stages. It notes that there is not yet great clarity about this conception, but that it is gaining wide recognition:

(Unity by stages) implies that the end cannot be seen from the beginning, and that unity must be pursued in terms of movement and process. It does imply that we know the direction in which we wish to move; and that we take definite steps to break down the barriers which at present stand in the way of visible unity.[4]

The Joint Working Group report acknowledges that the prerequisite for unity by stages is agreement in faith. This agreement in faith involves not only the work of dialogues but the reception of that work by the churches, and the support of common prayer and practical collaboration. Unity by stages makes possible limited eucharistic sharing. It will eventually call for consensus on authority in the church, the gospel and its implications, justification/salvation, the sacraments, the ministry and its ordering, the development of means of common worship and work, and genuine renewal by Anglicans and Lutherans.[5]

The Lutheran–Episcopal Agreement of 1982 is a clear and official response of the churches involved to the ecumenical methodology of unity by stages. The churches recognized a level of unity between them that permits not only interim eucharistic sharing (for too often the Agreement is seen only in that narrow light) but common prayer, study, and witness. It is also an open–ended stage in that the churches recognize that they are challenged by this stage of unity to see whether they are able to proceed further on the journey toward visible unity.

As one looks at the pilgrimage from visible disunity to visible unity, is it possible to plot where U.S. Episcopalians and Lutherans are now and what might be the next steps on the way to full communion? Such questions take into account that what is at stake is a process, a movement. The churches do not expect to pass from immediate disunity into full unity. Rather, they are prepared to undertake a common journey that will move them away from greater disunity and little unity and toward lesser disunity and greater unity. What is involved is unity in truth, the elimination of divisive differences and the achievement of fellowship. What is not involved is merger, mutual absorption, homogeneity, or total agreement on all aspects of Christian faith and life.

First it must be admitted that the four churches involved in the agreement are not where they were in 1982. In that year the churches had before them the work of three dialogues. An international Anglican–Lutheran dialogue, sponsored by the Lambeth Conference and the LWF, between 1970 and 1972 pursued work in five areas: sources of authority, the church, the Word and Sacraments, apostolic ministry, and worship. The final report (the Pullach Report) recorded considerable agreement in all these areas, noting certain qualifications regarding the historic episcopate. If this topic remained a controver-

sial area, the gap between differing positions was seen as greatly
narrowed by a common acknowledgment that apostolic mission and
episcopacy are more fundamental and inclusive than apostolic succession in the form of the historic episcopate.[6]

At this same time, 1969–1972, a U.S. Lutheran–Episcopal Dialogue
met under the sponsorship of the joint Commission on Ecumenical
Relations of the Episcopal Church and the Division of Theological
Studies of the Lutheran Council in the U.S.A. Significant agreement
was noted in Holy Scripture, worship, the centrality of preaching and
the Eucharist, and baptism and confirmation. Agreement on apostolicity and *episkope* was partial, but it allowed the dialogue to affirm
mutually the apostolicity of each other's ordained ministry.[7] Because
of agreement on fundamental aspects of church life and doctrine, the
dialogue recommended a selective and local eucharistic sharing under specific circumstances, and the continuation of joint theological
study.[8]

A second series of U.S. Lutheran–Episcopal Dialogue, under the
sponsorship of the Standing Commission on Ecumenical Relations of
the Episcopal Church and the Division of Theological Studies of the
Lutheran Council in the U.S.A. met from 1976 until 1980. In its final
report, the dialogue included joint statements on the gospel, apostolicity, justification, Eucharist, and the authority of Scripture.
Although the representatives of the Lutheran Church–Missouri
Synod attached separate recommendations, the representatives of the
American Lutheran Church, the Association of Evangelical Lutheran
Churches, and the Lutheran Church in America approved the following recommendations: (1) mutual recognition of the respective church
bodies as true churches, (2) a call for interim eucharistic hospitality,
(3) a request for joint worship under certain circumstances, (4) a
recommendation of cooperation in the publication and circulation of
dialogue materials, (5) a suggestion of local covenants between Lutheran and Episcopal congregations, and (6) an encouragement for a
third series of national dialogue.

In 1982, these three Lutheran churches and the Episcopal Church
by convention action adopted the Lutheran–Episcopal Agreement. As
point 1 of the agreement makes clear, this agreement is rooted in the
work of the three dialogues. The churches are officially giving their
judgment that all three dialogues have produced theological work
that demonstrates to them a "substantial progress" in correcting past
misunderstandings and identifying areas of common misunderstanding. As a result of that favorable evaluation of the dialogues'
work, the agreement draws out certain implications for the churches,

namely, they can recognize each other as churches of the gospel, they can encourage the development of a common Christian life, they can establish a relationship of interim sharing of the Eucharist, and they can establish a third dialogue for outstanding questions. It is true that the agreement is not identical with the recommendations from any of the three dialogues. Yet the agreement is related to the work of the dialogues. The agreement is a refinement of the dialogues' work, adapted to where the churches believed they could responsibly move in 1982. It is not uncommon for dialogues to push churches beyond where those churches are prepared to go in one step.

At the 1982 conventions, two developments occurred simultaneously. The churches made an official response to the dialogues. Such a response is the first official word from churches about a dialogue, but it is only a tentative word that must be tested by the churches. In 1982 the churches made a *response* to the dialogues *and* began a *process of reception.* Reception includes all the phases and aspects of a process by which a church makes the results of an ecumenical dialogue or statement a part of its faith and life.[9] In such a process the results of dialogue are given an authoritative character in the churches that they had earlier lacked. From 1982 until the present these three Lutheran churches and the Episcopal Church have been involved in this ongoing process of reception. Most indications to date are that this has been an affirming process. While reception is not a uniform process, at times it can be painful. Even with the risk of new tensions and even divisions, these Lutheran and Episcopal churches have shown that they are prepared to face it. Clearly more can be done. The process has not ended. Nevertheless, these churches have, by and large, grown closer together within the last three years than they were before. In 1986 the work of the earlier dialogues, interpreted through the Lutheran–Episcopal Agreement, has become more of a reality in the ongoing lives and faith of these four churches.

The challenge now is how these churches can move from the official response of 1982 and the partial but successful reception since then to another stage in the journey toward unity. Here they are legitimately looking to the dialogue for guidance. As the dialogue endeavors to answer this summons, it may be aided by a framework and description of a process suggested by the International Lutheran–Roman Catholic dialogue in its report, *Facing Unity.*[10]

Whatever final decisions the churches make about *Facing Unity,* it demands serious consideration for the ecumenical method it proposes. If it is to be rejected, the onus falls on us to find another, and presumably better, way. No doubt even those who are favorable to

Facing Unity will have many suggestions for modification before this particular method will win the approval of churches.

The *Facing Unity* method was developed in the context of Lutheran–Roman Catholic dialogue. But there is no need to limit the model to only those two traditions. In fact, even the participants in the dialogue recognized that their model might have wider applications. A question before the Lutheran-Episcopal dialogue is whether or not the method of reconciliation proposed in *Facing Unity* can, with appropriate modification, be a resource for greater Lutheran–Episcopal unity.

Among the many strengths of *Facing Unity* are the following: recognition (1) that unity will be a unity in diversity; (2) that the theologically based agreements of a dialogue should work through divergences to the point where they lose their church-divisive character; (3) that remaining differences based on a fundamental agreement on the apostolic faith are legitimate; (4) that church fellowship through theological agreement is compatible with unity in "reconciled diversity" and "a communion of communions"; (5) that unity must assume concrete forms in suitable structures, leading to common life and joint actions, and (6) that a process is involved that includes all areas of the churches.

Facing Unity sees three major phases on the way to church fellowship: community of faith, community in sacraments, and community of service. Movement through these phases is by mutual recognition and reception. The first phase is community in confessing the one apostolic faith. Characteristics of this phase include a joint witness to the apostolic faith, unity of faith in diversity of its forms of expression, and the removal of doctrinal condemnations. The last item is not relevant to Lutheran–Episcopal discussions. Certainly the three dialogues between Lutheran and Episcopalians, as implemented and interpreted through the Lutheran–Episcopal Agreement, disclose that most Lutherans and Episcopalians would acknowledge by mutual recognition and reception that they have indeed passed through this first phase. Lutherans and Episcopalians do jointly witness to the same apostolic faith with their agreements in the dialogues on Scripture, justification, baptism, the Lord's Supper, apostolicity, and ministry. At the same time, this unity in the same faith does not mean uniformity in the way that is articulated and expressed.[11] This, too, is recognized by Lutherans and Episcopalians. Further evidence that U.S. Lutherans and Episcopalians have arrived at a community in confessing the apostolic faith is the common statement on the gospel that has been produced by the third series of Lutheran–Episcopal

197

Dialogue. This document confirms the agreements identified in the earlier dialogues.[12]

As a result of this joint understanding of and witness to the apostolic faith, Lutherans and Episcopalians in the United States began in 1982 to move into the second phase, a commitment in sacramental life. This community in sacramental life is defined by the Lutheran–Episcopal Agreement and has been experienced since 1982. In order to move beyond this partial community in sacraments and toward a community in structured life, the third phase, not all open questions need be resolved, but steps of mutual commitment and integrity are required. Are not all churches, if they confess the same faith and share a common understanding of the sacraments, entitled or obligated to enter into a structured fellowship that commits the churches on all levels not only to an occasional fellowship but to a fully lived-out fellowship?

Answers to this question are deeply related to consensus about the gospel and ministry in the church. Let us assume that on the basis of the four dialogues, including the third series in the U.S., a mutually sufficient word of consensus of agreement in the Gospel can be given to the churches. The remaining question then becomes one of ordained ministry. There, too, areas of agreement already exist about the ordained ministry and the exercise of *episkope* in the church. These agreements are found in the work of the earlier dialogues and in some Lutheran and Anglican responses to BEM. These agreements have been experienced since 1982 in forms of cooperation between ordained ministries that are neither comprehensive nor full but nevertheless significant. Episcopalian and Lutheran bishops together have approved interim sharings of the Eucharist, clergy of both churches have stood together, not in place of each other, at the altar. They worked together in councils of churches, attended each other's conventions and synods, engaged in social service and evangelization, and discharged their public responsibility. Thus it could be argued that a preliminary form of joint exercise of ministry and *episkope* has come to be practiced between Lutherans and Episcopalians.

As is generally recognized, the difficulty of further advance centers around the historic episcopate. Differences here between Lutherans and Episcopalians have been reduced, but they remain. Simply put, the issue is as follows: Episcopalians have not seen the possibility of full communion without the full integration of ministries, including the historic episcopate. Lutherans have insisted that the historic episcopate cannot become a necessary condition for full communion.[13] Ways out of this cul-de-sac have not been obvious.

Is it time, on the basis of the *dialogue* and *reception* to date, for the third series of dialogue in the U.S. to challenge the churches to a bold but responsible step whose purpose would be to provide a new relationship between these churches rather than resolving old issues? This step would move the churches toward a community of structured life and allow a greater expression of sacramental sharing. In and of itself it would not result in full communion, but it would bring the churches closer to that goal. It could take a form similar to the following:

The third series of Lutheran–Episcopal Dialogue recommends that:

1. The Episcopal Church in the United States by means of official response and a process of reception recognize the role and intention of the Unaltered Augsburg Confession and Luther's Small Catechism as true witnesses to the gospel and acknowledge the ordained Lutheran ministry of these Lutheran churches and those in that ministry who exercise *episkope* in these churches as sufficient under the gospel for the faith and life of the church, noting that this ordering is neither the only order nor the most adequate order, and is in need of renewal.

2. The Lutheran churches, by means of official response and a process of reception acknowledge the intent of and significance of the office of *episkope* in the Episcopal Church in the United States as an effective sign of continuity of the church in faith and mission and sufficient under the gospel for the faith and life of the church, noting that this order is neither the only order nor the most adequate order, and is in need of renewal.

3. As a result of these mutual responses and establishment of a process of reception, the Episcopal Church in the United States and the Lutheran churches demonstrate this agreement in the gospel and in an ordering of the church by committing themselves to a process leading to a common office of *episkope* in their churches so that neighboring Lutheran and Episcopal bishops, on the basis of a jointly exercised *episkope*, would ordain new ministries together.

Some words of explanation about the three parts of this proposal could provide greater clarity.

In accepting these recommendations, the ECUSA does not become a Lutheran church. The Augsburg Confession and Small Catechism would not become symbolic books of the ECUSA. But the ECUSA would recognize the role and intention of these documents as witnesses to the gospel. In such a recognition, the ECUSA would be

199

accepting the Augsburg Confession and Small Catechism together as a criterion and hermeneutical key for understanding the Reformation and as legitimate confessions of the Christian faith. As a result, churches in which these documents occupy a central place and possess a binding authority would be acknowledged as the church of Jesus Christ.

Likewise, in accepting these recommendations the Lutheran churches would not surrender their historic stress on the teaching on CA 7 as their understanding of the church. These churches are placing no specific ordering of the church over the gospel, nor are they adopting a position of only one possible polity for the church.

Thus it should not be concluded from these recommendations that there is a total agreement on the role and intention of these Lutheran confessional documents, or on the place and significance of the office of oversight in the church. This is agreement on the reality and importance of the Augsburg Confession and the Small Catechism, and on the office of oversight, in the faith and life of the church, but it is acknowledged that they have been differently interpreted, experienced, and expressed in both the Anglican and Lutheran traditions. Although they acknowledge these realities differently, these churches are now prepared for the greater visible unity of the church to take specific steps to demonstrate these realities together. In taking these steps, the different understandings of their realities by Episcopalian and Lutherans are not completely removed.

However, in the commitment to a common office of oversight there is common agreement about the following. In any liturgical celebration initiating this process and in the subsequent joint ordinations, these views are excluded: reordination, supplementary ordination, reconciliation of ministries, and mutual commissioning. What is involved in joint ordinations by Lutheran and Episcopal bishops is a gift of grace of the Holy Spirit received in common by Episcopalians and Lutherans. A common and collegially ordained ministry is a gift of the Spirit that allows both traditions to proceed toward full communion. The question is not what one partner has given the other. This would be a step that would grow out of the jointly exercised *episkope*. The step itself would be a process accomplished by joint ordinations that would be confessional, epicletic, communal, and juridical. The result would be the gradual establishment of a common ordained ministry between Lutherans and Episcopalians in this country.

If this common ordained ministry were created, it would appear that Lutherans and Episcopalians could quickly move to full communion.[14]

13

RELATIONS BETWEEN
THE CHURCH OF ENGLAND AND SWEDEN
BY
WILLIAM A. NORGREN

Anglican-Church of Sweden relations were topics of discussion in nineteenth-century meetings of the two Convocations of the Church of England, the General Convention of the Episcopal Church in the U.S.A., and the Lambeth Conference.[1] Our story begins in earnest in 1909 with the appointment by the archbishop of Canterbury of a commission in pursuance of Resolution 74 of the Lambeth Conference of 1908. It was to correspond with the Swedish Church through the archbishop of Uppsala on the possibilities and conditions of "an alliance of some sort." The members of the commission proceeded to Sweden in the same year and met at Uppsala with the archbishop, several bishops (all were invited), present and former members of the Chapter of Uppsala, and a lay member of the Swedish Academy. The main topics of discussion, according to the report of the commission published in 1911, were:

First day:	Episcopal Succession in both countries
Second day:	The Diaconate
	Confirmation
	Doctrinal force and authority of the "Confessio Augustana" in the Church of Sweden
	The doctrine of the Confessio with regard to the Holy Communion
	The Relation of the Church in Sweden to Lutheran bodies in other countries

	Doctrine of the Church of Sweden as to the holy ministry and the constitution of the Church
Third day:	Forms of consecration and ordination in the Church of Sweden
	Swedish Churches in the U.S.A.
	Conclusion

Soon after the proceedings opened, a Swedish bishop declared that there was no difficulty as to the first three articles of the Lambeth Quadrilateral. The fourth article would be a question for discussion. A report on the Swedish episcopate dealt with its nature and character as shown in historical documents, and called attention to some debatable points. It is summarized in Appendix II of the Report. The rest of the first day was occupied by discussion of objections raised to the validity of Anglican orders concerning the consecration of Bishop Barlow and Archbishop Parker, and the intention of the Anglican Church as judged by its forms of ordination. The Anglican position on these objections was stated in terms of the reply of the archbishops of Canterbury and York to the apostolic letter *Apostolicae Curae* of Leo XIII. Some further questions were asked about the role of the sovereign in the Church of England.

The second day began with the diaconate and its disuse in Sweden. On the Swedish side, according to the Confessio, it is not necessary that all churches should have the same organization, but that there was "a kind of diaconate" in process of development. In the seventeenth century it had been the practice to ordain candidates first to be deacons and then to make them priests upon admission to a benefice.

A variety of historical practice regarding confirmation was reported. The Anglicans expressed regret that the laying-on-of-hands by a bishop was not prescribed, and that, with priests confirming, the bishops were not brought into contact with successive generations of young people. The commission later concluded that there had been and still was some disposition to revise the existing form and to bring into closer accordance with the Swedish formularies of 1575 and with Danish use. But it was evident that "any attempt on our part to press the imposition of hands as a condition of inter-communion would be inopportune."

The doctrinal force and authority of the "Confessio Augustana" were explained in terms of the church law of 1686: "In our kingdom...all shall individually and collectively confess the Christian doctrine and faith which are founded in God's Holy Word, the prophetic and Apostolic Scriptures of the Old and New Testaments, and set out in the three chief creeds, the Apostolic, the Nicene, and the Athanasian, and likewise in the unaltered Augsburg Confession of the year 1530, accepted in the Council of Uppsala in 1593, and explained in the whole so-called Book of Concord; and all who in the teaching profession enter any office in churches, academies, or schools, must, at their appointment, bind themselves to that doctrine and confession of faith." There is no record in the report that the Anglicans were asked to expound the doctrinal force and authority in their church. Anglicans did ask whether, in view of Article X of the "Confessio," any objection would be felt to the words of distribution in the English 1662 liturgy, which, though in harmony with the terms of Article X, are held by some to admit of more than one interpretation. It was replied that this comprehensiveness of the English liturgy might be regarded in many quarters, though not universally, as an advantage rather than otherwise.

It was explained that full intercommunion existed between the Church of Sweden and other churches that accepted the "Confessio," including admission to Holy Communion and interchange of pulpits. There was, however, no actual case of a clergyman ordained elsewhere holding a benefice in Sweden. The church law stipulated, "No one may enter upon the priesthood who is not regularly and lawfully able and chosen, and, by his bishop, found suitable, approved, and ordained." The practice was to allow a man ordained by royal permission, or in the Augustana Synod in the U.S.A., "to be a co-minister or chaplin," but not an incumbent.

The doctrine of the ministry and the constitution of the church of Christ are expounded at length, beginning with Article VII of the Confessio, which states the two attributes constitutive of a church and adds that traditions and ceremonies need not be in all places alike. Differences in the constitution of the church, episcopal or presbyterian, etc., and in the organization of the holy ministry, need not ruin the true unity of the church. No particular organization of the church and of its ministry is instituted *jure divino*. However, "We do not only regard the peculiar forms and traditions of our Church with the reverence due to a venerable legacy from the past, but we realize in them a blessing from the God of history accorded to us." Quotations from the *Kyrkoordning* of Laurentius, adopted in 1571, and from the Uppsala Möte of 1593, on the office of a bishop, are used to illustrate this statement:

Since this ordinance was very useful and without doubt proceeded from God the Holy Ghost (who gives all good gifts), so it was generally approved and accepted over the whole of Christendom, and has since so remained, and must remain in the future, so long as this world lasts, although the abuse, which has been very great in this as in all other useful and necessary things, must be set aside....So now must a bishop have oversight over all that are under his government, especially the clergy, that they may rightly and duly set forth God's word among the common men, rightly administer the Sacraments, preach and hear the catechism at the proper season, hear confession when it is proper, exhort and bring the people to common prayers, visit and console the sick, bury the dead, and faithfully and diligently perform all else that the ministry of the Church and the priestly office justly demands....It belongs also to the bishop's office that he, in his diocese, shall ordain and govern with priests, and whatsoever else is required, as S. Paul writes to his disciple Titus, whom he had sent as such an overseer to Crete: "For this cause (says he) left I thee in Crete, that thou mightest provide for what is lacking, and occupy the cities there with priests, etc." And for these reasons a bishop was called *ordinarius* or *ordinator*, which means in Swedish a sender or ordainer. Regarding this matter of taking order with priests, S. Paul writes to Timothy: "Lay hands suddenly on no man."

The report on this topic concludes with an explanation that by *jure humano*, Swedish theologians meant "something which is not directly ordered by our Lord, but prescribed by the Church, in accordance with the guidance of the Holy Spirit."

The third day's discussions led to Appendix III to the report, on Swedish forms of consecration and ordination. Information was also given on the Augustana Synod, which the Church of Sweden looked upon as a daughter church.

The conclusions at the end of the Anglican report are that the Church of Sweden is, of any church in Europe, most like their own in history and organization. The fellowship between the two churches was particularly manifested in the time of Bishop Henry Compton of London and Bishop Jesper Svedberg of Skara in the eighteenth century. The latter had the oversight both of the Swedish congregation in London and those on the Delaware River in the U.S. Interchange of ministries in the latter region was frequent, and the two churches treated one another as sister churches. On the basis of the evidence before them, the commissioners concluded that (1) "the succession of bishops has been maintained unbroken by the Church of Sweden, and that it has a true conception of the episcopal office, though it does not as a whole consider the office to be so important as most English Churchmen do," (2) "the office of priest is also rightly conceived as a divinely instituted instrument for the ministry of the Word and Sacraments, and that it has been in intention handed on throughout the whole history of the Church of Sweden." On the basis of these conclusions, the commissioners recommended that members of the "National Church of Sweden, otherwise qualified to receive the Sacrament in their own Church, might be admitted to Holy Communion in ours." They took note of the fact that it is within the competence of diocesan bishops to allow use of churches for Swedish marriages, burials, and the like, and suggested that permission be given occasionally to Swedish ecclesiastics to give addresses. They hoped that the step they proposed would lead to fuller and more constant intercourse between the two churches, and eventually to intercommunion in a fuller sense.

The Lambeth Conference of 1920 welcomed the report and, accepting its conclusions on the succession of bishops of the Church of Sweden and the conception of the priesthood set forth in its standards, recommended the proposals. Lambeth added two recommendations of its own: (1) if any Anglican province found local irregularities in the order or practice of the Church of Sweden outside that country, they might legitimately postpone such action until they were satisfied that these irregularities has been removed. (2) In the event of an invitation being extended to Anglican bishops to take part in the consecration of a Swedish bishop, the invitation should, if possible, be accepted, subject to the approval of the Metropolitan. They also recommended that in the first such instance, more than one of their bishops should take part "as an evident token of the restoration of closer relations between the two Churches."

In 1922 the Conference of Bishops of the Church of Sweden replied to the Lambeth acceptance of the commission's recommendations. They approved of Anglican reception of Holy Communion in the Church of Sweden and recommended that invitations to take part in Anglican episcopal consecrations should be accepted, subject to the approval of the archbishop of Uppsala. The reply, however, stressed the point that "essential agreement, proved by the confessional documents of the communion in question," must exist on "the spirit and the main points of Christian faith." They acknowledged that the direct acceptance of the CA had not always been considered necessary, citing the fact that, from the seventeenth century, a situation of intercommunion had existed in North America between Anglicans and the Church of Sweden. Two centuries later, after 1866, Swedish immigrants were sometimes recommended to go to the Episcopal Church in the U.S.A. if they found no Swedish Lutheran community.

The reply repeated the declaration of the position laid before the commission in 1909 concerning the organization and ministry of the church. Of decisive importance, however, was whether and how far the two communions agreed as to the context of the message of salvation, founded on divine revelation. The difference as to the emphasis laid on the doctrine of the ministry, it is said, might point to a discrepancy in matters that have a more central position. So might the difference which, according to the confessions of both churches, existed in their conception of the Lord's Supper, a judgment that was made more difficult by the fact that within the Anglican Church itself different doctrines were held on these two questions. The reply concluded on this point that "without any wish to belittle the difference that exists between the two Churches, we do not hesitate to pronounce as our opinion that during the course of the preparatory negotiations, and so far as we have gradually got to know more about the Anglican Church, our impression of that unity which binds the two Churches together in what is deepest and most central, has become predominant. In the Church and the congregation of Christ, as in every living body, real concord is not characterized by uniformity, but by unity in diversity."

Prescinding from detailed definition, the reply called attention to two points "more decisive than all others, with regard to the purity of Christian doctrine—viz., the recognition of Scripture as *norma normans* both with regard to life and doctrine, and the building of our salvation on God's grace alone received by faith." In the following exposition of revelation and of faith and grace, it was said, "The revelation is throughout essentially a revelation of God's prevenient and unconditional grace, precedent to and independent of all human endeavor—that is, a revelation of the love of God, which, while condemning sin, searches for the sinner and restores him with His forgiveness. What we want to express by this is not only one, not even the most central, of those Christian doctrines which have grown out of the divine revelation, but the fundamental direction and meaning of God's whole activity for salvation, whereby He has revealed Himself to us, and has, in spite of our sin, opened to us in Jesus Christ His paternal bosom. The revelation has no other meaning that could be put on a level with this: everything else that we derive from it is only a consequence of this." There is more along this line, but the reply concluded that this same conception was contained in the sixth, eleventh, twelfth, and thirteenth of the Thirty-nine Articles. Despite "the shades of opinion that may exist, there is an essential unity in that fundamental conception which we have briefly indicated."

The closing paragraphs returned to the topic of confirmation. The bishops said they had no difficulty in using the laying-on-of-hands in confirmation, unless it was supported by arguments that would in any way question its character as an adiaphoron. But they also called attention to the "very great importance" the Church of Sweden attached to instruction of first communicants in the fundamentals of the Christian faith—"a requirement that does not seem to be paid the same attention in the Anglican practice of Confirmation." The bishops were of the opinion "that both Churches may have something to learn from each other."

Actions subsequent to the work of the Anglican Commission and to the Swedish Bishops' Reply include recognition by the Lambeth Conference of 1930 that Anglican bishops had taken part in a consecration in Uppsala (1920) and that a Swedish bishop had taken part in a consecration in Canterbury (1927). On a limited number of occasions since that time, such interconsecration has continued. In 1954, after considering the report of a committee under the chairmanship of Bishop G.K.A. Bell, both Houses of Convocation in full Synod of the Church of England recognized the succession of the Swedish episcopate and approved the steps proposed by the 1909 Commission.

In 1961 the Lower House of Canterbury heard a report of a committee to review relations between the churches of England and Sweden, in light of the new situation created by the ordination of women in Sweden in 1960. The resulting resolutions reaffirmed that Swedish clergy should be permitted to preach, and recommended that they would be given permission to celebrate Holy Communion according to their own rite or assist at the Anglican rite when in Anglican churches. Female priests were excluded from these provisions.

The same report also dealt with the question of invitations to share in episcopal consecrations, and sounded a cautionary note, lest acceptance of an invitation to participate in Swedish consecrations be seen as endorsement of the ordination of women. But the committee ultimately felt that the decision was the archbishop's. There were in fact no invitations from 1959 onwards, with the Church of Sweden respecting Archbishop Fisher's view (expressed verbally to the Archbishop of Uppsala in London) that once women had been ordained, such invitations could not be accepted. With the new situation after the General Synod decision of 1975 that there were "no fundamental objections" to the ordination of women, the House of Bishops discussed the situation afresh in 1976 and approved the resumption of participation in consecrations, the first occurring later that year.

CONCLUSION

The documents produced by the commission of 1909 and the Swedish bishops in 1922 speak for themselves. Their conclusions are important because of their affirmation of basic unity in fundamental doctrine, even with the differences that exist. These conclusions are echoed in the reports of the conversations between England and Finland (1934) and Latvia and Estonia (1938). (See the section below on other Scandinavian churches.) It is worthy of note in this connection that the content of the third clause of the Bonn Agreement between Anglicans and Old Catholics (1931) appears in the reports on Finland, Latvia, and Estonia: "Intercommunion does not require from either Communion the acceptance of all doctrinal opinion, sacramental devotion, or liturgical practice characteristic of the others but implies that each believe the other to hold all the essentials of the Christian faith."

We in America need to view the English-Swedish documents in the context of two European national churches. Significantly, English missionaries had a share in the conversion of West Gothland, and the Englishman Sigfried or Sigurd baptized Olaf Skotkönung at Husaby in 1008 A.D. The Church of Sweden has, therefore, a special bond with the Church of England, and tends to look on England as a mother rather than a sister church. The considerable similarity between the two churches inevitably draws them together, even though fellowship is limited by the distance between them.

It will be seen that, although the 1909 report contains interesting material concerning the doctrine of the faith, it does not provide a systematic or extensive treatment. The 1922 Swedish Bishops' Response does show a growing acquaintance with the faith and practice of the English church. Such growth has never ceased between these churches. The Anglo-Scandinavian Theological Conferences, only semiofficial in character, have brought together a group of theologians and clergy from the Church of England and from the churches of Sweden, Norway, Denmark, and Finland regularly since 1929, to learn about each other's theological traditions and discuss differences and theological problems.

Perhaps a closing word about the occasional participation of these churches in each other's episcopal consecrations will be fitting. It seems to me that this forms a sign of and testimony to the basic unity in the fundamental doctrine that these churches were able to recognize in each other. Participation in each other's consecrations is, therefore, not to be taken simply as an expression of church unity or a sharing in the historic episcopate, but primarily as a sign or testimony that each of these churches recognizes the catholicity and apostolicity of the other and claims this identity.

NOTE ON OTHER SCANDINAVIAN CHURCHES

The Lambeth Conference of 1930 asked the archbishop of Canterbury to appoint a Church of England committee to examine relations with the Church of Finland. In 1933 and 1934 the commission met representatives of the Church of Finland. A joint report was issued in 1934 stating "that on the most fundamental points of doctrine there is agreement. Such relations between the two Churches as we recommend do not require from either Communion the acceptance of all doctrinal opinion or of all sacramental or liturgical practice characteristic of the other, but imply that each believes the other to hold the most fundamental doctrines of the Christian faith. We are of the opinion that both Churches hold the most fundamental doctrines of the Christian faith." It was therefore recommended "that if the Archbishop of Turku shall invite the Archbishop of Canterbury to appoint a bishop to take part in the consecration of a bishop in the Church of Finland, he shall commission a bishop for such a purpose; and in the same way if the Archbishop of Canterbury shall ask the Archbishop of Turku to appoint a bishop to take part in the consecration of a bishop in the Church of England, he shall commission a bishop for such a purpose." The Anglican delegation also recommended that communicants of the Church of Finland be welcome to communion in the Church of England. In 1935 the recommendations were accepted by the convocations of Canterbury and York. The first Anglican took part in a Finnish consecration in 1951.

The Committee on Unity of the Church at the Lambeth Conference of 1930 also suggested that a commission might then consider further other Scandinavian churches. In 1937 the archbishop of Canterbury received a joint request from the archbishop of Latvia and the bishop of Estonia to arrange a conference similar to the one held with the Church of Finland. Delegates of the three churches met at Lambeth in 1936 and at Riga and Tallinn in 1938 and issued a Joint Report. It, also, stated that "on the most fundamental points of doctrine there is agreement" and that all doctrinal opinion or sacramental or liturgical practice need not be agreed. They agreed on inter-consecration of bishops, and the Anglican delegation recommended admission of communicants of the churches of Latvia and Estonia to communion in the Church of England, taking note that the churches of Latvia and Estonia would be ready to admit to communion communicant members of the Church of England. Additionally, as with the English-Finnish commission before, it was recommended that whenever there is a conference between bishops of the Anglican Communion and bishops of other churches in communion with it, bishops of the churches of Latvia and Estonia should be asked to attend it, and vice versa. The convocations of Canterbury and York approved the recommendations in 1937.

A 1951 report from a committee appointed by the archbishop of Canterbury for conversations with the churches of Norway, Denmark, and Iceland led to resolutions in the convocations of Canterbury and York welcoming baptized and communicant members of these churches to receive communion in the Church of England when cut off from the ministrations of their own churches. The question of episcopal succession was a difficulty because the three churches had not maintained it, and they were not interested in expressing unity through interconsecration.

The Lambeth Conference of 1948 welcomed the steady growth in friendship between the Scandinavian churches and the Anglican Communion. It called attention to the resolutions of 1920 on relations with the Church of Sweden and recommended that they be formally brought to the notice of the provinces of the Anglican Communion, which had not yet considered them. It is uncertain whether provinces took any action.

NOTES

Preface

1. Porvoo (see "Abbreviations," p. 13).
2. See James E. Griffiss and Daniel F. Martensen, eds., *A Commentary on Concordat of Agreement* (Minneapolis: Augsburg, 1994).

Chapter 1. L. William Countryman

1. *Oxford Classical Dictionary*, 2nd ed., *s.vv.* "Clubs, Greek" by Marcus Niebuhr Tod and "Clubs, Roman" by George Hope Stevenson.
2. On John, see the review of literature in Robert Kysar, *The Fourth Evangelist and His Gospel* (Minneapolis: Augsburg, 1975), pp. 249–259. On Eucharist and Agape, see Josef A. Jungmann, *The Early Liturgy* (Notre Dame: Univ. of Notre Dame, 1959), pp. 29–38. Contrast the more recent discussions and literature in Cheslyn Jones et al., eds., *The Study of Liturgy* (New York: Oxford, 1978), pp. 170–176.
3. Jungmann, pp. 74–86; Jones et al., pp. 95–110. Contrast the hints about the earliest catechesis in Heb. 6:1–6.
4. Cf., e.g., the relatively unfriendly treatment of the development in Hans von Campenhausen, *Ecclesiastical Authority and Spiritual Power in the Church of the First Three Centuries* (London: Adam & Charles Black, 1969), pp. 149–177; or the less theoretically oriented discussion in Robert M. Grant, *Augustus to Constantine* (New York: Harper & Row, 1970), pp. 63–68, 145–160.
5. Papias' dictum survives in Eusebius, *Church History* 3.39.4.
6. On the apostolate, cf. L. William Countryman, "Christian Equality and the Early Catholic Episcopate," *ATR* 63 (1981):127–34. Hippolytus seems to assume ordination as a normal practice, not as anything new or controversial.
7. See the good study by Carl A. Volz, "The Confession-Making Process in the Early Church," *Studies: The Confession-Making Process* (distributed by the Division of Theological Studies, Lutheran Council in the U.S.A., copyright 1975), pp. 9–14. For areas where my presentation differs, see L. William Countryman, "Tertullian and the Regula Fidei," *The Second Century* 2 (1982):208–27.

8. *Interpreters Dictionary of the Bible*, 5 vols. (Nashville: Abingdon, 1966, 1976), *s.v.* "Canon of the NT" by F. W. Beare.

9. *Ibid*. See also Robert M. Grant, *A Historical Introduction to the New Testament* (New York: Simon & Schuster, 1972), pp. 25–38.

10. It is possible that one might include a fifth institution, that of provincial or metropolitical organization. This seems, however, less continuous (despite a beginning on it in the role of James the Just), less universal (early in Egypt and perhaps Africa; late in some other areas, such as Spain), and less theological in nature. The heyday of this institution begins not before the fourth century.

11. So, for example, such pioneering works as Amos N. Wilder, *Early Christian Rhetoric* (Cambridge: Harvard, 1971) and Norman Perrin, *Rediscovering the Teaching of Jesus* (New York: Harper & Row, 1976); also the large recent bibliography on parables.

12. Nora K. Chadwick, *The Age of Saints in the Early Celtic Church* (London: Oxford, 1961), pp. 77–78.

13. I have used the translation of Burton Scott Easton (reprint) (Archon Books, 1962).

14. Quoted in Kenneth E. Kirk, *The Vision of God* (London: Longmans Green, 1931), p. 361.

15. Cf. Melanchthon's complaint: "...the bishops either force our priests to forsake and condemn the sort of doctrine we have confessed, or else, in their unheard of cruelty, they kill the unfortunate and innocent men. This keeps our priests from acknowledging such bishops." BC 214.

Chapter 2. Robert J. Goeser

1. Some material from the first half of this essay appeared in "The Historic Episcopate and the Lutheran Confessions" in *Lutheran Quarterly* 1:214–232 (1987). See also Goeser, "Word, Ministry, and Episcopacy according to the Lutheran Confessions," *Lutheran Quarterly* 4:45–60 (1990), and "Classical Lutheran Approach to Ministry," a paper given at the ELCA Consultation of Teaching Theologians, 1990.

2. WA 12:191, 19–20. "*...et Episcopi papales nolint dare verbi ministros, nisi tales, qui verbum aboleant et Ecclesiam perdant....*"

3. WA 12:191, 23–27. "*...et orationibus ac manuum impositionibus universitati commendare et confirmare, atque eos tum pro legitimis Episcopis et ministris verbi agnoscere et colere....*"

4. WA 12:194, 14–20.

5. WA 12:191, 16–18, 21.

6. WA 12:194, 33–39. "*Iam si et hic vos scrupulus terret, vos non esse certo Ecclesiam dei: Respondeo, Ecclesiam non moribus sed verbo cognosci....At ubiubi verbum dei cum cognitione Christi est, inane non est, quantumvis sint infirmi moribus externis, qui illud habent.*"

7. WA 15:720, 11–13.

8. *Ibid.*, line 14.

9. WA 15:721, 1–2.

10. WA 15:721, 3–5. "*Ordinare non est consecrare. Si ergo scimus pium hominem, extrahimus eum et damus in virtute verbi quod habemus, auctoritatem praedicandi verbum et dandi sacramenta. Hoc est ordinare.*"

11. WA 17¹:511, 3–5.

12. See Erich Vogelsang, *Die Anfänge von Luthers Christologie* (Berlin: Walter deGruyter, 1929).

13. Hellmut Lieberg provided a fine summary of the differences between the two positions in *Amt und Ordination bei Luther und Melanchthon* (Göttingen: Vandenhoeck und Ruprecht, 1962), pp. 25–26: "Der römische ordo übertrug die Vollmacht zur Darbringung des Messopfers. Dieses hatte satisfaktorischen Charakter. Der Messpriester, der es darbrachte und gerade zu diesem Werk geweiht worden war, hatte so eine Mittlerstellung zwischen Gott und Mensch inne. Hierdurch wurde das Kreuz Christi seine alleinige Heilsmittlerschaft, sein allein sühnnendes und einmaliges Opfer verdunkelt und der ganze Charakter der Gnadenmitteldarbietung ins Gegenteil der eigentlichen Stiftungsintention Gottes verkehrt. In der Funktion des satisfaktorischen Priestertums trat die Richtung vom Menschen zu Gott bestimmend hervor und verderbte den gesamten Kultus, der somit unter den Gesichtspunkt des meritorischen Werks des Menschen trat und seine Begründung in der freien Gabe und dem Geschenk Gottes verlor....Das Messopfer nun war auf den ordo gestützt, der seinerseits wiederum von diesem her seine charakteristische Prägung empfing. Die Entstellung und Pervertierung der Messe, des heiligen Abendmahls, aus einer Heilsgabe Gottes an die Menschen zum meritorisch-satisfaktorischen Opferwerk, das der Mensch Gott darbringt, bedingte die Entstellung des Amtes zu einem Opferpriestertum. Hiergegen bestimmt Luther den wahren Charakter des Amtes als *ministerium verbi, nicht sacerdotium.*"

14. Ernst Bizer, *Fides ex Auditu* (Neukirchen: Buchandlung der Erziehungsvereins, 1961).

15. Lieberg, *Amt und Ordination*, pp. 25–29.

16. *Corpus Reformatorium*, Melanthonis *Opera* (Halle: Schwetschke et filium, 1834), 1:763.

17. *Ibid.*, 1:766.

18. "Erstlich die Prediger belangend muß man bekennen, daß ein iglicher Prediger schuldig ist, das Hauptstück christlicher Lahr zu predigen, vom Glauben an Christum, und dasselbig nicht bergen aus einiger Ursach." *Ibid.*, 1:764. "Dieweil nun die Prediger im Predigtamt gewesen, sind sie schuldig gewesen, die Wahrheit zu vertheidigen, und hat sie Gottes Geboth gedrungen, ihr Amt zu thun, Papst und Bischöfe machten was sie wollten." *Ibid.*, 1:766.

19. *Ibid.* Translation by Goeser.

20. Philip Melanchthon, *Loci Communes*, C. L. Hill, tr. (Boston: Meador, 1944), pp. 130–143.

21. WA 26:195.

22. WA 26:196.

23. WA 197:12.

24. Ibid., 235:9.

25. Ibid., line 12.

26. Ibid., lines 26–39.

27. Lieberg, Amt und Ordination, p. 183.

28. Hermann Pfister, Die Entwicklung der Theologie Melanchthons unter dem Einfluß der Auseinandersetzung mit Schwärmgeistern und Widertäufern (Freiburg: Deutsche Pax-Christi Bewegung, 1968), p. 117.

29. Franz Lau and Ernst Bizer, A History of the Reformation in Germany (London: Black, 1969).

30. See Bernd Moeller, Imperial Cities and the Reformation (Philadelphia: Fortress Press, 1972), Midelfort and Edwards, tr., pp. 41–115; also Martin Brecht, "Die gemeinsame Politik der Reichstädte und die Reformation" in Zeitschrift der Savigny-Stiftung für Rechtsgeschichte 94 (1977): 180–263.

31. Here, too, there were doctrinal differences. The Franconian cities were mainly Lutheran, the Swabian cities were oriented toward the Swiss and to Bucer (Moeller, Imperial Cities, op. cit.).

32. One of the earliest theological confessions was that in the third section of Luther's Bekenntnis vom Abendmahl Christi (1528), WA 26:499ff. (LW 37: 360ff.). Some of this is reworked in the Schwabach Articles (WA 30³:86).

33. All of Charles' dynastic holdings took priority over the empire, and even at Augsburg his goal was to assure his brother's succession to the imperial throne. See Wolfgang Reinhard, "Das Augsburger Bekenntnis im politischen Zusammenhang," in Das Augsburger Bekenntnis in drei Jahrhunderten (Weissenborn: Anton Konrad Verlag, 1980), ed. Horst Jesse.

34. Moeller, Imperial Cities, op cit.

35. Wilhelm Maurer, "Erwägungen und Verhandlungen über die geistliche Jurisdiction der Bischöfe vor und während des Augsburger Reichstags von 1530," in Zeitschrift der Savigny-Stiftung für Rechtsgeschichte 86 (1969).

36. Maurer, "Erwägungen und Verhandlungen," p. 350.

37. Wilhelm Maurer, "Die Entstehung und erste Auswirkung von Artikel 28 der Confessio Augustana" in Volk Gottes, Bäumer and Dolch, eds. (Freiburg: Herder, 1967), pp. 361–394.

38. Henry E. Jacobs, The Book of Concord, vol. 2 (Philadelphia: 1888), p. 176.

39. Ibid., p. 83.

40. Ibid., p. 94.

41. WA 17¹, p. 511 (n. 1).

42. Jacobs, The Book of Concord, p. 88.

43. Ibid. pp. 89–90.

44. Maurer, "Erwägungen und Verhandlungen," p. 353. What makes this critique so significant is that it disavows any attack on the secular power of the prince bishop (Jacobs, *The Book of Concord*, p. 89). One hears, of course, the Saxon respect for order.

45. Maurer, "Erwägungen und Verhandlungen," p. 351.

46. Wilhelm Gussmann, *Quellen und Forschungen zur Geschichte des Augsburgischen Glaubensbekenntnisses* (Leipzig: Teubner, 1911), and Maurer, "Erwägungen und Verhandlungen," p. 366 (n. 35).

47. Maurer, "Erwägungen und Verhandlungen," p. 366.

48. *Ibid.*

49. *Ibid.*, p. 367.

50. Maurer observes that the passion that breaks out in these complaints marks the gulf between pastor and feudal lord, and in light of it there was no chance of success for the compromise plan (*ibid.*, p. 368).

51. Klaus Rischar, "Johann Eck auf dem Reichstag zu Augsburg 1530" (Münster: 1968), and Rischar, "Johann Eck in seinem Kampf gegen die Täufer auf dem Reichstag zu Augsburg 1530," in *Mennonitische Geschichtsblätter* 26 (N.F. 21) (1969):44–54.

52. John Oyer, *Lutheran Reformers against Anabaptists* (The Hague: M. Nijhoff, 1964), pp. 152–153. Also Melanchthon, *Werke in Auswahl* (Studienausgabe) (Gütersloh: C. Bertelsmann Verlag, 1951), vol. 1, pp. 272–295.

53. Oyer, *Lutheran Reformers*, p. 155.

54. Maurer, "Erwägungen und Verhandlungen," p. 374.

55. *Ibid.*, p. 375.

56. WA Br 5:1709.

57. Gussman, *Quellen und Forschungen*, vol. 1, part 1, p. 338.

58. Maurer, "Erwägungen und Verhandlungen," p. 389.

59. *Ibid.*, p. 398.

60. Gussmann, *Quellen und Forschungen*, pp. 315–319.

61. Wilhelm Maurer, *Historischer Kommentar zur Confessio Augustana*, vol. 1 (Gütersloh: G. Mohn, 1976), BC 78.

62. T. G. Tappert (editor), *Book of Concord* (Philadelphia: Muhlenberg Press, 1959), p. 81.

63. BC 82.

64. BC 84.

65. BC 212.

66. BC 84.

67. Maurer says that appeals to episcopal jurisdiction (even when referring to the power of the Word) are nullified by the equalization of bishop or pastor (*"episcopi seu pastores"*) at decisive places—CA 28:69 and 79 (Maurer, "Erwägungen und Verhandlungen," p. 351).

68. Jacobs, *The Book of Concord*, p. 88.

69. *Ibid.*, pp. 89–90.

70. BC 330.

71. BC 331.

72. Clyde Manschreck, ed. and tr., "Melanchthon on Christian Doctrine" (*Loci Communes*, 1555) (New York: Oxford University Press, 1965), pp. 262–263.

73. Melanchthon, *Selected Writings*, Leander Hill, tr. (Minneapolis: Augsburg, 1962), p. 136.

74. *Ibid.*, p. 137.

75. The material briefly summarized here is from two major works by Peter Fraenkel, *Testimonia Patrum* (Geneva: E. Droz, 1961), esp. pp. 110–161, and "Revelation and Tradition" in *Studia Theologica* 13 (Lund: C.W.K. Gleerup, 1959):97–133.

76. Ruth Rouse and Stephen Neill, eds., *A History of the Ecumenical Movement 1517–1948*, 2nd ed. (London: S.P.C.K., 1967), pp. 56–58.

77. Norman Sykes, *Old Priest and New Presbyter* (Cambridge: University Press, 1956), p. 17.

78. *Ibid.*, p. 27.

79. *Ibid.*

80. Richard Hooker, *Of the Laws of Ecclesiastical Polity* (Everyman's Library: London, 1963), vol. 1, pp. 299–333.

81. *Ibid.*, p. 109.

82. Quoted in Sykes, *Old Priest*, p. 20.

83. Sykes quotes an important passage in which Hooker allows "that the whole church might even change the episcopal form of polity" (*Old Priest*, p. 69). The passage quoted is from the *Laws*, Bk. 7, v, 8.

84. Sykes, *Old Priest*, p. 66.

85. Quoted in Sykes, *Old Priest*, p. 74.

86. *Ibid.*

87. Quoted in Sykes, *Old Priest*, p. 78.

88. *Ibid.*, pp. 89–94.

89. *Ibid.*, pp. 142–146 and 152–3. See also Norman Sykes, *William Wake*, 2 vols. (Cambridge: University Press, 1957).

90. Sykes, *Old Priest*, pp. 146–147.

91. Sykes, *Old Priest*, pp. 154–158, and Rouse and Neill, *Ecumenical Movement*, pp. 160–161. See also H. P. Thompson, *Into All Lands* (London: S.P.C.K., 1951), and C.F. Pascoe, *Two Hundred Years of the S.P.G.* (London: S.P.C.K., 1901).

92. See Charles Hole, *The Early History of the Church Missionary Society* (London: Church Missionary Society, 1896).

93. Israel Acrelius, *A History of New Sweden*, tr. Reynolds (Philadelphia: Historical Society of Pennsylvania, 1874), p. 362. Acrelius was provost of the Swedish Mission in America from 1749 to 1756.

94. Quoted in H. E. Jacobs, *A History of the Evangelical Lutheran Church in the United States* (New York: Scribner's, 1907), 5th ed., pp. 279–280.

95. Vernon Storr, *The Development of English Theology in the Nineteenth Century 1800–1860* (London: Longmans, Green and Co., 1913), pp. 250–251. For similar explanations of the origins of the Oxford movement see: Bernard Reardon, *From Coleridge to Gore* (London: Longman, 1971), ch. 3; Owen Chadwick, *The Victorian Church* (London: A. and C. Black, 1972), part. 2, chs. 1–3 and 8.

96. Newman in *Tracts for the Times* (London: 1840), Tract 1, p. 3.

97. Sykes, *Old Priest*, p. 210.

98. Tract 7, p. 2.

99. Tract 20, p. 3.

100. Yngve Brilioth, *The Anglican Revival* (London: Longmans, Green and Co., 1933), pp. 180–210.

101. *Ibid.*, p. 183.

102. Quoted in Brilioth, *The Anglican Revival*, p. 201.

103. Leighton Frappell, "'Science' in the Service of Orthodoxy: The Early Intellectual Development of E. B. Pusey," Perry Butler (ed)., *Pusey Rediscovered* (London: S.P.C.K., 1983), pp. 1–14.

104. *Ibid.*, p. 21.

105. *Ibid.*, p. 26.

106. Brilioth, *The Anglican Revival*, p. 183.

107. Heinrich Hermelink, *Das Christentum in der Menschheitgeschecht*, 3 vols. (Tübingen: J. B. Metzler und R. Wunderlich, 1951).

108. *Ibid.*, vol. 1, p. 144.

109. Emanuel Hirsch, *Geschichte der Neuern Evangelischen Theologie*, vol. 5 (Gütersloh: G. Mohn, 1960), pp. 103–115.

110. For a discussion of Hengstenberg, see Hirsch, *Evangelischen Theologie*, pp. 118–130.

111. See the survey in the introduction to Theodore Tappert, *Lutheran Confessional Theology in America 1840–1880*, (New York: Oxford University Press, 1972).

112. Hirsch, *Evangelischen Theologie*, pp. 185–190.

113. Tappert, *Confessional Theology*, p. 13.

114. James T. Addison, *The Episcopal Church in the United States 1789–1931* (New York: Scribner's, 1951), pp. 275–276.

115. I have been helped in posing this issue from the Anglican side by Norman Sykes, *Old Priest and New Presbyter*, and E. C. Rich, *Spiritual Authority in the Church of England* (London: Longmans, Green and Co., 1953); Stephen Sykes, *The Integrity of Anglicanism* (New York: Mowbrays, Seabury, 1978); and Reginald Fuller, "Anglican Self-Understanding and Anglican Traditions," in *Tradition and Lutheranism and Anglicanism*, Günther Gassmann and Vilmos Vajta, eds. (Strasbourg: Strasbourg Institute for Ecumenical Research, 1972).

116. Joseph Burgess, "The Historical Background of Vatican I," in *Teaching Authority and Infallibility in the Church* (Minneapolis: Augsburg, 1978).

117. *Ibid.*, p. 294.

118. *Ibid.*, p. 296.

Chapter 5. L. William Countryman

1. I am not, however, willing to detach the issue of sacramental validity from the life of the Christian community. While God's grace is available freely and without precondition, the sacraments are covenanted rites of the community and are not to be privatized.

2. In this respect, I think we must take care that our vision is not limited only to Lutherans and Anglicans. While we cannot make decisions for other bilateral dialogues, we can at least try to avoid moving in directions that might make an emerging Lutheran-Anglican accommodation a barrier to larger unity in the church.

3. I am not suggesting either that the lists are exhaustive or that every Lutheran or Episcopalian would agree with my presentation of their group—only that such sentiments are in fact to be heard within it.

4. Is this a point of difference between Anglicans and Lutherans? Does the longstanding anxiety of Danes, for example, about having any Swedish bishops participate in the laying-on-of-hands at their ordinations, imply that the Lutheran tradition accepts that churches in communion with one another may maintain mutually exclusive networks of ordination? If so, this may, from an Anglican perspective, be a graver hindrance to full communion than most of those on which we have spent more time in our conversations. Cf. p. 98.

5. This and the following materials belong to a project I have had in hand for a long time and which I hope to complete in 1990.

6. The germ of truth behind this distortion, I think, is that the missionary character of apostolic ministry does imply that a single person can bring the church to a new place, as, for example, when Augustine of Canterbury was consecrated bishop and authorized, contrary to the canons, to consecrate other bishops in England by himself. Yet even in this case, there was an existing Christian community that acknowledged his vocation to such work and consented to his original ordination.

7. I do not see this as meaning that the ELCA could not receive ministers from other Lutheran churches without the historic episcopate; only that all ordinations within the ELCA in the future would include the historic episcopate.

8. Re-ordination, of course, suggests anxiety or doubt about the reality of past ministrations. I do not see how it can answer our present needs. There have been models, of course, of a kind of general merging of ministries in the inaugurating of new united churches. Insofar as these tend to be deliberately ambiguous about what is being done, I think they are rather unsatisfactory—the gestural or ritual equivalent of mumbling in oral languages.

Chapter 6. Eric W. Gritsch

1. *To the Christian Nobility of the German Nation*, 1520. WA 6:407, 29–30; LW 44:128.

2. WA 6:408, 11–13; LW 44:129.

3. *Concerning the Ministry*, 1523. WA 12:189, 25–27; LW 40:34. What a "right" (*Recht*) is can be interpreted in several ways. But for Luther the right of the community is anchored in his understanding of the local church as expression of the church catholic. See also Peter Brunner, "Vom Amt des Bischofs," in *Pro Ecclesia, Gesammelte Aufsätze zur dogmatischen Theologie* (Berlin and Hamburg: Lutherisches Verlagshaus, 1962), 241–242.

4. *Instructions for the Visitors of Parish Pastors in Electoral Saxony*, 1528. WA 26:197, 16–19; LW 40:271.

5. WA 26:197, 20–21; 200:28–34; LW 40:271.

6. Luther's confession of faith ("until my death") in *Confession Concerning Christ's Supper*, 1528. WA 26:504, 30–33; 505, 11–13; LW 37:364, 365.

7. In 1538, Luther published Jerome's letter to the presbyter Euagrius, which argued for the equality of priest and bishop. WA 50:339–343. For the consistency of Luther's views on the matter, see Brunner, "Vom Amt des Bischofs," 253–256.

8. *Exhortation to All Clergy Assembled in Augsburg*, 1530. WA 30²:342, 4, 8–16; LW 34:50–51. Quotation, 50.

9. For a detailed study of the origin of the Augsburg Confession, its two parts, and twenty-eight articles, see Wilhelm Maurer, *Historical Commentary on the Augsburg Confession*, tr. H. George Anderson (Philadelphia: Fortress, 1986), esp. pp. 6–57.

10. BS; BC; AC; AP.

11. Maurer, *Historical Commentary*, p. 59. Interpreters of CA 28 and CA 14 have rightly viewed the office of bishop in the context of the demand for the freedom of the gospel. See Leif Grane, *The Augsburg Confession: A Commentary*, tr. John H. Rasmussen (Minneapolis: Augsburg, 1987), 151–158, 241; Friedrich Mildenberger, *Theologie der lutherischen Bekenntnisschriften* (Stuttgart/Berlin/Köln/Mainz: Kohlhammer, 1983), pp. 103–108. That CA 5, 14, and 28 prefer a hierarchically functioning ministry has been demonstrated by Eric W. Gritsch and Robert W. Jenson in *Lutheranism: The Theological Movement and Its Confessional Writings* (Philadelphia: Fortress, 1976), 110–123.

12. Maurer, *Historical Commentary*, p. 60.

13. *Ibid.*, p. 61. Text in BS 120:18–35.

14. BS 120:20, 27.

15. Maurer, *Historical Commentary*, p. 64.

16. *Ibid.*, p. 70.

17. German text. BC 81:2; BS 120.

18. Latin text. BC 82:8; BS 121.

19. Latin text. BC 82:11; BS 122.

20. Latin text. BC 83:18; BS 123.

21. Italics added. The German text is clearer by deleting "except," thus including in the ministry of Word and Sacrament the power of the keys. BC 84:21; BS 123–124.

22. Latin text. BC 85:29; BS 125.

23. *Ibid*.

24. BC 86:34; BS 126.

25. Latin text. BC 89:51; BS 128.

26. Latin text. BC 93:69; BS 131.

27. Latin text. BC 93:71—94:74; BS 131–132.

28. Latin text. BC 93:76–78; BS 132.

29. WA Br 5:477, 79–80; LW 49:381.

30. Letter to Melanchthon dated July 21, 1530. WA Br 5:492, 10–11; 17–19; LW 49:383.

31. WA Br 5:492, 27–31; 493, 38–53; 494, 116; LW 49:385–390.

32. Some compromises were made at the Regensburg Colloquy, but conservatives on both sides refused to accept any convergences. See Jill Raitt, "From Augsburg to Trent" in *Justification by Faith: Lutherans and Catholics in Dialogue VII*, H. George Anderson, T. Austin Murphy, Joseph A. Burgess, eds. (Minneapolis: Augsburg, 1983), pp. 200–217.

33. German and Latin texts in Herbert Immenkötter, *Die Confutatio der Augustana vom 3. August 1530*, Corpus Catholicorum 33 (Münster: Aschendorff, 1979), 199:20–200:2. English translation in J. M. Reu, ed., *The Augsburg Confession: A Collection of Sources with an Historical Introduction* (Chicago: Wartburg, 1930), p. 361.

34. BC 281:4; BS 397.

35. 283:13–14; BS 400.

36. BC 284:23; BS 402–403.

37. BC 285:27; BS 403.

38. Latin text, CA 5. BC 31:2; BS 58.

39. CA 14. BC 36; BS 69.

40. Maurer, *Historical Commentary*, pp. 191–192.

41. *Infiltrating and Clandestine Preachers*, 1532. WA 30³:518, 21–23; LW 40:384.

42. Latin text, CA 7. BC 32:2; BS 61.

43. AP 14, italics added. BC 214:2; BS 296–297.

44. *Treatise on the Power and Primacy of the Pope*, 1537. BC 330:61; BS 489.

45. BC 331:67; BS 491. Augustine's example is cited: If there are two Christians on a ship, one of whom baptized the other, and the latter, after his baptism, absolved the former.

46. BC 332:74; BS 493.

47. Article 10. BC 314:1; BS 457–458.

48. BC 314:3; BS 458. Luther referred to St. Jerome's report that the church in Alexandria was governed by priests and not by bishops.

49. BC 316–317; BS 463–464.

50. *Exempel, einen rechten christlichen Bischof zu weihen: Geschehen zu Naumburg Anno 1542, Januar 20.* WA 53:219–260.

51. Text of *Wittenbergische Reformation* in *Corpus Reformatorum: Philippi Melanchthonis opera,* Carl B. Bretschneider and H. E. Bindseil, eds. (Halle: Schwetschke, 1840–1860), 5:579–606. Quotation, 597.

52. *Ibid.,* 602.

53. See the historical survey by Bernhard Lohse, "The Development of Offices of Leadership in the German Lutheran Churches: 1517–1918" in *Episcopacy in the Lutheran Church? Studies in the Development and Definition of the Office of Church Leadership,* Ivar Asheim and Victor R. Gold, eds. (Philadelphia: Fortress, 1970), pp. 51–71. The study of sixteenth-century Lutheran episcopacy has recently stressed the "guard office" (*Wächteramt*) that could not be constitutionally maintained, because of the political events leading to a territorial fusion of church and state. See Gerhard Tröger, "Bischoff III: Das evangelische Bischofsamt," in *Theologische Realenzyklopädie,* Gerhard Krause and Gerhard Müller, eds. (Berlin/New York: De Gruyter, 1976–), 6:691.

54. See Kurt Schmidt-Clausen, "The Development of Offices of Leadership in the German Lutheran Churches: 1918–the Present," in Asheim and Gold, *Episcopacy in the Lutheran Church?* pp. 72–115. Ernst Benz, *Bischofsamt und apostolische Sukzession im deutschen Protestantismus* (Stuttgart: Evangelisches Verlagswerk), p. 153, lamented the fact that Lutheran apostolic succession, embodied in Zinzendorf, did not become the model of leadership. He called the lack of such a model "a charismatic impoverization" (*charismatische Verarmung*).

55. See Eric W. Gritsch, "Lutheran Teaching Authority: Past and Present," in *Teaching Authority and Infallibility in the Church: Lutherans and Catholics in Dialogue VI,* Paul Empie, T. Austin Murphy, and Joseph A. Burgess, eds. (Minneapolis: Augsburg, 1978), pp. 144–145.

56. Martin Parvio, "The Post-Reformation Developments of the Episcopacy in Sweden, Finland, and the Baltic States," *ibid.,* pp. 133–134.

57. In the sixteenth century, Laurentius Petri, the first evangelical archbishop of Sweden, came close to the notion that the episcopacy exists *iure divino*; he regarded the office of bishops as being a particular creation of the Holy Spirit. His views did not prevail. *Ibid.,* p. 131. For a summary of Lutheran discussions of episcopacy, see Jerald C. Brauer, "Afterword," *ibid.,* pp. 197–211.

58. BEM 29:38. The latest American response, from the no longer existing Lutheran Church in America, simply states that "there is no Lutheran consensus on these matters [threefold pattern of ministry]." See *The Response of the Lutheran Church in America* (Department of Ecumenical Relations, New York, 1984), p. 7.

59. "Protestant principle" and "Catholic substance" are terms indicating objections to identifying the "ultimate concern" of "justification by faith alone" with the church's creation, its historical tradition of piety, its order, or other human elements. See Paul Tillich, *Systematic Theology*, 3 vols. (Chicago: Univ. of Chicago, 1956), 1:37; 3:223. Jaroslav Pelikan, *Obedient Rebels* (New York: Harper & Row, 1964) calls "Catholic substance" that which Luther sought to reform rather than abolish. *Ibid.*, pp. 13, 17.

60. See, for example, the convergence between Avery Dulles and George Lindbeck, "Bishops and the Ministry of the Gospel," in *Confessing One Faith: A Joint Commentary on the Augsburg Confession by Lutheran and Catholic Theologians*, George W. Forell and John F. McCue, eds. (Minneapolis: Augsburg, 1982), 147–148; and the argument against such a convergence by Robert Goeser, "The Historic Episcopate and the Lutheran Confessions," *Lutheran Quarterly* 1 (new series, 1987):226–229. Dulles and Lindbeck contend that for the CA, "no other alternative was conceivable" ("Historic Episcopate," p. 229). Most recently a critique of a Lutheran episcopate concluded with a call for an "evangelical episcopate" embodied in "men and women of God" who would need "no other mandate than that already provided for them by the Scripture, the Confessions of their church, and the call of the Christians they are summoned to lead....Such an episcopate is desperately needed." See Joseph A. Burgess, "An Evangelical Episcopate?" in *Called and Ordained*, Todd W. Nichol and Marc Kolden, eds.,(Minneapolis: Fortress, 1990), p. 149.

61. CA, Preface. BC 26:13; BS 46–47.

62. *Lutheran-Episcopal Dialogue: A Progress Report* (Maxi Book, 1972), p. 22.

Chapter 7. Walter R. Bouman

1. Transcript of the discussion of LED III, Tuesday afternoon, 28 January 1986.

2. *Constitutions and Canons for the Government of the Protestant Episcopal Church in the United States of America*, 1982, p. 8.

3. *Ibid.*, Title III (The Ministry), canon 21, sec. 1(a), p. 95.

4. *Ibid.*, Title IV (Ecclesiastical Discipline), canon 1, sec. 1(4), p. 111.

5. Stephen Sykes, *The Integrity of Anglicanism* (New York: Seabury, 1978), p. 44.

6. *Ibid.*, p. 36.

7. According to the rite of Ordination, a Lutheran ordinand is addressed and questioned as follows:
   The Church in which you are to be ordained confesses that the Holy Scriptures are the Word of God and are the norm of its faith and life. We accept, teach, and confess the Apostles', the Nicene, and the Athanasian Creeds. We also acknowledge the Lutheran Confessions as true witnesses and faithful expositions of the Holy Scriptures. Will you therefore preach and teach in accordance with the Holy Scriptures and these

creeds and confessions? (*Occasional Services* [Minneapolis: Augsburg, 1982], p. 194.

8. Cf. John H. Westerhoff III, *Will Our Children Have Faith?* (New York: Seabury, 1976). Westerhoff indicated that in the 1960s the most significant voices in religious education recognized that "the church teaches most significantly through nurture in a worshiping, witnessing community of faith," (p. 4). Despite mounting evidence to the contrary, however, they continued to advocate a "schooling-instructional paradigm" for religious education (pp. 6–10). Westerhoff expressed the educational vision as follows:

By their rites will you know them is more than mere rhetoric, for no aspect of corporate life is more important than its rituals. Worship, therefore, is at the center of the church's life; indeed, the word orthodoxy means "right praise"—as well as "right belief." Ritual or cultic life sustains and transmits the community's understandings and ways....Liturgy needs to become a major aspect of Christian education, but before that will be possible the character and role of rites and rituals need to be properly understood, (pp. 54–55).

9. Marion J. Hatchett, *Commentary on the American Prayer Book* (New York: Seabury, 1981), p. 25.

10. BCP, p. 13.

11. CA 24; BC 60:34.

12. BC 249.

13. Hatchett, *Commentary*, pp. 47–88.

14. See Philip H. Pfatteicher, *Festivals and Commemorations* (Minneapolis: Augsburg, 1980). *Manual on the Liturgy* by Philip H. Pfatteicher and Carlos Messerli (Minneapolis: Augsburg, 1979), pp. 41–76, has shorter biographies, more like those in Hatchett.

15. BC 445–446.

16. Geoffrey Wainwright, *Eucharist and Eschatology* (London: Epworth, 1971).

17. Hatchett, *Commentary*, p. 320.

18. *Ibid.*, p. 342.

19. Cf. Marianne H. Micks, *The Future Present* (New York: Seabury, 1970), pp. 141–158; Gerhard Lohfink, *Jesus and Community* (New York: Paulist, 1984), pp. 23–25; and Stephen Sykes, "the Sacraments," *Christian Theology*, Peter Hodgson and Robert King, eds. (Philadelphia: Fortress, 1985), pp. 274–301, and esp. the excellent bibliography on p. 301.

20. Hatchett, *Commentary*, p. 386.

21. BEM, Eucharist ¶13.

22. Cf. CA 24, BC 58–60:21–34, and AP 24, BC 252-268.

23. AP 24, BC 252:19 and 256:35.

24. J. G. Davies, *A Select Liturgical Lexicon* (Richmond: John Knox, 1965), p. 48.

25. CA 28, BC 94:77.

26. AP 28, BC 383:12–14.

27. Robert Jenson, "Sacraments of the Word," *Christian Dogmatics,* vol. 2, Carl Braaten and Robert Jenson, eds. (Philadelphia: Fortress, 1984), p. 311.

28. CA 7, BC 32:2–3.

29. Sykes, *Integrity,* p. 36.

30. *Ibid.,* p. 47.

Chapter 8. J. Robert Wright

1. Eric W. Gritsch and Robert W. Jenson, *Lutheranism* (Philadelphia: Fortress, 1976), pp. 5–6.

2. *Ibid.,* p. 172.

3. Arthur Carl Piepkorn, *Profiles in Belief,* vol. 2 (San Francisco: Harper & Row, 1978), p. 10.

4. *Ibid.,* pp. 43–44.

5. D. W. H. Arnold and C. G. Fry, *The Way the Truth and the Life: An Introduction to Lutheran Christianity* (Grand Rapids: Baker, 1982), p. 167.

6. *Ibid.,* pp. 160–170.

7. *Evangelical Lutheran Church in America Constitution, Bylaws, and Continuing Resolutions* (Minneapolis: Augsburg, 1991), p. 19.

8. *Ecumenism,* p. 9.

9. Quotations in the paragraph above are from *Occasional Services,* a companion to *Lutheran Book of Worship* (Minneapolis: Augsburg, 1982), pp. 194, 225, 219.

10. George W. Forell and J.F. McCue, eds., *Confessing One Faith: A Joint Commentary on the Augsburg Confession by Lutheran and Catholic Theologians* (Minneapolis: Augsburg, 1982), p. 334.

11. *All Under One Christ,* report of the Roman Catholic/Lutheran Joint Commission (Geneva: LWF, 1981, sec. 18, reprinted in *Lutheran/Roman Catholic Discussion on the Augsburg Confession,* ed. Harding Meyer (Geneva: LWF Report 10, 1982), p. 57.

12. Cardinal Jan Willebrands, "Confessio Augustana—A Form of Encounter," *Lutheran/Roman Catholic Discussion on the Augsburg Confession.* Documents 1977–1981, ed. Harding Meyer (Geneva: LWF Report 10, 1982), p. 57.

13. Vilmos Vajta in *Confessio Augustana 1530–1980: Commemoration and Self-Examination,* ed. Vilmos Vajta (Geneva: LWF Report 9, 1980).

14. *Ibid.,* p. 89.

15. "The Augsburg Confession reread in the Present Ecumenical Context: A Report on a Consultation," published in *The Augsburg Confession in Ecumenical Perspective,* ed. Harding Meyer (Geneva: LWF Report 6/7, 1980), p. vii.

16. *Ibid.,* p. ix.

17. Paraphrased from Edmund Schlink, "The Ecumenical Character and Claim of the Augsburg Confession," published in Meyer, *Augsburg Confession*, p. 2.

18. See my essay, "Martin Luther: An Anglican Ecumenical Appreciation," in *Anglican and Episcopal History* 56 (September 1987):319–329.

19. *The Augsburg Confession: A Commentary* (Minneapolis: Augsburg, 1987), pp. 161–240. See also *Confessing One Faith*, Forell and McCue, eds., p. 286.

20. Further, see Robert E. Hood, *Social Teachings in the Episcopal Church* (Harrisburg/Wilton: Morehouse, 1990).

21. Heiko Oberman, *Forerunners of the Reformation* (New York: Holt, Rinehart, Winston, 1966).

22. *The Augsburg Confession in Ecumenical Perspective*, ed. Meyer, pp. 30–31, 39–41.

23. Thomas Tentler, *Sin and Confession on the Eve of the Reformation* (Princeton: Princeton Univ., 1977).

24. All references to the CA are from BC.

25. This is quoted from a text statement made by the Sixth Assembly of the LWF (meeting at Dar es Salaam in 1977) and published in *Lutheran-Roman Catholic Discussion on the Augsburg Confession: Documents 1977–1981*, ed. Harding Meyer (Geneva: LWF Report 10, 1982), p. 27.

26. *Confessing One Faith*, p. 338.

27. A statement by the Executive Committee of the LWF in 1981, published in Meyer, *Lutheran-Roman Catholic Discussion* , p. 72.

28. A statement by Jan Cardinal Willebrands in his article "Confessio Augustana—A Form of Encounter," Meyer, *ibid.*, p. 57.

29. Vilmos Vajta, *Confessio Augustana 1530–1980*, p. 120.

30. A statement by Yves Congar in 1982, published in *Diversity and Communion* (London: SCM, 1984), p. 146.

31. Heinrich Fries, writing in 1979 and cited in *ibid.*, p. 148.

32. Piepkorn, *Profiles*, p. 10.

33. *Ibid.*, p. 47.

34. A statement by Walter Kasper in "The Augsburg Confession in Roman Catholic Perspective," published in Meyer, *The Augsburg Confession in Ecumenical Perspective*, p. 163.

35. My paraphrase of Arnold and Fry, *The Way*, p. 167.

36. Wolfhart Pannenberg, "The Confessio Augustana as a Catholic Confession and Basis for the Unity of the Church," published in *The Role of the Augsburg Confession: Catholic and Lutheran Views*, ed. Joseph A. Burgess (Philadelphia: Fortress, 1980), p. 42.

37. Harding Meyer, "The *Augustana* Accepted by Rome? What Lutheran and Catholic Theologians Can Contribute to This Goal," written in 1977 and published in *ibid.*, p. 69 (internal quotation marks removed).

38. Ordination vow from *Occasional Services*, p. 194.

39. Heinrich Fries and Karl Rahner, *Unity of the Churches: An Actual Possibility* (Philadelphia: Fortress; New York: Paulist, 1985).

Chapter 9. Richard Norris

1. P. 37, quoting the Helsinki Report.

Chapter 10. William G. Rusch

1. In regard to the concept of full communion, see the preface to the Concordat of Agreement and note 1 in *TFC & Concordat*, p. 97.

2. *Ibid.*, pp. 19–23, and esp. comments by Stephen Sykes on p. 21.

3. See the reference to the comments of Edmund Schlink in the third part of this essay.

4. See *Lutheran-Episcopal Dialogue: A Progress Report* (Cincinnati: Forward Movement, 1973), pp. 20–22.

5. See *Lutheran-Episcopal Dialogue: Report and Recommendations* (Cincinnati: Forward Movement, 1981), pp. 39–41.

6. *Ibid.*, pp. 62–63.

7. See *Growth in Agreement*, H. Meyer and L. Vischer, eds. (New York: Paulist; Geneva: WCC, 1984), pp. 23–26.

8. *Anglican-Lutheran Dialogue: The Report of the Anglican–Lutheran European Regional Commission* (London: S.P.C.K., 1983), pp. 14–20.

9. *Ibid.*, p. 30.

10. Niagara, pp. 24–33.

11. *Ibid.*, pp. 41–44.

12. For a fuller description of this ecumenical consensus, see *Confessions in Dialogue: A Survey of Bilateral Conversations among World Confessional Families*, Nils Ehrenström and Günther Gassmann, eds., rev. ed. (Geneva: WCC, 1975), esp. pp. 180–195, and *Growth in Agreement*, esp. pp. 511–512, for further reference.

13. Edmund Schlink, *The Coming Christ and the Coming Church* (Philadelphia: Fortress, 1967), p. 233.

14. *Baptism, Eucharist and Ministry*, Faith and Order Paper 3 (Geneva: WCC, 1982).

15. See the official responses to BEM, e.g., *Churches Respond to BEM*, vols. 1–6, edited by Max Thurian, Faith and Order Papers 129, 132, 135, 137, 143, and 144 (Geneva: WCC, 1986–1988), and *Baptism, Eucharist and Ministry 1982–1990: Report on the Process and Responses*, Faith and Order Paper 149 (Geneva: WCC, 1990).

16. BEM, p. 32.

17. *Ecumenical Perspectives on Baptism, Eucharist and Ministry*, Max Thurian, ed., Faith and Order Paper 116 (Geneva: WCC, 1983).

18. *Ecumenical Perspectives*, pp. 129–139.

19. *Facing Unity: Models. Forms and Phases of Catholic-Lutheran Church Fellowship* (Geneva: LWF, 1985)

Chapter 11. Michael Root

1. I will assume that the question is immediately relevant only to the ELCA and not to the Lutheran Church–Missouri Synod. No substantive changes in the analysis would need to be made, however, to include the LCMS.

2. I will, throughout, use the terms "communion" and "fellowship" interchangeably as denoting the same set of relationships. Both terms are translated into German with the term *Kirchengemeinschaft*. For brevity's sake, I will often omit the adjective "full."

3. The phrase "perfection of communion" is used by the Second Anglican-Roman Catholic International Commission to refer to this eschatological reality. See *Church As Communion,* ¶11.

4. The history of the Lutheran discussion is traced in Eugene L. Brand, *Toward a Lutheran Communion: Pulpit and Altar Fellowship,* LWF Report 26 (Geneva: LWF, 1988).

5. In the version of this essay presented to the dialogue in 1990, this unease was not mentioned and a general rule was proposed: The burden of proof is on an assertion that something is a necessary element in full communion if it does not already exist as a unifying element among either the Lutheran or Anglican churches. I now believe that this general rule gives too normative a role to the present shape of the Lutheran and Anglican communions.

6. An exception to this consensus might be the international Anglican-Roman Catholic statement *Church as Communion* (see the appendix to this essay, no. 8). While not absolutely clear, it seems to include some form of universal primacy as a constitutive element of ecclesial communion. One could include such a primacy in the described consensus under "right ordering of ministry," but one should add that Lutherans and Anglicans have not included universal primacy in the descriptions of communion that they have worked out together. For a strong statement of the universal primacy of the successor of Peter as a constitutive element of ecclesial communion, see the letter to the Roman Catholic bishops from the Congregation for the Doctrine of the Faith, "Some Aspects of the Church Understood as Communion," *Origins* 22 (1992):108–112.

7. Some Lutherans may object that unity in ministry is not explicitly mentioned in the description of the unity of the church in CA 7. On the one hand, CA 7 cannot be read in isolation from the rest of the CA. CA 5 is unambiguous in its assertion that "God instituted the office of the ministry." Thus, as a *jure divino* aspect of the church's structure, this office must be seen as presupposed by activities referred to in CA 7. On the other hand, it is not insignificant that the ministry is not explicitly mentioned in CA 7. The ordained ministry, however essential it may be

to the identity of the church, is subordinate to the activities for which it exists, the proclamation of the Word and the celebration of the sacraments.

8. See André Birmelé, "The Leuenberg Agreement from 1973 to 1988," in *The Leuenberg Agreement and Lutheran-Reformed Relationships: Evaluations by North American and European Theologians,* William G. Rusch and Daniel F. Martensen, eds. (Minneapolis: Augsburg, 1989), p. 49.

9. A complicated situation would arise if, say, the ECUSA were to realize exchangeability of clergy with a church with which the ELCA was not willing to enter into such a relation. The ELCA would then be forced either in fact to accept such an exchangeability at one remove, through the ECUSA, or deny the exchangeability of a particular group of Episcopal clergy, i.e., those who had transferred from the third church.

10. This paragraph condenses a more detailed argument I have made in "Bishops as Points of Unity and Continuity," in *Episcopacy: Lutheran-United Methodist Dialogue II,* Jack M. Tuell and Roger M. Fjeld, eds. (Minneapolis: Augsburg, 1991), pp. 118–125.

11. The post-Reformation discussion of episcopacy has, I think, been skewed by a one-sided emphasis on succession at the expense of collegiality. A bishop's ministries of oversight, unity, and continuity are finally one ministry in such a way that the loss of collegial unity is to be taken with the same kind of seriousness as the loss of succession in the laying-on-of-hands. However significant the maintenance of episcopal succession in the laying-on-of-hands in the churches of England and Sweden may be, it must be set next to their loss of communion with the larger body of Western Christendom. That a lack of collegial communion is a defect in any ministry has recently been increasingly recognized. In the participation of bishops from one church in episcopal installations or consecrations of another, I would place at least equal emphasis on the widening sphere of collegiality as on entrance into a line of succession in the laying-on-of-hands.

12. Peter Brunner, "The Realization of Church Fellowship," in *The Unity of the Church: A Symposium,* papers presented to the Commission on Theology and Liturgy of the LWF (Rock Island, Ill: Augustana, 1957), p. 18. The translation has been slightly altered.

13. The ECUSA clearly favors such a growth in its call for a unity of *episcopoi* as an aspect of communion (see the appendix to this essay, no. 17).

14. This problem is discussed in André Birmelé, "International Bilateral Theological Dialogues by the LWF: Are They Compatible with Each Other?" in *Communio and Dialogue: A Report from the Consultation on Ecumenical Dialogues,* Venice, 24–28 September, 1991, Eugene L. Brand, ed. (Geneva: LWF, 1992), pp. 17–27.

15. Elaboration and textual support for these comments can be found in "The Relation between 'Satis Est' and Full Communion: An Opinion from the Institute for Ecumenical Research, Strasbourg," in *A Commentary on "Ecumenism: The Vision of the ELCA,"* William G. Rusch, ed. (Minneapolis: Augsburg, 1990), pp. 105–118.

16. In *Documents of Lutheran Unity in America*, Richard C. Wolf, ed. (Philadelphia: Fortress, 1966), p. 510.

17. See, e.g., with explicit reference to Anglican-Lutheran discussions, Mary Tanner, "The Goal of Unity in Theological Dialogues Involving Anglicans," in *Einheit der Kirche: Neue Entwicklungen und Perspektiven*, Günther Gassmann and Peder Nørgaard-Højen, eds. (Frankfurt a.M.: Verlag Otto Lembeck, 1988), esp. pp. 74–78; and David F. Ford, "In the Light of Our Common Mission, What Needs To Be Reformed in Our Respective Expressions of Episcopé?," in *Papers of the Consultation*, an Anglican-Lutheran Consultation on "Episcopé in Relation to the Mission of the Church Today," Niagara Falls, 24 September–3 October 1987 (Geneva: LWF, 1988), pp. 146–147. My impression is that the questions about the description of full communion reported at the first meeting of the Anglican-Lutheran International Continuation Committee (appended to Niagara, p. 61) reflected this Anglican concern about the nature of the ecumenical goal. At its meeting in September and October, 1989, the Continuation Committee decided that a reformulation of the description of full communion was not necessary.

18. See Michael Kinnamon, *Truth and Community: Diversity and Its Limits in the Ecumenical Movement* (Grand Rapids: Eerdmans; Geneva: WCC, 1988), p. 86.

Chapter 12. William G. Rusch

1. See "Einheit der Kirche I, Einigungsbestrebungen," by Harding Meyer, in *Ökumene Lexikon*, pp. 285–303.

2. *The Lutheran Episcopal Agreement: Commentary and Guidelines* (Philadelphia: Lutheran Church in America, 1983), p. 13.

3. *Anglican-Lutheran Relations: Report of the Anglican-Lutheran Joint Working Group*, pp. 13–14.

4. *Ibid.*, p. 14.

5. *Ibid.*, pp. 15–16.

6. See the summary in *Confessions in Dialogue* by Nils Ehrenström and Günther Gassmann, pp. 14–17.

7. *Lutheran-Episcopal Dialogue: A Progress Report*, p. 21, section 4 and p. 22.

8. *Ibid.*, pp. 23–24.

9. See William G. Rusch, *Reception: An Ecumenical Opportunity* (Philadelphia: Fortress, 1988), esp. p. 31.

10. *Facing Unity*, also entitled *Einheit vor uns*, was published in 1985 by the LWF and the Secretariat for Promoting Christian Unity of the Roman Catholic Church. *Facing Unity: Models, Forms and Phases of Catholic-Lutheran Church Fellowship* (Geneva: LWF, 1985).

11. See *ibid.*, pp. 27–36.

12. See *Implications*.

13. The Pullach Report, pp. 87, 89; *Lutheran-Episcopal Dialogue: A Progress Report*, pp. 21–22, 34–35, 41–44; *Lutheran-Episcopal Dialogue: Report and Recommendations*, pp. 39–44.

14. These last several paragraphs were written before the completion of *TFC & Concordat*. Many of the ideas in these paragraphs found their way into the final dialogue report.

Chapter 13. William A. Norgren

1. *Publications Mentioned:*

The Church of England and the Church of Sweden: Report of the Commission Appointed by the Archbishop of Canterbury (London: A. R. Mowbray, 1911).

"The Answer of the Swedish Bishops in 1922," *Church in Fellowship: Pulpit and Altar Fellowship Among Lutherans*, ed. Vilmos Vajta (Minneapolis: Augsburg, 1963), pp. 181–188. Also, *Documents on Christian Unity 1920–1924*, ed. G. K. A. Bell (1924).

The Church of England and the Church of Finland: A Summary of the Proceedings at the Conference held at Lambeth Palace, London, on October 5th and 6th, 1933, and at Brandö, Helsingfors, on July 17th and 18th, 1934 (London: S.P.C.K., 1934). Also, *Documents on Christian Unity, 1930–1948*, ed. G. K. A. Bell.

Conferences between Representatives Appointed by the Archbishop of Canterbury on Behalf of the Church of England and Representatives of the Evangelical Lutheran Churches of Latvia and Estonia (London: S.P.C.K., 1938).

The Church of England and the Churches of Norway, Denmark and Iceland: Report of a Committee Appointed by the Archbishop of Canterbury in 1951 (London: S.P.C.K., 1952).

Other Books:

Arthur Carl Piepkorn, "Anglo-Lutheran Relations," *Pro Ecclesia Lutherana* 2 (no.1) (1934?):58–69 (described as "Part I").

"The Anglo-Scandinavian Theological Conferences," *Scandinavian Churches: A Picture of the Development and Life of the Churches of Denmark, Finland, Iceland, Norway and Sweden*, ed. Leslie Stannard Hunter (London: Faber & Faber, 1963), pp. 184–189.

Gunnar Rosendal, *The Catholic Movement in the Swedish Church*, Hale Sermon (Evanston: Seabury-Western Seminary, 1951).

G. Mott Williams, *The Church of Sweden and the Anglican Communion* (London: A. R. Mowbray, 1910).

C. B. Moss, "Episcopacy in the Church of Sweden," *Episcopacy Ancient and Modern*, Claude Jenkins and K. D. MacKenzie, eds., pp. 321–333.

Episcopacy in the Lutheran Church? Ivar Asheim and Victor R. Gold, eds. (Philadelphia: Fortress, 1970).

Einar Molland, "From the Scandinavian Standpoint," *Union of Christendom*, ed. Kenneth MacKenzie (London: S.P.C.K., 1938).

Carl Lyttkens, *The Growth of Swedish-Anglican Intercommunion between 1833 and 1922*, Bibliotheca Theologiae Practicae, 24 (Lund: Gleerups, 1970).

Suzanne B. Geisler, "A Step on the Swedish Lutheran Road to Anglicanism," *Historical Magazine of the Protestant Episcopal Church*, March 1985.

A. G. Herbert, "The Scandinavian Communions," *Union of Christendom*, ed. Kenneth MacKenzie (London: S.P.C.K., 1938). Bibliography is at the end.

H. M. Waddams, *The Swedish Church* (London: S.P.C.K., 1946).

J. Howard Swinstead, *The Swedish Church and Ours* (London: S.P.C.K., 1921).

LIST OF CONTRIBUTORS

The Rev. L. William Countryman
Professor of New Testament
The Church Divinity School of the Pacific
Berkeley, California

The Rev. Walter R. Bouman
Edward C. Fendt Professor of Systematic Theology
Trinity Lutheran Seminary
Columbus, Ohio

The Rev. Jerald C. Brauer
Emeritus Professor
University of Chicago Divinity School
Chicago, Illinois

The Rev. Paul E. Erickson
Bishop (retired)
Illinois Synod of the Lutheran Church in America
Chicago, Illinois

The Rev. Robert J. Goeser
Emeritus Professor
Pacific Lutheran Theological Seminary
Berkeley, California

The Rev. Eric W. Gritsch
Emeritus Professor
Gettysburg Theological Seminary
Gettysburg, Pennsylvania

The Rev. Daniel F. Martensen
Associate Director
Department for Ecumenical Affairs
Evangelical Lutheran Church in America
Chicago, Illinois

The Rev. William A. Norgren
Ecumenical Officer (retired)
The Episcopal Church, U.S.A.
New York, New York

The Rev. Richard Norris
Professor of Church History
Union Theological Seminary
New York, New York

The Rev. John H. Rodgers, Jr.
Dean
Episcopal School for Ministry
Ambridge, Pennsylvania

The Rev. Michael Root
Research Professor
Institute for Ecumenical Research
Strasbourg, France

The Rev. William G. Rusch
Executive Director
Department for Ecumenical Affairs
Evangelical Lutheran Church in America
Chicago, Illinois

The Rev. J. Robert Wright
Professor of Ecclesiastical History
General Theological Seminary
New York, New York